NOT
SO!

NOT
SO!

Popular Myths About America from Columbus to Clinton

Paul F. Boller, Jr.

OXFORD UNIVERSITY PRESS

NEW YORK   OXFORD

Oxford University Press

Oxford   New York
Athens   Auckland   Bangkok   Bombay
Calcutta   Cape Town   Dar es Salaam   Delhi
Florence   Hong Kong   Istanbul   Karachi
Kuala Lumpur   Madras   Madrid   Melbourne
Mexico City   Nairobi   Paris   Singapore
Taipei   Tokyo   Toronto

and associated companies in
Berlin   Ibadan

Copyright © 1995 by Paul F. Boller, Jr.

First published in 1995 by Oxford University Press, Inc.
198 Madison Avenue, New York, New York 10016

First issued as an Oxford University Press paperback, 1996

Oxford is a registered trademark of Oxford University Press

Library of Congress Cataloging-in-Publication Data
Boller, Paul F.
Not so! : popular myths about America from Columbus to Clinton
by Paul F. Boller, Jr.
p. cm.   Includes bibliographical references and index.
ISBN 0-19-509186-8
ISBN 0-19-510972-4 (Pbk.)
1. United States—History—Errors, inventions, etc. I. Title
E178.6B64   1995   973—dc20

1 3 5 7 9 10 8 6 4 2
Printed in the United States of America

For
Paul and Karen
David and Patty

Preface

The chronicles of American history are strewn with myths, legends, fables, folklore, misinformation, and misconceptions. Some of the myth-making is inadvertent, but much of it is deliberate. Patriotism and filiopietism have set many a tall tale in motion, but so have political partisanship and ideological zeal. The bent for simplism, as well as just plain sloppy reporting, has also added to the mischief. Decontextualism—the moralizing passion for judging past generations by present-day standards—has been at work, too. ("Understanding the past," as Paul Fussell reminds us, "requires pretending that you don't know the present.")[1] And paranoia has sometimes entered the picture, for some mentalities automatically transmute the contingent and unforeseen into conspiratorial design. Some of the myths are innocuous enough; others, though, stand in the way of our getting a good insight into what went on in the past and on how we got to where we are now.

What follows is an analysis of what seem to me to be the most popular—and most enduring—myths shaping contemporary thinking about the American past. I do not regard my choices as definitive, but I do think that any list that omitted the items appearing here would be woefully incomplete.

In politics, one person's myth may be another's verity, but in history there are no absolutes. When it comes to controversial issues, the historian deals with probabilities, not finalities. I hope I have made this clear in what I say here.

Texas Christian University, Fort Worth   P. F. B., Jr.
December 1994

Grateful acknowledgment is made to the following
for permission to quote material in copyright:

Elmer Kelton, "Politically Correct or Historically Correct?"
The Roundup Magazine, September–October 1993, pp. 7, 9.
Reprinted by permission of Elmer Kelton.

Arthur Schlesinger, Jr., "Was America a Mistake?"
Atlantic Monthly, September 1992, p. 22.
Reprinted by permission of Arthur Schlesinger, Jr.

Stanley Weintraub, *Long Day's Journey into War*
(Penguin Books, 1991), p. 525.
Reprinted by permission of Stanley Weintraub.

Contents

NOT
SO!

CHAPTER I

Columbus and
the Flat-Earthers

In daring to sail westward in 1492, hoping to reach the Indies, Christopher Columbus was challenging the prevailing belief of his day that the earth was flat.

Not so.

Most educated people in Columbus's day believed that the earth was round, not flat, and the problem Columbus faced in seeking support for his "Enterprise of the Indies" centered on the size, not the shape, of the earth. The Bible itself was vague about the earth's size and shape, but learned men, both in antiquity and in the Middle Ages, took for granted the earth's sphericity. "In the first fifteen centuries of the Christian era." wrote historian Jeffrey Burton Russell in 1991, "nearly unanimous scholarly opinion pronounced the earth spherical, and by the fifteenth century all doubt had disappeared."[1] In 1480, William Caxton (England's famous printer) wrote that in the absence of obstacles a person could walk all around the earth "lyke as a flye goth round aboute a round apple." His opinion was unexceptionable.[2]

It was Washington Irving, author of the influential *Life and Voyages of Christopher Columbus* (1828), who first encouraged, in a dramatic fashion, the idea that Columbus had to overcome the opposition of the flat-earthers when he requested financial support for his ambitious undertaking from the court of Spain. In 1486, according to Irving, Columbus appeared before a council of learned ecclesiastics in Salamanca—professors of astronomy, geography, and mathematics, as well as church dignitaries and learned friars—to explain and defend his proposal to sail west. He had a difficult time at the meeting, wrote Irving, for he was only an obscure navigator with no pretensions to learning, while his interrogators formed an erudite assembly embodying the religious and scientific consensus of 15th-century Christendom.[3]

The Salamanca sages, reported Irving, bombarded Columbus with hostile questions. "To his simplest proposition, the spherical form of the earth," he wrote, they "opposed figurative texts of scripture. They observed that in the Psalms the heavens are said to be extended like a skin, that is, according to commentators, the curtain or covering of a tent, which among the ancient pastoral nations, was formed of the skin of animals; and that St. Paul, in the Epistle to the Hebrews, compares the heavens to a tabernacle, or tent, extended over the earth, which they thence inferred must be flat." Columbus's unfriendly inquisitors also confronted him gleefully with a passage from Lactantius, a 4th-century Christian apologist, who dismissed the notion of a spherical earth as patently absurd. "Is there anyone so foolish," they quoted Lactantius as asking, "as to believe that there are antipodes with their feet opposite to ours; people who walk with their heels upward, and their heads hanging down? That there is a part of the world in which all things are topsy turvy; where the trees grow with their branches downward, and where it rains, hails and snows upward?" The Salamanca cognoscenti, Irving added, also brought the opinions of the great St. Augustine to bear on the matter. Augustine, they told Columbus, held that the "doctrine of the antipodes," that is, the belief that there were inhabited lands on the opposite side of the globe, implied that there were people in the world who were not descended from Adam, thus contradicting the Bible's assertion that all men were descended from one common parent. Columbus was devoutly religious, Irving noted, but at times he feared he would be convicted of heresy as well as of error. Still, he held his ground and courageously refused to abandon his belief in the earth's sphericity.[4]

Irving's was a charming tale, but, as historian Samuel Eliot Morison, an expert on Columbus, pointed out years ago, it was "pure moonshine."[5] Columbus may have been innovative, but it wasn't because he believed the earth was round. Most Catholic scholars shared his belief; Lactantius, a 4th-century convert to Christianity, along with Cosmas Indicopleustes, a 6th-century Greek writer, were notable exceptions. Even the opponents of Copernicus (who objected to his putting the Sun rather than the Earth at the center of the planetary system) thought the Earth was ball-shaped. What concerned Columbus's critics at Salamanca was the size, not the shape, of the earth; they thought he underestimated the distance between Spain and the Indies, and in this they were, of course, right. Soon after the meeting, though, Columbus was put on the royal payroll, and in 1492 he was able to sail westward. But he might not have done so had he known that the ocean was far wider (as his critics maintained) than he had calculated.

The Irving myth that church scholars in Columbus's day were flat-earthers soon became conventional wisdom in the United States. Champions of Darwinian evolution in the late 19th century took to the myth with special enthusiasm, for they were eager to demonstrate that the religious opponents of Darwin's theory in their own day were just as benighted as Columbus's foolish foes had been four centuries before. In *The History of the Conflict Between Religion and Science* (1876), New York University scientist John W. Draper wrote that although intelligent sailors like Columbus were inclined to a belief in "the globular figure of earth," this idea was, "as might be expected . . . received with disfavor by theologians." Draper went on to report that "its irreligious tendency was pointed out by the Spanish ecclesiastics and condemned by the Council of Salamanca."[6] Andrew D. White, president of Cornell University, made the same erroneous point in his popular *History of the Warfare of Science and Theology in Christendom* (1896). Following Irving's lead, White described how "sundry wise men of Spain" confronted Columbus with "the usual quotations" from the Bible and Augustine, and how, even after Columbus's voyages greatly strengthened the theory of the earth's sphericity, the "Church by its highest authority solemnly stumbled and persisted in going astray." It took Magellan's famous voyage around the world in 1519 to give science the victory, according to White, but even then the Church dragged its heels when it came to accepting the roundness of the earth.[7]

Draper and White—and countless other writers, down to our times—got it all wrong. In accepting the authority of Irving, they went egregiously astray themselves. "The curious result," observed historian Russell, was "that White and his colleagues ended by doing what they accused the church fathers of, namely, creating a body of false knowledge by consulting one another instead of the evidence."[8]

Why the persistence of the flat-earth error into the 1990s? "Our determination to believe the Flat Error," suggested Russell, "arises out of contempt for the past and the need to believe in the superiority of the present." It was, he thought, the "most stubborn remaining variety of ethnocentrism."[9]

CHAPTER 2

Pre-Columbian America

Until Columbus reached the New World the people he called "Indians" lived in peace and harmony with nature and with one another.

Not so.

The Spanish (and later the French and English) conquest of the New World following Columbus brought death, destruction, exploitation, and slavery with it, but it is sentimental condescension to hold that until Columbus the Indians lived idyllic lives of "balanced and fruitful harmony," as one writer put it, with the natural world and each other. "One should not pull the pendulum all the way over," warned Alvin M. Josephy, Indian specialist, "and pretend that pre-Columbian America was a paradise with no ills or vices—which . . . it was not."[1]

There were, to be sure, peaceful tribes in pre-Columbian America, like the Hopis of the Southwest and the Slaves of subarctic Canada. Most Indian tribes, however, were familiar, long before Columbus, with the kinds of wickedness that had beclouded European (and Asian and African) history for centuries: aggression, warfare, torture, persecution, bigotry, slavery, tyranny. By the time of the Columbus Quincentenary in 1992, however, it had become orthodox wisdom with many Americans to look back on the pre-Columbian Indians as morally superior to the 16th-century Europeans who came in Columbus's wake and to lament rather than celebrate the so-called "discovery of America." (Columbus, not

Adam, was apparently the original sinner: "In Chris's landfall, we sinned all.") The pre-Columbian Indians had their virtues, of course, and their achievements, particularly in the arts and agriculture, were tremendous. But they also knew war, conquest, torture, exploitation, and despotism long before Columbus, and their treatment of the natural world fell far short of the standards demanded by conscientious environmentalists in the United States in the 1990s.

Was John Collier, the New Deal's Commissioner of Indian Affairs, being accurate when he asserted that the pre-1492 Indians lived in "perfect ecological balance with the forest, the plain, the desert, the waters and animal life"?[2] Not exactly. It is certainly true that Indians who lived on a primitive level did less damage to the environment than those who developed more complex economies, but even simple hunters and gatherers, who moved around a lot in their quest for food, left a lot of garbage behind them. Small semi-nomadic tribes, moreover, practiced "slash and burn" agriculture that involved making a clearing in a forest by stripping the bark along the base of trees, letting them die, and then burning them. More complex Indian societies, of course, altered the environment even more drastically. The Maya of Central America, according to some scholars, overused the land and deforested the countryside, thereby bringing about climatic and ecological changes that contributed to their own decline. In building large cities, moreover, and in developing networks of roads and canals, the Maya, as well as the Aztecs and Incas, "left marks on the landscape that were still visible centuries later."[3]

As for animals, there is no doubt that many tribes prior to Columbus, did their hunting selectively, not wastefully. But some tribes, like the Arapaho of eastern Colorado, used a pell-mell system in seeking game. They started grass fires on the prairies in order to stampede herds of bison into death traps, and then butchered the best animals and left the rest for the vultures. Some anthropologists, moreover, believe that the hunting methods of early immigrants from Asia contributed to the extinction of several animal species, including the horse (genus *Eohippus*), that once roamed North America. The European invaders, to be sure, behaved even more recklessly than the Indians as they took over the New World, but the pre-Columbian Indians were by no means environmental purists, and many of them eventually took up the European ways of dealing with plants and animals after Columbus's landfall.[4]

When it came to social arrangements, most pre-Columbian Indian tribes were no more free, open, and egalitarian than the European monarchies of the 15th century. Some tribes, to be sure, were fundamentally peace-loving and even democratic in their ways, but most of them were authoritarian in structure, with a privileged few ruling the roost and calling the tune, just as in Europe. Inca civilization, according to Peruvian novelist Mario Vargas Llosa, was a "pyramidical and theocratic society" with a "totalitarian structure" in which the individual had no importance and virtually no existence." Its foundation he noted, was a "state religion that took away the individual's free will and crowned the authority's decision with the aura of a divine mandate that turned the Tawantinsuy [Inca empire] into a beehive."[5] Mayan civilization and Aztec society—and countless far less sophisticated Indian cultures—were similarly despotic in nature, though none of them practiced state terrorism on as large a scale as the Inca did.

Among the pre-Columbian Indians there was a dearth of what some U.S. moralizers in the 1990s regarded as "politically correct behavior." There was, for one thing, plenty of "elitism" with little or no empowerment for the less privileged. Among the Natchez, for example, a small elite, consisting of a chief (the Great Sun), his relatives (Suns), nobles, and honored men, ran things as they pleased, while the masses, called "stinkards" (French translation of a Natchez term), did as they were told. There was also "ageism" among some Indian tribes. The Crees and the Chippewayans of Central Canada abandoned or even strangled senior citizens who couldn't keep up with tribal migrations. Sexism, too, was rife, as it was with the European conquerors. Women in some of the subarctic groups did most of the heavy work—dragged the toboggans, built the shelters, gathered the firewood and didn't get to eat until the men had finished their meals. Cruel and unusual punishments, moreover, were not at all uncommon in pre-Columbian America. Some of the tribes in the Iroquois Confederacy punished adultery by having the male offender's ears or lips cropped or the end of his nose cut off. For murder the penalty was death, and if the murderer fled, a male member of his family was killed in his place.[6]

Neither war nor slavery was unknown in pre-Columbian America. Highly complex civilizations like the Aztec, Maya, and Toltec were, as Texas writer Elmer Kelton noted, "built on a sea of blood, on massive human sacrifice, on warfare, brutal conquest and enslavement." But it wasn't only the sophisticated societies of Central and South America which resorted to violence.[7] "Warfare was common on both continents," according to Alvin Josephy, "and was a principal preoccupation among some Indian societies."[8] The Natchez of Mississippi, for one, were chronically warlike. "War was a man's proper occupation," observed anthropologist Oliver LaFarge of the Natchez. "Their fighting was deadly, ferocious, stealthy if possible, for the purpose of killing—men, women, or children, so long as one killed—and taking captives, especially strong males, whom one could enjoy torturing to death."[9] Indian tribes everywhere tended to regard outsiders with suspicion—as barbarians, "sons of she-dogs," enemies, alien spirits—and deserving of death. Cheyennes fought Crows mainly because they were different, and the Crows fought back for the same reason. Pawnees similarly fought the Sioux and the Cheyennes, while the Blackfeet, it is said, fought just about everybody. The warring tribes slaughtered men, women, and children, sometimes in disputes over hunting grounds, but sometimes simply because their foes belonged to other tribes. "Certainly since there has been recorded history—or even Indian legends," wrote Kelton, "there has been incessant intertribal warfare. The carnage was sometimes unspeakable in its horrors, long before Columbus ever got his feet wet."[10]

Many Indian tribes were so busy fighting one another that they were unable to put up an effective defense against the European invaders arriving after Columbus. Some Indians, in fact, sided with the invading whites because they wanted to get even with rival chiefs and bands that had been abusing them. Hernán Cortés conquered the mighty Aztec empire with fewer than six hundred men not only because of better weapons, but also because the Tlascalans and other native peoples who were being exploited by the Aztecs were willing to help the Spaniards. "There is not one foot of land in this country," declared Kelton, "that in the past has not been claimed by one Indian tribe or another, in most cases a succession of tribes in the ebb and flow of history, the cycles of conquest and defeat. It has been bought with blood, over and over again." The European invasion of the New World, in short, "did not introduce conquest and subjugation to this continent. That was already here. It only brought a new set of conquerors, far more numerous, and far better armed."[11]

Indian warfare brought slavery (common on both continents), ritual torture, and human sacrifice with it. The Tahltans of western Canada, who fought constantly with their neighbors, killed their male prisoners, but enslaved the women. On the Northwest coast, Indian chiefs who obtained slaves by capture liked to show their indifference to mere possessions by killing them with a special club known as the "slave killer." The Iroquois tortured men they captured in battle but made use of women and children as slaves. The Mayan city-states, which seem to have engaged in continual warfare, ritually tortured their prisoners and then decapitated them. The Aztecs also went in for torture and sacrifice. Their belief that human blood and the human heart contained the vital energy for the sun's motion and the earth's fertility produced religious ceremonies in the capital city, Tenochtitlán, in which people captured in wars against surrounding cities and towns were sacrificed to the gods. For major events (installing an emperor or dedicating a new temple), thousands of captives, including women and children, proceeded through the streets, ascended the 114 steps of the great pyramid, and then were pressed down on the killing stone at the top so a priest could plunge the obsidian knife into their chests, tear out the still pulsing heart, and raise it to the sun. Their bodies were then sent rolling down the steps to be picked up by old men from the local temple and carried through the streets for dismemberment, distribution, and consumption. At one ceremony involving 20,000 captives, one of the priests finally collapsed from sheer exhaustion after hours of cutting out the bleeding hearts of the sacrificial victims. Like the Aztecs, the Mundurucú societies of the Amazon went in for cannibalism as well as ritual torture.[12] Their treatment of prisoners, according to anthropologist Louis Faron, "ranged from the exotic mutilation of shrinking heads to eating parts of the corpse." After removing the brains and teeth of prisoners and closing their eyes with beeswax, the Mundurucú boiled the head and strung cords through the mouth and out of the nostrils.[13]

"Neither Cortés, nor Columbus, nor any other conquistador entered a static, timeless and peaceful world of innocents," wrote historian Hugh Thomas in his absorbing study *Conquest: Mon-*

tezuma, Cortés, and the Fall of Old Mexico (1993). "The Tainos whom Columbus encountered seemed happy. But they had themselves come to the Caribbean Islands as conquerors and had driven out, or rather had driven into the west end of Cuba, the primitive inhabitants, the so-called Guanahatabeys (also known as Casimiroids). They themselves were menaced by the Caribs who, coming from the South American mainland, had been fighting their way up the lesser Antilles. The Caribs had already conquered the so-called Igneri culture in what are now called the Windward islands, and were beginning to threaten the Leewards, perhaps even Puerto Rico."[14] Despite the dramatic clash of cultures after the arrival of the Spanish in the New World, historian Arthur Schlesinger, Jr., thought that in certain respects there was "little difference between the Europe and Mexico of 1492: little difference in the uses of power, in prescriptive inequalities, in coercion and torture, in imperialism and violence and destruction, in (to leap centuries forward to contemporary standards) the suppression of individual freedom and human rights. The record illustrates less the pitiless annihilation of an idyllic culture by a wrecking crew of aliens than it does the criminality of all cultures and the universality of original sin. Cruelty and destruction are not the monopoly of any single continent or race or culture."[15]

Without question, the Europeans treated the native population brutally after arriving in the New World. But they treated each other brutally, too; and the Indians themselves also dealt brutally with one another. Two wrongs do not make a right, of course, but awareness of both wrongs may help to guard against the feelings of moral superiority in judging other people that have always produced a great deal of misery in the world. Contempt for others in other times and places is not an especially promising basis for morality in any time or place.

Visiting Havana in the early 1990s, historian Schlesinger asked Fidel Castro how he viewed the Quincentennial. "We are critical," the Cuban leader told him, "Columbus brought many bad things." "If it weren't for Columbus you wouldn't be here," Schlesinger reminded him. "Well," said Castro, "Columbus brought good things as well as bad."[16]

CHAPTER 3

The Puritans and
Religious Freedom

The Puritans came to the New World to establish "a city on a hill" based on religious freedom.

Yes and no. The Puritans who founded Massachusetts Bay Colony in the early 17th century wanted to establish what John Winthrop, the governor, called "a city upon a hill," but they did not base it on religious freedom as we understand it today.

Freedom, for Winthrop and the other Massachusetts Puritans, did not mean the right of people to worship as they pleased. For them it meant something more exalted: self-perfection, that is, emancipation from one's selfish impulses and evil inclinations and action in accordance with moral law and the will of God. In a lecture, "A Model of Christian Charity" (1630), which Winthrop gave just before the Puritans left England, he called on his co-religionists to found a "Christian Commonwealth" in the New World which would be a kind of "city upon a hill" for the rest of the world to admire and perhaps imitate. Dedicated to God, the new colony would see to it that the "care of the public must oversway all private respects" and that the inhabitants strive "to do justly, to love mercy, to walk humbly with our God."[1]

The moral freedom to which Winthrop committed Massachusetts was intimately bound up with the Puritan theology and polity that inpired the migration. Puritan theology was basically Calvinistic; it centered on predestination, original sin, and salvation by the grace of God. Puritan polity was Congregational, that is, it looked on the church as an assembly of the believers (all of whom had experienced conversion) who had voluntarily come together to organize their congregation and then to elect their minister and elders for governing the congregation. The Puritans tried hard to "purify" the Church of England, in which they had been reared, and purge it of the vestiges of the Roman Catholic Church from which England had been separated years before. They disliked the Anglican Church's hierarchical organization, with its bishops and archbishops; they also objected to the way the Anglican Church regarded all citizens, even those who had never experienced conversion, as church members. Their preference was for self-governing congregations of true believers.

The Puritans failed to reshape the Church of England to their own liking, so they headed for America to found a colony of their own, based on their own conviction of what was right and proper when it came to religion. After founding Massachusetts Bay Colony they saw to it that everyone who settled there attended and supported the Congregational church and its doctrines and lived in accordance with its moral code. And they required evidence of an authentic conversion experience for elevation to church membership and to the political privileges (the right to vote and hold office) that came with it. The "city upon a hill" they established was, in short, quintessentially Puritan. Its founders never dreamed of tolerating religious opinions and practices which departed from those of the Puritan establishment. When Roger Williams denounced "soul yokes" and called for "soul liberty," that is, the right for the people to worship as they pleased, the Puritan authorities sent him off into the "howling wilderness." And when Anne Hutchinson, a devout Puritan (like Williams), came up with some outlandish religious views of her own, they sent her packing too. Neither Williams nor Hutchinson, in their opinion, cherished the kind of moral freedom on which the founders of Massachusetts had based their colony.

The Puritans were irked by demands for "soul liberty," that is, for the freedom to practice a religion of one's own choosing. This kind of religious liberty—with its absence of external restraints and constraints on beliefs and practices—was, they insisted, a negative and inferior kind of freedom. Inner freedom (liberation from irrational impulses), not external freedom (doing as one pleased), was what counted. John Winthrop, governor of Massachusetts Bay Colony for many years, called the ability to do as we please a "natural corrupt liberty" which was "common to man with beasts and other creatures" and needed to be severely limited by the civil and ecclesiastical authorities. For the true Christian, he said, moral liberty, that is, the liberty to do what is "good, just, and honest," which comes from faith in Christ, was the only liberty worth taking seriously.[2] Winthrop's clerical brothers heartily agreed with his view of the matter. Exclaimed Thomas Shepard, minister of the Church in Cambridge: "'Tis Satan's policy to plead for an indefinite and boundless toleration." Urian Oakes, president of Harvard, announced that the kind of religious freedom Roger Williams demanded was the "first born of all Abominations." And Nathaniel Ward, pastor at Ipswich, said that the only freedom that people like Williams possessed was "free liberty to keepe away from us."[3]

The Puritans weren't entirely wrong in their views of freedom. Surely the inner freedom they emphasized—liberation from excessive self-concern—is indispensable for civilized intercourse. (Psychologically, we recognize today, people are only truly free when they forget themselves in their absorption in love, work, and play.) Still, the external freedom which they depreciated—absence of external coercion—is also crucial to individual creativity and social comity. The two freedoms go together, and the task of civilization is to achieve a proper balance between them.

CHAPTER 4

Roger Williams's
Soul Liberty

Roger Williams was a religious liberal who favored separation of church and state.

Not exactly.

Williams advocated separation of church and state, to be sure, but not because he was a religious liberal.

Williams was in fact a devout Puritan. He took for granted the fundamental beliefs of 17th-century Puritans: predestination, original sin, salvation by grace, the doctrine of the elect, the second coming of Christ, and the centrality of the Bible for Christian believers. Religion was his abiding passion. He called for church-state separation not because he was lukewarm about religion but because he cared about it so much. Where secular humanists today favor church-state separation because they don't want the church meddling with the state, Williams favored it because he didn't want the state meddling with the church. He thought that when the state got involved in religious matters the result was invariably insincerity, hypocrisy, worldliness, and worst of all, intolerance and persecution.

Vernon L. Parrington was primarily responsible for the image of Roger Williams as a kind of 20th-century liberal whose interests were more political than religious. In his exuberant (and, for a long time, influential) *Main Currents in American Thought* (1927–30), Parrington described Williams as a "transcendental mystic" and a "Christian freethinker," who was in many ways a forerunner not only of John Locke and the natural rights philosophy but also of William Ellery Channing's Unitarianism and Ralph Waldo Emerson's transcendentalism. He was, Parrington declared, "the repository of the generous liberalisms of a vigorous age."[1]

Parrington could not have been more mistaken. Williams insisted on religious freedom primarily for theological, not secular, reasons. His ideal was a church so pure that, like the earliest Christian congregations, it consisted only of men and women who had experienced conversion and showed signs of grace. There had been no such church on earth, in Williams's opinion, since the early Christian era, and there never would be another such church until Christ's return; therefore, there was no reason for any eccleslastical organization—Protestant or Catholic—to present itself as the "true church" and seek the assistance of the state in imposing its beliefs and practices on citizens at large. Williams eventually became a "Seeker," that is, one who had dedicated his life, in an imperfect world, to an endless quest for spiritual insight. But he did so within the framework of Puritan theology.

In Massachusetts Bay Colony, where Williams arrived as a preacher from England in 1631, the magistrates attempted to enforce religious uniformity on the inhabitants, just as civil authorities in England and in most of the nations of Western Europe did during the 17th century. But to Williams "forced worship stinks in God's nostrils," and he was so openly critical of the Puritan establishment that in 1635 he was thrown out of the colony. In Providence, which he founded in 1636, there was no established church; his colony was based, as he put it, on "that grand cause of freedom of conscience." Governments he thought, were set up to protect lives and property and to maintain the civil peace, and they should have no say-so when it came to "spirituall and Soul-causes." Williams's let-alone policy when it came to spiritual and soul-causes (including Quakerism, with which he was in hearty disagreement) went pretty far. He asked that "a permission of the most *Paganish, Jewish, Turkish,* or *Antichristian consciences* and *worships* be granted to *all* men in all *Nations* and *Countries.*" It was an extraordinary view for the 17th century, especially for a committed Christian like Roger Williams.[2]

If Williams had been simply the modern liberal Parrington thought he was, he would have nothing to tell us that we don't already know. But since he was a passionate believer who at the same time denied that anyone, including himself, knew so much about eternal truth that he was obliged to enforce his views on others, he raises the question of whether this is true for politics as well as for religion. The 20th century has been an age of what George Orwell called "smelly little orthodoxies," and it still has something to learn from the God-intoxicated founder of Providence Plantations. Williams would have been appalled by the persistence of what he called "the bloudy tenent of persecution" in the modern world. But he would have known why: the belief by ideologues of various persuasions that they have final answers to the big questions about human existence in their grasp and consequently the obligation to force their views on the rest of the world. There do not seem to be many people like Williams in any age: passionate believers who prefer debate to coercion.[3]

CHAPTER 5

Sex and
the American Puritan

The colonial American Puritans were prim, proper, and prudish prigs.

Not exactly.

It was 19th-century Victorian Americans, not colonial Puritans, who were unbelievably fastidious when it came to things of the flesh. For them, legs became limbs, stockings became hose, breasts became bosoms, bulls became male cows or gentlemen cows, and cocks became roosters or hen's husbands.[1] In the years before the Civil War, it is recorded, a newspaper in Charleston, South Carolina, refused to print birth notices; a woman in New Orleans never changed clothes without turning her picture of Andrew Jackson to the wall; and one woman saw to it that the books of male and female authors, unless married, were properly separated on her bookshelves. The *New York Herald* singled out Dickens and Dumas as "Trashy Literature" about this time, not fit to be read by respectable people, and excoriated the polka as "one of the most indecent, immodest and scandalous exhibitions ever brought from Europe." Peregrinating the United States in 1837 and 1838, Captain Frederick Marryat, popular British novelist, came across a girls' school which featured a piano in the living room whose legs (limbs?) were carefully clothed "in modest little trousers with frills at the bottom of them!" The Brit was astonished.[2]

The colonial Puritans would have been astonished too. There was nothing priggish about them. They expressed themselves frankly and forthrightly, not shyly and shamefacedly, when it came to earthy matters. In 1713, the first Harvard student publication, *The Tell Tale*, discussed the question "Whether it be Fornication to lye with one's Sweetheart (after Contraction) before marriage." And in 1766, during the first organized student revolt on record, Asa Dunbar (Henry Thoreau's grandfather) confronted a senior tutor at Harvard and proclaimed: "Behold, our butter stinketh and we cannot eat thereof. Now, give us, pray thee, butter that stinketh not."[3]

The colonial Puritans did, to be sure, have a strict moral code; they insisted on chastity before marriage and fidelity within marriage. But they never went tiptoeing around nervously and speaking in whispers when it came to sex. They glorified marriage and sexual union within marriage and took an exceedingly dim view of celibacy. The Rev. John Cotton once vigorously denounced a recently married couple in Boston who, he said, "immediately upon marriage, without ever approaching the *Nuptial* Bed," agreed to live apart from the rest of the world, "and afterwards from one another, too." He called it "blind zeal," for he said, "*it is not good that man should be alone.*" Another clergyman told his congregation that "the use of the Marriage bed" was "founded in man's Nature." A Boston congregation even expelled one of its members, James Mattock, because "he denied conjegal fellowship unto his wife for the space of two years. . . ."[4]

The Puritans were realistic. They recognized the power of the sexual drive and did what they could to keep it within the bounds of marriage. If married men arrived in Massachusetts Bay Colony without their wives, the magistrates ordered them to leave at once or arrange to bring their wives over as soon as possible. They also permitted divorces for people whose spouses were impotent or abusive. The divorce laws in Puritan New England in the 17th century were the easiest in the Western world.

What about the "Saints," that is, Puritans who had had conversion experiences, made public confessions of faith, and been admitted to church membership? In the records of churches in colonial Massachusetts, there are hundreds of confessions of premarital sexual relations, but if the experience of grace by would-be (but fallible) Saints seemed authentic, they were admitted to the church membership without any further ado. There were laws against premarital sex, to be sure, but the magistrates seem not to have enforced them strictly. The Puritans concentrated on preventive measures: encouraging early marriages and seeing to it that single people did not live alone. At Harvard, though, the Puritan boys enjoyed reading erotic lines from Shakespeare and they especially liked a poem by Robert Herrick that began with the line, "Gather ye rosebuds while ye may."[5]

Herrick's lines eventually became off-limits for pious Americans. In the early part of the 19th century, a series of religious revivals swept the country which not only produced a tremendous increase in Protestant church membership but also had a profound effect on middle-class American culture. Evangelical Protestantism, as it was called, tended to be ascetic in nature; it inculcated a series of prohibitions (don't drink, don't play cards, don't gamble, don't dance, don't swear, don't break the Sabbath), and was especially repressive when it came to sex. Respectable people, according to evangelical ideals, were serious, conscientious, and hard-working, and concerned themselves with the "higher" things of life. Victorian Americans, as historians call them today, were eager to show off their carefully cultivated refinement and good taste, especially to European visitors who might be inclined (as many Europeans were) to think of Americans, especially Westerners, as crude, ignorant, loudmouthed, and ill-mannered.[6]

Some of America's Victorians seem to have overdone it. At least Frances Trollope, an Englishwoman who lived in the United States for a time and wrote a book about her American experiences, thought so. In *Domestic Manners of the Americans* (1832), she recounted, almost in disbelief, her encounters with prudish people in Cincinnati and elsewhere. Once, she reported, she mentioned Alexander Pope's satirical poem, "The Rape of the Lock," to a young man, and he became extremely upset. "The very title!" he exclaimed. "Shakespeare, madam, is obscene," he went on to tell her, "and thank God, *we* are sufficiently advanced to have found it out! If we must have the abomination of stage plays, let them at least be marked by the refinement of the age in which we live." A little later a young German tourist came to Mrs. Trollope in search of some urgent advice. Though he was a gentleman with perfectly good manners, he had inadvertently offended some respectable people in Cincinnati for having used the word "corset" in front of some women. One old lady urged him to apologize, but, as he told Mrs. Trollope, he "felt himself greatly at a loss how to word it."[7]

While Mrs. Trollope was visiting Cincinnati, two ballet dancers from Europe put on a performance at one of the theaters there that, to her amazement, horrified respectable people in the city. Everyone "agreed that the morals of the Western world would never recover from the shock," reported Mrs. Trollope. "When I was asked if I had ever seen any thing as dreadful before, I was embarrassed how to answer, for the young women had been exceedingly careful, both in their dress and in their dancing, to meet the taste of the people." But, she went on, the "ladies altogether forsook the theatre; the gentlemen muttered under their breath, and turned their heads aside when the subject was mentioned; the clergy denounced them from the pulpit; and if they were named at the meetings of the saints, it was to show how deep the horror such a thing could produce. I could not but ask myself if virtue were a plant, thriving under one form in one country, and flourishing under a different one in another? If these western Americans are right, then how dreadfully wrong we are! It is a very puzzling subject."[8]

Mrs. Trollope's defense of the ballet infuriated Boston's *North American Review*. "What then is the puzzle?" the editors demanded to know. Then they described in some detail the outrageous performance which Mrs. Trollope had brazenly defended. "The attire of an opera dancer in Europe," they wrote, "which Mrs. Trollope judiciously designates as 'transparent,' appears to consist of flesh-coloured pantaloons, fitted as tight to the limbs as the skin they are designated to imitate, and over these, one single covering of gauze or some other transparent material stopping several inches *above* the knee. This is the *entire dress*, in which the opera dancers at London appear before mixed multitudes—before crowds of men and women assembled in the theatre. This is the dress, in which matrons and maidens of Great Britain behold, unblushing and delighted, the public appearances of persons of their own sex. So much for the dress. As for the dancing, particularly that part of it for which even Mrs. Trollope's lively and graphic pen could find no epithet more discriminative than 'remarkable,' it is remarkable indeed, and for two reasons;—first, that females not lost to shame, should be found to perform it, on the stage; and second, that they should find men and women of character to countenance the exhibition in the boxes.

The *pirouette*, in a word, is a movement, in which a woman, dressed as we have described, poising herself on one limb, extends the other to its full length, at right angles, and in this *graceful* attitude spins round, some eight or ten times, leaving her drapery, 'transparent' and short as it is at the best, to be carried up, by the centrifugal force imparted to it by the revolution of the dancer, as far as it will go. This we believe is an unexaggerated description of that scene, which Mrs. Trollope sneers at the ladies of Cincinnati for regarding with horror. Is there a father or a mother, a husband or wife, a brother or sister in Christendom . . . who would view it with anything but horror?"[9]

Prudishness, Mrs. Tollope noted amusedly, was not without its own special brand of playfulness. Typical, she said, was a light-hearted exchange between two young people, which she observed more than once. A young woman is making a shirt, for example, "which it would be a symptom of absolute depravity to name," so a young gentleman comes in and promptly asks her what she is making. "Only a frock for my sister's doll, sir," she says coyly. "A frock!" exclaims the gentleman, "not possible. Don't I see that it is not a frock? Come Miss Clarissa, what is it?" "'Tis just an apron, for one of our Negroes, Mr. Smith," she says demurely. "How can you, Miss Clarissa!" persists the gentleman. "Why is not the two sides joined together? I expect you better tell me what it is," "My!" cries the young lady, "why then, Mr. Smith, it is just a pillow-case." "Now that passes, Miss Clarissa!" cries the gentleman. "'Tis a pillow for a giant then. Shall I guess, Miss?" "Quit, Mr. Smith! behave yourself," cries the woman, "or I'll certainly be affronted." And, added Mrs. Trollope, "Before the conversation arrives at this point, both gentleman and lady are in convulsions of laughter. I once saw a young lady so hard driven by a wit, that to prove she was making a bag, and nothing but a bag, she sewed up the ends before his eyes, showing it triumphantly, and exclaiming, 'There now! what can you say to that?'"[10]

The evangelical prudishness that puzzled Mrs. Trollope—so different from the realistic view which colonial Puritans held—persisted well into the 20th century and left its mark everywhere on American culture. And then, suddenly, came the sexual revolution of the 1960s, putting an end, once and for all, to its dominance. Even Mrs. Trollope would have been shocked by the freewheeling nature of the so-called counterculture that emerged in the 1960s and '70s. So would the colonial Puritans. After all, as a clergyman told his congregation in old-time Boston: "God sent you not into this world as a Play-House, but a Work-house."[11]

CHAPTER 6

The Second and
the Fourth of July

The Continental Congress, meeting in Philadelphia, voted for independence from Great Britain on July 4, 1776.

Not so.

Congress voted for independence on July 2, 1776, not July 4. The following day, John Adams, one of the delegates from Massachusetts, wrote excitedly to his wife Abigail: "The second day of July 1776, will be the most memorable epocha in the history of America. I am apt to believe that it will be celebrated by succeeding generations as the great Anniversary Festival. . . . It ought to be solemnized with pomp, and parade, and shows, games, sports, balls, bonfires, and illuminations, from one end of this continent to the other, from this time forevermore." But in 1777, when American patriots celebrated the first anniversary of their independence, they did so on the fourth, not the second, and so it has continued until the present time.[1]

How did Adams manage to get it wrong? The answer is simple. On June 7, Richard Henry Lee, delegate from Virginia to the Second Continental Congress, submitted a resolution calling for independence, and it was on July 2 that Congress voted to adopt his resolution. Adams thought this would be the great day. On June 10, however, the delegates had appointed a committee to write up a statement giving reasons for independence, and on July 4, two days after the delegates voted to adopt Lee's independence resolution, they accepted the lengthy statement submitted by the committee which came to be called the Declaration of Independence.[2]

The committee that drafted the Declaration of Independence consisted of five members, including Benjamin Franklin, Thomas Jefferson, and John Adams, but in the end Jefferson wrote most of it. "The committee met, discussed the subject, then appointed Jefferson and me to make the draught, I suppose because we were the two first on the list," recalled Adams years later. "The subcommittee met. Jefferson proposed to me to make the draught," Adams remembered, and then recounted the little argument he and Jefferson got into. When Jefferson suggested Adams do the writing, the latter said firmly, "I will not." "You should do it," said Jefferson. "Oh! no," persisted Adams. "Why will you not?" asked Jefferson. "You ought to do it," "I will not," persisted Adams. "Why?" cried Jefferson. "Reasons enough," said Adams. "What can be your reasons?" Jefferson wanted to know. "Reason first—you are a Virginian, and a Virginian ought to appear at the head of this business," Adams explained. "Reason second—I am obnoxious, suspected, and unpopular. You are very much otherwise. Reason third—you can write ten times better than I can." "Well, said Jefferson, "if you are decided I will do as well as I can." "Very well," said Adams, "when you have drawn it up, we will have a meeting." Jefferson then wrote the Declaration of Independence, and the committee was so pleased with what Adams called Jefferson's "peculiar felicity of expression" that it was accepted with only minor revisions. And on July 4, the Philadelphia delegates, after deleting a paragraph in which Jefferson blamed King George III for the slave trade (and making a few other changes), voted to accept Jefferson's statement of the reasons why they had voted for independence two days before.[3]

July 4, the day the Continental Congress adopted Jefferson's declaration, rather than July 2, the day it adopted Lee's resolution, became the "great Anniversary Festival" that Adams had called for. It is easy to see why. Lee's resolution was matter-of-fact; Jefferson's statement, particularly the first part, was dramatic and moving. The Great Declaration which Jefferson wrote contained the natural-rights philosophy underlying the American Revolution and it elevated the War for Independence from a mere colonial rebellion to a war of liberation based on universal moral principles. "We hold these truths to be self-evident," Jefferson calmly told the world, "that all men are created equal, that they are endowed by their Creator with certain unalienable Rights, that among these are Life, Liberty and the pursuit of Happiness. That to secure these rights, Governments are instituted among Men, deriving their just powers from the consent of the governed. That whenever any Form of Government becomes destructive of these ends, it is the Right of the People to alter or to abolish it, and to institute new Government, laying its foundation on such principles and organizing its powers in such form, as to them shall seem most likely to effect their Safety and Happiness."

Although many Englishmen, and some Americans, too, scoffed at the philosophy Jefferson set forth in July 1776, countless people, in foreign lands as well as in America, were deeply moved by the powerful way he presented the case for government based on the consent of the governed and on respect for the rights of citizens. Condorcet, the great French *philosophe*, regarded Jefferson's Declaration as "a simple and sublime exposition of those rights so sacred and so long forgotten." And Jefferson himself never wavered in his conviction that the evidence for natural rights was "impressed on the sense" of every person. "We do not claim these under the charters of kings or legislators," he explained, "but under the King of kings."[4]

Twentieth-century scholars, however, have not for the most part shared Jefferson's confidence in an absolute basis for human rights. Discarding the whole notion of self-evident truths and natural rights (as well as the belief in a moral universe on which they were based) as illusory fictions, they have taken a historical rather than a metaphysical view of human rights and thus weakened their moral force. But as Yale philosopher Wilbur Urban used to exclaim: "How in hell can you have an ethics without a metaphysics?" Curiously enough, it was a Czech, not an American, who in the 1990s sought a surer foundation for human rights than a mere pledge of allegiance to ideas lingering from the past. Speaking in Philadelphia on July 4, 1994, Vaclav Havel, President of the Czech Republic, took account of the persistence of fierce tribal loyalties in the late 20th-century world (and the intolerance, strife, and persecution which these loyalties produced), and went on to say that the basis for a new world order must be universal respect for human rights. But such an imperative, he warned, was meaningless unless grounded in an environment that respected a sacred dimension: "the miracle of Being, the miracle of the Universe and the miracle of our own existence."

But what was the basis in the late 20th century for such a vision? President Havel found clues to what he was looking for in postmodern science as well as in ancient religions. In the "anthropic cosmological principle" he found the idea that human beings "are not at all just an accidental anomaly, the microscopic caprice of a tiny particle whirling in the endless depths of the universe," but, instead, "mysteriously connected to the universe" and "mirrored in it, just as the entire universe is mirrored in us." And from the "Gaia hypothesis" came the idea that the Earth was a kind of "megaorganism, a living planet," of which human beings were a part and on which they depended. The "anthropic principle" and the "Gaia hypothesis," Havel observed, "remind us of what we have long suspected . . . and what perhaps has always lain dormant within us as archetypes. That is, the awareness of our being anchored in the Earth and the universe, the awareness that we are not here alone nor for ourselves alone, but that we are an integral part of higher, mysterious entities against whom it is not advisable to blaspheme." Havel's conclusion was thoroughly Jeffersonian: "The Declaration of Independence, adopted 218 years ago in this building states that the Creator gave men the right to liberty. It seems man can realize that liberty only if he does not forget the One who endowed him with it."[5]

CHAPTER 7

George Washington's
Prayer at Valley Forge

General Washington prayed on his knees in the snow at Valley Forge during the American Revolution.

Not so.

Today just about every American knows that the story about Washington's chopping down a cherry tree is a fable, but some people are still taken in by the equally spurious story about Washington's praying at Valley Forge. Mason Locke ("Parson") Weems, an Episcopalian minister and popular writer who in 1800 published the first biography of Washington, made up both the cherry tree story and the Valley Forge tale. His story about the pious Quaker who abandoned his pacifism after overhearing the American commander utter a fervent prayer at Valley Forge is, however, not without charm.

"In the winter of 1777," wrote Weems soon after Washington's death, "while Washington, with the American army, lay encamped at Valley Forge, a certain good old FRIEND, of the respectable family and name of Potts, if I mistake not, had occasion to pass through the woods near headquarters. Treading his way along the venerable grove, suddenly he heard the sound of a human voice, which, as he advanced, increased on his ear; and at length became like the voice of one speaking much in earnest. As he approached the spot with a cautious step, whom should he behold, in a dark natural bower of ancient oaks, but the commander in chief of the American armies on his knees in prayer! Motionless with surprise,

29

Friend Potts continued on the place till the general, having ended his devotion, arose; and, with countenance of angelic serenity, retired to headquarters. Friend Potts then went home, and on entering his parlour called out to his wife, 'Sarah! my dear Sarah! all's well! all's well! George Washington will yet prevail!' 'What's the matter, Isaac?' replied she, 'thee seems moved.' 'Well, if I seem moved, 'tis no more than what I really am. I have this day seen what I never expected. Thee knows that I always thought that the sword and the gospel were utterly inconsistent; and that no man could be a soldier and a christian at the same time. But George Washington has this day convinced me of my mistake.' He then related what he had seen, and concluded with the prophetical remark—'If George Washington be not a man of God, I am greatly deceived—and still more shall I be deceived, if God do not, through him, work out a great salvation for America.'"[1]

The Potts story has been the most cherished of all the anecdotes about Washington's piety, though, interestingly, it was never alluded to by Quaker writers on Washington, not even those of a "Free Quaker" or non-pacifist persuasion. It has been repeated with countless variations since Weems first put it forward; scores of "witnesses" attesting to the event (many years later) have been unearthed by champions of the story; and many details have been added to Weem's original account by subsequent writers. Isaac Potts, according to later versions of the event, was a Quaker preacher; he saw "the tears flowing copiously" down Washington's cheeks during the prayer and he himself "bust into tears" as he told his wife (variously referred to as Sarah, Betty, and Martha) about his experience. In addition, good patriot that he had become, he thereafter "sent Washington many items concerning movements of the enemy."[2]

The Valley Forge story is utterly without foundation in fact. There was indeed a Quaker farmer named Isaac Potts who came into possession of a house in Valley Forge toward the end of the Revolutionary War, but he was nowhere near Valley Forge in the winter of 1777 when Washington was supposed to have been praying in the snow. Nevertheless, Washington's "Gethsemane," as the Valley Forge episode has been called, was eventually fixed in bronze on the Sub-Treasury Building in New York City and Potts's house itself was made into a shrine. It has also been celebrated in verse:

Oh! who shall know the might
Of the words he utter'd there?
The fate of nations there was turn'd
By the fervor of his prayer.
But wouldst thou know his name
Who wandered there alone?
Go, read enrolled in Heaven's archives,
The prayer of Washington.[3]

In June 1903, moreover, the cornerstone of the million-dollar Washington Memorial Chapel, commemorating the event, was laid in Valley Forge; in 1928 the United States government issued a batch of two-cent stamps showing Washington praying at Valley Forge; and in 1955 a private chapel for the use of U.S. Congressmen was opened in the Capitol, containing, as its chief feature, a stained-glass window above an oak altar depicting the kneeling figure of Washington at Valley Forge. Even "Parson" Weems, one guesses, would have been somewhat surprised by the solemn literalism with which many of his readers interpreted his exuberant narrative of *The Life of George Washington; with Curious Anecdotes, Equally Honourable to Himself, and Exemplary to His Young Country.*

Washington was in fact a typical 18th-century deist, like Benjamin Franklin and Thomas Jefferson, who believed in what he called a "Supreme Architect of the Universe." He was a member of the Anglican (later Episcopalian) church in Virginia, served on the vestry, attended services with a fair degree of regularity, and was convinced that religion was an indispensable basis for morality. But he was not especially pious. His references to God, in public addresses and in letters to relatives and friends, were all deistic in nature: Grand Architect, Governor of the Universe, Higher Cause, Great Ruler of Events, Supreme Architect of the Universe, Author of the Universe, Great Creator, Director of Human Events, and Supreme Ruler. He was not given to praying on his knees nor to referring to Jesus in public or in private. Nor did he partake of the sacrament of the Lord's Supper in his church. When he attended Christ Church in Philadelphia during his presidency, he invariably left just before communion (his wife stayed), and when the minister one Sunday referred to the poor example "those in elevated stations" were setting, he stopped going to the church at all on communion Sundays.[4]

On March 3, 1797, just before Washington left office as President, some Philadelphia clergymen, by pre-arrangement, presented him with a congratulatory address written in such a way as to elicit some remarks from him about his views on Christianity. But as one of the ministers ruefully admitted afterward, "the old fox was too cunning for them."[5] To the clergyman's disappointment, Washington simply reiterated his belief in the close association between religion and morality and then shifted to a favorite topic of his when speaking to religious groups: religious toleration. "I view with unspeakable pleasure," he told the clergymen, "that harmony and Brotherly Love which characterizes the clergymen of different parts of the United States, exhibiting to the world a new and interesting spectacle, at one the pride of our Country and the surest basis of universal Harmony."[6]

CHAPTER 8

George Washington's
False Teeth

Washington's dentures were made of wood.

No, they weren't.

The legend that Washington wore wooden dentures dies hard. When Presidents' Day was being celebrated on February 19, 1991, one New Yorker summed up what he knew about the Father of His Country: "I know he had wooden teeth."[1]

Washington's dentures were, in fact, made of ivory. A New York City dentist, John Greenwood, made several sets for the President and none of them contained any wood. For years Greenwood tried to save Washington's last remaining tooth, the first bicuspid in his left lower jaw. In 1789, when he made his first set of teeth for the President—carved from hippopotamus ivory, to which some human teeth (from a previous owner) were attached with gold rivets—he made a hole in the left lower plate which fitted snugly over the President's last natural tooth. In 1796, however, he had to extract the lone tooth, and after taking it out he put a wire through it so Washington could suspend it on his watch chain if he so desired. Later on, when the tooth came into Greenwood's possession, he had it encased in a gold locket and inscribed it thusly: "In New York 1790. Jn Greenwood made Pres Geo Washington a whole sett of teeth. The enclosed tooth is the last one which grew in his head."[2]

Washington exchanged several letters with his dentist. Not only did he discuss various problems with the dentures; he also complained that one set had turned black. Greenwood blamed it on the port wine Washington liked to imbibe; since the wine was sour, he said, it took all the polish and color out of the ivory. His advice was for Washington to take his dentures out after dinner and put them in some clean water, while wearing another set. He also suggested cleaning them with a brush and some chalk. If the blackness persisted, he said, Washington should try soaking the dentures in broth or pot liquor or porter (stout).[3]

Some of the dentures Washington used pushed his mouth out of shape. When Gilbert Stuart came to do portraits of the President, he emphasized the distortions of Washington's mouth. He did so partly because he and Washington never hit it off well during numerous sittings. The result, as historian James Thomas Flexner noted, was that Stuart's portraits "have encouraged the world to think of Washington as the hero with ill fitting false teeth."[4]

CHAPTER 9

The Founding Fathers and Democracy

The Founding Fathers believed in democracy.

No way.

The Founding Fathers, that is, the men who framed the Constitution, disagreed about many things, but on one point they were in complete agreement: that democracy meant mob rule and if unchecked would pose a grave threat to life, liberty, and property. They insisted on the consent of the governed, of course, and favored representative, that is, republican, government; but in the framework of government they devised in Philadelphia during the summer of 1787 they placed severe limitations on the possibility of the American people participating directly in their national government.

The framers of the Constitution made no secret of their distrust of democracy in the debates they got into over various clauses in the Constitution they were forming. "The voice of the people has been said to be the voice of God," announced New York's Alexander Hamilton at one point, "and however generally this maxim has been quoted and believed, it is not true in fact. The people are turbulent and changing; they seldom judge or determine right." Hamilton told his colleagues it was foolish to think that a "democratic assembly" would "pursue the common good" or that it was possible to have "a good executive upon a democratic plan." His advice was to place as many checks as possible in the Constitution on "the imprudence of democracy."[1]

Hamilton, to be sure, believed in high-toned government, and his cynicism about human nature in general was so outspoken that on one occasion it brought a protest from Virginia's James Madison. But he wasn't the only delegate to take an exceedingly critical view of democracy. Virginia's George Mason expressed grave doubts about the ability of the people to choose a chief executive wisely. It would be, he told his colleagues, "as unnatural to refer the choice of a proper character for chief Magistrate to the people, as it would, to refer a trial of colours to a blind man. The extent of the Country renders it impossible that the people can have the requisite capacity to judge of the respective pretensions of the Candidates."[2] Maryland's John F. Mercer agreed. "The people," he said, "cannot know and judge of the characters of the Candidates. The worst possible choice will be made."[3] James McHenry, Mercer's colleague from Maryland, declared that democracy was synonymous with "confusion and licentiousness," and Virginia's Edmund Randolph spoke of "the turbulence and follies of democracy."[4] At one point Connecticut's Roger Sherman and Massachusetts's Elbridge Gerry had a little exchange on the subject. "The people," said Sherman, "immediately should have as little to do as may be about the Government. They want information and are constantly liable to be misled." Responded Gerry: "The evils we experience flow from the excess of democracy. The people do not want virtue, but are the dupes of the pretended patriots." Then alluding to a farmers' uprising (Shays's Rebellion) the year before, he continued: "In Massachusetts it has been fully confirmed by experience that they are daily misled into the most baneful measures and opinions by the false reports circulated by designing men, and which no one on the spot can refute."[5]

The Founding Fathers took an aristocratic view of politics. They believed that the upper classes should assume leadership in government and politics because the masses of people lacked the capacity to govern wisely. "The people ever have been and ever will be unfit to retain the exercise of power in their own hands," declared William Livingston, delegate from New York; "they must of Necessity delegate it somewhere. . . . But further, as prejudices always prevail more or less, in all popular governments, it is necessary that a check be placed somewhere in the hands of a power not immediately dependent upon the breath of the people, in order to stem the torrent, and prevent the mischiefs which blind passions and rancorous prejudices might otherwise occasion." Edmund Randolph, like Livingston, saw dangers in "the democratic parts of our constitution."[6]

What "democratic parts"? Randolph was probably thinking of the House of Representatives. In arranging for the people of the different states to vote directly for members of what came to be called the Lower House of Congress, the Constitution-makers did make one concession to democracy and majority rule. Everywhere else, though, they severely limited popular rule. The state legislatures were to elect U.S. Senators (serving longer terms than Representatives); an Electoral College, whose members were chosen by the states, was to pick the President; and the President himself was to choose Federal judges with the advice and consent of the Senate. But the Founding Fathers, it is important to remember, feared despotism as well as democracy. Distrusting human nature (especially in positions of power) as they did, they carefully put together a government of checks and balances which they hoped would limit the powers of federal officials, no matter how they were chosen, in all three branches of government. Still, there is no question but that they deliberately limited the "democratic parts" of the Constitution which they drew up for the American people in 1787.

There was nothing unusual in the Founding Fathers' distrust of democracy; it was conventional wisdom in the 18th century. Even well into the 19th century, in the United States as well as Western Europe, the word "democracy" had unsavory connotations (mob, rabble, anarchy), especially among conservatives. Thomas Jefferson did not use the word either in the Declaration of Independence or in any of his public pronouncements while he was President. (During his presidency a newspaper in Baltimore called itself *The Republican; or, Anti-Democrat.*) Even Andrew Jackson avoided the word in the public statements he made while in the White House. And for years the party of Jefferson and Jackson called itself the Republican party, though on a local level some party groups began calling themselves "democratic" or "democratic-republican" in the early 19th century. In 1840, the party of Jefferson and Jackson referred to "the Democratic faith" in resolutions adopted at its national convention, but also to "their Republican fellow citizens." Not until 1844 did the party finally jettison the word "Republican" and call itself "the American Democracy" in one of the resolutions adopted at its national convention that year. From then on, it was the Democratic party. In 1854, the newly formed party of Abraham Lincoln resurrected Jefferson's old word and called itself the Republican party. Years later, Woodrow Wilson referred to the United States as a democracy in public statements made during World War I. He was the first President to do so and after that it became customary to call the country a democracy.[7]

In the 1950s, the ultraconservative John Birch Society insisted vehemently that the United States was a republic, not a democracy. If by republic the Birchers meant representative government, there was some truth in their contention. In the Constitutional Convention, and in the *Federalist* (the series of articles by Jay, Hamilton, and Madison urging ratification of the 1787 document), it was taken for granted that the new government was republican (representative) in nature. Still, as historian Charles Beard pointed out years ago, the Constitution itself nowhere officially proclaims the United States to be a republic. There is one clause, it is true, in which the Constitution guarantees each state a republican form of government, but it does not explain what that means. And though it became customary in the early years of the new nation to refer to the United States as a republic in official and diplomatic papers, there was no constitutional sanction for the practice. As far as the Constitution is concerned, Beard insisted, the country is simply "The United States of America."[8]

The United States, as conservatives have long insisted, is undoubtedly a republic. But with the democratization of the Constitution by various amendments (as, for example, the 17th Amendment, providing for the direct election of senators) during the 19th and 20th centuries, it has gradually become a democracy as well. Today the terms are virtually interchangeable.

CHAPTER 10

The Declaration, the Constitution, and Natural Rights

The Constitution guarantees to American citizens life, liberty, and the pursuit of happiness.

No, it doesn't.

It's the Declaration of Independence, not the U.S. Constitution, which proclaims, as a self-evident truth, that all men are created equal, that they are endowed with certain inalienable rights, including life, liberty, and the pursuit of happiness, and that governments are instituted to secure these rights and must rest on consent of the governed.

It's amazing how many educated Americans confuse the Great Declaration with the U.S. Constitution. On September 16, 1993, Jack Faris, president of the National Federation of Independent Business, criticized President Clinton's health-care plan by saying: "We checked the Constitution, and we don't see where it gives you the right to universal health insurance. The Constitution says we have the right to life, liberty, and the pursuit of happiness. That's what small business is about. Well, this [plan] is reducing our pursuit of happiness." Faris had every right, of course, to complain about Clinton's health plan, but it is clear that he didn't check the Constitution carefully. If he had, he would have discovered that it says nothing about pursuit of happiness and that it doesn't even mention inalienable natural rights in general.[1]

It has been customary to say that the Declaration of Independence was liberal, even radical, and far-reaching in its sentiments, while the Constitution was sober-minded, cautious, and conservative. There is some truth in this contention, but it is also important to note that there is an unmistakable continuity between the liberal Declaration and the conservative Constitution. The Constitution, for one thing, singles out several basic objectives, just as the Declaration did, and among these are: "establish Justice," "promote the general Welfare," and "secure the Blessings of Liberty to ourselves and our Posterity." For another, the Constitution takes for granted the Declaration's natural-rights philosophy and, in attempting to safeguard the American people's inalienable rights, forbids the federal government to do certain things: suspend the writ of habeas corpus; pass bills of attainder or ex post facto laws; grant titles of nobility.

The so-called Bill of Rights (the first ten amendments to the Constitution, added in 1791) takes the same natural-rights approach. It does not contain a list of rights which the government presumes to confer on citizens, as did, for example, the Soviet Constitution of 1936. What it does is to accept the people's inalienable natural rights as a given, even before the formation of government, and concentrate on spelling out with some precision the various ways in which the federal government should keep its hands off citizens' rights. The new federal government, according to the Bill of Rights, is not to interfere with the American people's free exercise of religion or with their freedom of speech, press, and assembly; nor is it to subject them to such flagrant violations of their inherent rights as unreasonable searches and seizures, double jeopardy, deprivation of life, liberty, or property without due process of law, excessive bail, and cruel and unusual punishments. Just to be sure that the intent of the Bill of Rights is absolutely clear, the framers even included one sweeping assertion: "The enumeration in the Constitution of certain rights, shall not be construed to deny or disparage others retained by the people" (9th Amendment).

The natural-rights philosophy on which the United States was founded came in for vehement criticism from conservatives at the time of the American Revolution. British Tories, as well as American Loyalists, ridiculed the idea of inalienable rights as dangerous nonsense and pointed out that some of the Revolutionary leaders (like Thomas Jefferson) were slave-owners even though they professed to believe in natural rights. The conservative hostility to natural rights continued undiminished into the 19th century. When abolitionists like William Lloyd Garrison appealed to natural rights in condemning the institution of slavery, proslavery apologists like John C. Calhoun went to great lengths to demonstrate that liberty was a privilege, earned by superior people, not a natural right, possessed by all human beings. Once, just before the Civil War, conservative Boston lawyer Joseph Choate scornfully dismissed the natural-rights ideas of the Declaration of Independence as "glittering generalities." But transcendentalist writer Ralph Waldo Emerson quickly retorted: "Say, rather, GLITTERING UBIQUITIES!"[2]

Choate, not Emerson, seems to have triumphed with 20th-century historians and social analysts. Modern scholarship has not taken kindly to ubiquities, glittering or otherwise. Sociologist William Graham Sumner, for one, conceded that the natural-rights doctrine had been useful in the struggle against arbitrary government, but he insisted that its usefulness had long since passed, and, with the coming of Darwinism, it was necessary to take a more realistic view: that rights of any kind were the achievements of society, not a gift of nature, and that they emerged as folkways during the long course of social evolution and then, when deemed essential to social viability, developed into mores, carrying a moral sanction for observance. The historical view of human rights which Sumner took in the late 19th century gradually became standard wisdom in the scholarly world during the 20th century.[3]

Still, American historians could not help acknowledging the enormous appeal of the natural-rights philosophy throughout U.S. history. From the Revolutionary period onward, they recognized, whenever minority groups—abolitionists, feminists, Populists, trade unionists, democratic socialists—sought to expand their influence and broaden their opportunities in the American system, they inevitably appealed to the philosophy of the Declaration of Independence to justify their stand. By the 20th century, moreover, many conservatives also found themselves turning to the natural-rights doctrine in their resistance to the expansion of government activity during the Progressive and New Deal periods of our history. Business leader John Faris may have mislocated his beloved phrase "pursuit of happiness," but he knew exactly what he was doing when he cited it.

CHAPTER 11

The Religion of
Thomas Paine

Thomas Paine was an atheist.

No, he wasn't.

In one of his books, Theodore Roosevelt contemptuously dismissed Paine as "a filthy little atheist," but he could not have been more wrong. Paine was not, so far as we know, unusually diminutive nor spectacularly sleazy, and if we take him at his word, no atheist. But Texas newspaper columnist Molly Ivins also got it wrong—she called him a "splendid atheist"—in one of her pieces appearing in September 1993. The misconception persists.[1]

Paine was a deist, like George Washington and Thomas Jefferson. He believed in a Great Creator and Grand Architect of the Universe and in life eternal too. And like Jefferson, he believed that God had endowed human beings with the natural right to life and liberty and that human institutions should respect and nourish these God-given rights.[2]

Why, then Paine's reputation as an atheist? Mainly because his lengthy treatise, *Age of Reason*, appearing in 1794 and 1795, was a blast against organized religion. Paine was a warm supporter of the French Revolution (until it descended into a reign of terror) and, appalled by the close ties between the church and the Old Regime in France, he concluded that organized religion had for centuries been one of the main enemies of freedom. But Paine wrote *Age of Reason* to counteract atheism as well as orthodoxy, for he feared that in the general overturn of established religious institutions and practices in

France during the Revolution people might "lose sight of morality, of humanity, and of the theology that is true."[3]

What was the "true theology" for Paine? He summed it up briefly in his book: "I believe in one God, and no more, and I hope for happiness beyond this life." He went on to say that religious duties consisted of "doing justice, loving mercy, and endeavoring to make our fellow creatures happy." And though he was a deist, not a Christian, he spoke respectfully of Jesus: "He was a virtuous and an amiable man" and "the morality he preached and practiced was of the most benevolent kind." Paine thought the Quakers came closer than any other Christian group to following in Jesus' footsteps.[4]

But *Age of Reason* mostly accentuated the negative. In it, Paine announced that he most emphatically did not believe in the creeds professed by the Jewish, Roman, Greek, Turkish, Protestant, or any other organized religion, and he announced defiantly: "My own mind is my own church." All national church establishments, Christian, or otherwise, he went on to say, were "no other than human inventions, set up to terrify and enslave mankind, and monopolize power and profit." Then he went after the Bible. He rejected it as the word of God, questioned the historical authenticity of the events recorded in it, subjected the ideas it contained to scathing criticism, and went through the Old Testament and the New, book by book, reducing most of their ideas to absurdity. He had good words only for the Psalms and the Book of Job, both of which, he acknowledged, contained a great deal of sentiment reverentially expressed about the power and benignity of the Almighty. The Old Testament, in short, was mostly a mélange of "obscene stories, voluptuous debaucheries, cruel and tortuous executions, and unrelenting vindictiveness," and the New Testament, with its miracles, degraded "the Almighty into a character of showman, playing tricks to amuse and make the people stare and wonder." For Paine, Jesus was not divine; he was no more the son of God than was any other human being. And though his moral teachings were splendid, similar systems of morality had been preached by Confucius and some of the Greek philosophers years before him. Furthermore, the Christian church had set up a system of religion utterly contradictory to the character of the person whose name it bore. "It has set up a religion of pomp and of revenue, in pretended imitation of a person whose life was humility and poverty."[5]

Was there, then, to be no word of God? Was there to be no divine revelation for humanity? There was indeed, Paine hastened to say. "The WORD OF GOD IS THE CREATION WE BEHOLD," he exclaimed, "and it is this *word*, which no human invention can counterfeit or alter, that God speaketh universally to man." "God's power," said Paine, "is found in the immensity of the universe; his wisdom in the unchangeable order by which the incomprehensible whole" was governed; his munificence in the abundance with which he filled the Earth; and his mercy in not withholding that abundance even from the unthankful. "In fine," said Paine, "do we want to know what God is? Search not the book called Scripture, which any human mind might make, but the Scripture called creation."[6]

Paine's *Age of Reason* delighted free-thinkers and appalled Christian believers everywhere. Devout people in the United States called it "The Devil's Prayer Book" and excoriated Paine as an atheist, infidel, sot, adulterer, reptile, monster, and "lily-livered rogue." In 1801, when President Jefferson invited him to return to the United States from France on a government vessel there was an outburst of indignation among the orthodox in America. "What!" exclaimed a Boston newspaper, "invite to the United States that lying, drunken, brutal infidel, who rejoiced in the opportunity of basking and wallowing in the confusion, devastation, bloodshed, rapine, and murder in which his soul delights!"[7]

When Paine finally returned to the United States in 1802 to live out his remaining years, he was treated like a pariah. Even the Quakers held him at arm's length. In 1809, he died in Greenwich Village in poverty and obscurity, still hoping for the final triumph of a religion of reason in America. He would doubtless have been chagrined by the resurgence of religious "fundamentalism" in the United States toward the end of the 20th century. But he probably would also have been disappointed by the spread of atheism among urban peoples in the Western world as technology gradually replaced nature as the center of things.

CHAPTER 12

Thomas Jefferson and
Sally Hemings

Thomas Jefferson took Sally Hemings, an attractive young slave women at Monticello, as his mistress and had five children by her.

Almost certainly not.

It is biographer Fawn Brodie who is largely responsible for the current belief in the Sally Hemings legend. In her 1974 bestseller, *Thomas Jefferson: An Intimate Life*, Brodie resurrected an old wives' (and husbands') tale about Jefferson which was first put into circulation by Jefferson's enemies while he was President: that a few years after the death of his wife Martha in 1782 he took Sally Hemings, one of his slave girls, as his mistress and fathered five children by her. To the Hemings story (which has surfaced periodically since Jefferson's day), Brodie added an embellishment of her own. Jefferson's relations with Sally, she insisted, were marvelously tender and deeply satisfying and secretly brought the two of them much happiness for thirty-eight years.

Brodie developed the romantic angle by reading creatively between the lines and uncovering delicious Freudian slips here and there in Jefferson's writings. Her aim, she announced, was to humanize Jefferson and to disprove the charge of his critics that his "blood is very snow-broth." For the tenderness of Jefferson's relations with Sally, she has no evidence whatsoever. For the assertion that Sally was Jefferson's concubine for many years, she relied on rumors that were circulating when Jefferson became President. But there is no hard evidence for the Jefferson-Hemings involvement.

Twentieth-century historians—including experts on Jefferson like Dumas Malone, Merrill Peterson, and biographer Willard Sterne Randall—have never taken the story seriously.[1]

It was James T. Callender, a notoriously scurrilous political journalist (he called John Adams a "British spy" and said George Washington was a shameless Revolutionary profiteer), who first put the Hemings story into circulation. Miffed because he did not receive an appointment as postmaster in Richmond under the Jefferson administration, he started attacking the President in the pages of Virginia's *Richmond Recorder*. On September 1, 1802, he announced: "It is well known that the man whom *it delighteth the people to honor* keeps, and for many years has kept, as his concubine, one of his own slaves. Her name is SALLY. . . . By this wench Sally, our president has had several children. . . . The AFRICAN VENUS is said to officiate, as housekeeper at Monticello." The Federalist press took up Callender's story about "Black Sal" with relish and spread it widely throughout the land accompanied by satirical poems dedicated to "Dusky Sally" and to "the Sage of Monticello." Jefferson's friends and neighbors denied the tale, but Jefferson himself remained silent. His policy was to ignore personal attacks—his political foes called him inter alia, an atheist, free lover, and dangerous radical—on the theory that "the man who fears no truth had nothing to fear from lies." He did, though, indirectly deny the truth of Callender's story in letters to two of his friends.[2]

But Callender's story lived on. In 1848, William Wells Brown, a former slave, published a poem called "Jefferson's Daughter," and in 1853 he came out with a novel entitled *Clotel, Or the President's Daughter*, based on the Callender story. In 1873, moreover, two former Monticello slaves (one of them Sally's son), in interviews with S. F. Wetmore for Ohio's *Pike County Republican*, backed up the story told by Callender. But the testimony of the two former slaves—Madison Hemings, Sally's son, and Israel Jefferson—given in old age, was exceedingly shaky. In *The Jefferson Scandals: A Rebuttal* (1982), Virginius Dabney, Pulitzer Prize-winning journalist, carefully analyzed the Wetmore interviews and, like historian Dumas Malone (who won a Pulitzer Prize for his multi-volumed biography of Jefferson), found them misleading, full of inaccuracies, possibly doctored up by the interviewer, and clothed in improbable prose.[3]

In refuting Callender's story, Dabney cited a letter which Jefferson wrote his Secretary of the Navy, Robert Smith, in 1805, in which, by admitting to one indiscretion in his youth (he tried to seduce Betsey Walker, wife of a friend), he denied by implication the story about Sally which his political foes were making so much of. "You will perceive," Jefferson told Smith, "that I plead guilty to one of their charges, that when young and single I offered love to a handsome [married] lady. I acknowledge its incorrectness. It is the only one founded on truth among all their allegations against me." Dabney found convincing, too, the testimony of Edmund Bacon, longtime overseer at Monticello, who, in an interview with the Rev. Hamilton W. Pierson, president of Cumberland College in Princeton, Kentucky, in 1862, had this to say about Sally's daughter Harriet: "He [Jefferson] freed one girl some years ago before he died, and there was a great deal of talk about it. She was nearly white as anybody, and very beautiful. People said he freed her because she was his own daughter. She was not his daughter, she was ————'s daughter. I know that. I have seen him come out of her mother's room many a morning when I went up to Monticello very early."[4]

Who was the person coming out of Sally's room "many a morning"? Dabney believed it was one of Jefferson's nephews: either Peter or Samuel Carr. In *The Jefferson Scandals*, Dabney reproduced a conversation (recorded in 1868) which Jefferson biographer Henry S. Randall had with Thomas J. Randolph, Jefferson's grandson, in which the latter declared that Sally was the mistress of Peter Carr and that Sally's sister Betsy was the mistress of Samuel. From "these connections," Randolph added, "sprang the progeny which resembled Jefferson." One day, Randolph told Randall, he came across a newspaper containing "some very insulting remarks about Mr. Jefferson's mulatto children," and he handed Peter the paper and pointed to the article about Jefferson in it. Peter read it, according to Randolph, "tears coursing down his cheeks, and then handed it to Samuel. Samuel also shed tears. Peter exclaimed, 'Arn't you and I . . . a couple of ——— pretty fellows to bring this disgrace on poor old uncle who has always fed us! We ought to be ——— by ————!'" Dabney pointed out that Ellen Randolph Coolidge, Jefferson's granddaughter, provided additional testimony for the Carr boys' involvement. In a long letter to her husband on October 24, 1858, dealing with the "yellow children" at Monticello, she reported that when her brother Thomas was a young man he once heard Peter Carr say, with a laugh, that "the old grandfather [Thomas Jefferson] had to bear the blame for his and Sam's . . . misdeeds."[5]

Why did Jefferson keep mum about all this? Jefferson's unwillingness to deny the Hemings story publicly is readily explained, Dabney thought, by the fact that if he had gone public he would have implicated other members of his family. "Bear in mind," wrote Dabney, "that his father-in-law, John Wayles, was widely regarded as the sire of Sally Hemings and five other children by the slave Betty Hemings, and that these illegitimates were therefore the half-sisters and brothers of Jefferson's beloved wife. Consider also that his two nephews, Peter and Sam Carr, were in all likehood the progenitors of other groups of mulattoes at Monticello, including Sally's children. In proclaiming his own innocence, Jefferson could hardly have avoided implicating his close kin. He chose to suffer in silence."[6]

Virginius Dabney—and Dumas Malone—have made a powerful and well-nigh irrefutable case against Callender, but it is unrealistic to think they have succeeded in consigning the Hemings tale to oblivion. (Producers of the movie *Jefferson in Paris,* in 1995, expectably featured the old chestnut about Sally.) Some 20th-century blacks—overlooking the fact that Callender hardly meant his allegation as a compliment—cherished the Hemings tale because it linked black people with one of America's great historical figures. And some 20th-century whites also liked the story because it enabled them to add the Sage of Monticello to the list of famous Americans whom they enjoy belittling. But all of the myth-cherishers failed to take account of the fact, well documented, that Jefferson fell deeply in love with Maria Cosway, a married woman, when he was American envoy to France in the 1780s, and that, as Jefferson biographer Willard Sterne Randall put it in 1993, "it is impossible to believe that Jefferson abandoned his love for Maria Cosway to force his affections on even the most beautiful adolescent slave girl."

CHAPTER 13

Thomas Jefferson on Government

Thomas Jefferson is the author of the much-quoted statement: "That government is best that governs least."

Not so. He may have believed it but he never said it.

It was John O'Sullivan, one of the founders and editors of the *United States Magazine and Democratic Review*, who first made the statement. In the introduction to the very first issue of the journal in the fall of 1837, O'Sullivan announced, "The best government is that which governs least," and then went on to develop the idea at length. "No human depositories," he said, "can with safety, be trusted with the power of legislation upon the general interests of society so as to operate directly or indirectly on the industry and property of the community. Such power must be perpetually liable to the most pernicious abuse, from the natural imperfection, both in wisdom of judgment and purity of purpose, of all human legislation, exposed constantly to the pressure of partial interests; interests which, at the same time that they are essentially selfish and tyrannical, are ever vigilant, persevering, and subtle in all the arts of deception and corruption. In fact, the whole history of human society and government may be safely appealed to, in evidence that the abuse of such power a thousand fold more than overbalances its beneficial use."[1]

More than a decade after O'Sullivan wrote these words, Henry David Thoreau picked out the first sentence of the *United States Magazine* editor's assault on government and used it, without indicating its source, in his famous essay justifying civil disobedience when a government demands unethical behavior on the part of citizens. Later on, writers began attributing the statement to Jefferson and it gradually became one of the most popular quotations ever put in the great Virginian's mouth. The erroneous attribution is not surprising. Long before O'Sullivan, Jefferson had voiced sentiments similar to O'Sullivan's, both publicly and in private. For example, in his First Inaugural Address, on March 4, 1801, he called for a "wise and frugal government which shall restrain men from injuring one another, which shall leave them otherwise free to regulate their own pursuits of industry and improvement, and shall not take from the mouth of labor the bread it has earned. This is the sum of good government, and this is necessary to close the circle of our felicities."[2]

But neither O'Sullivan nor Jefferson was completely loyal to the weak-government philosophy they preached. O'Sullivan's journal gave voice to the powerful nationalism of the early 19th century and promoted a vigorous territorial expansionist policy for the young American republic. In an article that O'Sullivan himself probably wrote for the *United States Magazine* in the summer of 1845 he came up with some more famous words: "our manifest destiny to overspread the continent allotted by Providence for the free development of our yearly multiplying millions."[3] Jefferson also supported territorial expansion, and as President, he turned out to be anything but a minimalist when it came to federal action. He approved the purchase of Louisiana from France in 1803, even though the U.S. Constitution nowhere authorizes the acquisition of new territory by the federal government. He also sponsored the Lewis and Clark overland exploring expedition of 1804–06. In his Second Inaugural Address, in March 1805, moreover, he recommended amending the Constitution so the federal government could spend money on roads, canals, the arts, manufactures, and education.[4] And in 1807, in an effort to force Britain and France (then at war) to respect America's trading rights, he sponsored the Embargo Act prohibiting the export of any goods from the United States by land or sea. When "embargo breakers" thumbed their noses at the federal government and shamelessly defied the law, he supported the Force Act in 1809 permitting federal officials without warrant to seize goods they suspected were intended for foreign ports. Cried an irate New Hampshire poet:

Our ships all in motion,
Once whiten'd the ocean
They sail'd and return'd with a Cargo;
Now doom'd to decay
They are fallen a prey,
To Jefferson, worms, and EMBARGO.[5]

Sometimes people are remembered more for what they say than for what they do.

CHAPTER 14

James Madison and
Congressional Power

James Madison the "Father of the Constitution," feared that Congress was becoming too powerful.

No, he didn't.

Madison's worry was always about the concentration of powers in any one branch of government, whether legislative, executive, or judicial.

It was President George Bush who first put the story in circulation that Madison was fearful of congressional aggrandizement. As a Republican, Bush continually clashed with a Congress dominated by Democrats and he thought he was scoring points with the American people (and members of Congress) when he reminded them that James Madison, commonly thought of as "the Father of the Constitution," had the same problem with Congress as he did.

Bush cited Madison in a speech at Princeton on May 10, 1991, in which he talked about the recent Gulf War, to which he had committed U.S. forces under a U.N. resolution, an action which most members of Congress supported, though with some misgivings about the President's reluctance to consult with them about his decision to go to war. As President of the United States, he announced, he had the "inherent power" to commit American forces to battle on his own, even though he had great respect for Congress and preferred to work cooperatively with the national legislators whenever possible. "So, while a President does bear special foreign policy obligations," he continued, "those obligations do not imply any liberty to keep

Congress unnecessarily in the dark." Having made these grudging concessions to the legislative branch of government, Bush went on to twit Congress for its unruly behavior. "Although our founders," he said, "never envisioned a Congress that would churn out hundreds of thousands of pages' worth of reports and hearings and documents and laws each year, they did understand that legislators would try to accumulate power." At this point he cited Madison, "Princeton's son," who, he said, had warned that "the legislative department is everywhere extending its impetuous vortex." Added Bush triumphantly: "That was Mr. Madison speaking, not Mr. Bush speaking."[1]

In citing Madison, President Bush, perhaps unwittingly, decontextualized the Father of the Constitution. Madison wasn't referring to Congress under the Constitution when he penned those words, as Bush seemed to think, but to the Congress that existed under the Articles of Confederation and which ran the country until its critics saw to it that a new Constitution was framed in 1787 and ratified by the states in 1788. Madison's criticism of the Confederation's Congress appeared in *Federalist* No. 47 and was written and published in 1788, before the Constitution was ratified and the new government, with an entirely new kind of Congress, was launched on the last day of April 1789. And Madison's whole point was that too much power in any one place in government was dangerous. "The accumulation of all powers, legislative, executive, and judiciary in the same hands," he wrote, "whether of one, a few or many, and whether hereditary, self appointed, or elective, may justly be pronounced the very definition of tyranny."[2]

Madison himself had experience in Congress as well as in the White House. A member of the House of Representatives, he played a major role in the first four Congresses that met under the newly adopted Constitution. In the first Congress (1789–91), he took the lead in promoting organizational and economic legislation that got the new government off to a good start, all the time working closely with George Washington, the first President. He also took the initiative in formulating amendments to the Congress that became the Bill of Rights and promoting their acceptance by Congress. "He is our first man," pronounced Massachusetts's Fisher Ames, one of Madison's colleagues in the House.[3]

On June 1, 1812, when Madison was President and the United

States was on the verge of war with Britain, he sent a message to Congress summing up the nation's grievances against Britain and then declared that the decision as to whether the country should continue to put up with British aggression or choose forcible resistance was "a solemn question which the Constitution wisely confides to the legislative branch of government." Congress then voted for war and Madison signed the war declaration on June 18. The war went badly and the people began denouncing it as "Mr. Madison's War." But it wasn't just his war; it was Congress's war, too.[4]

CHAPTER 15

The War of 1812 and Vietnam

Until the Vietnam War of the 1960s and '70s, the United States never lost a war which it undertook.

Not so.

The War of 1812—young America's first declared war—was in many ways a disaster. Andrew Jackson, it is true, whipped the British at New Orleans in January 1815, and his victory led many Americans to look on the war itself as a glorious triumph over the British, but their memories were short. During the conflict the United States sustained several major defeats at the hands of the British, experienced the humiliation of having British troops invade Washington, and, in the end, achieved none of the objectives for which it fought. Jackson's victory itself came two weeks after a peace treaty (which ignored America's grievances against Britain) was signed at Ghent, Belgium, in December 1814. If the British hadn't been preoccupied much of the time with their far greater struggle with Napoleonic France, moreover, it is conceivable that the "War of 1812" (as Americans called it, though it lasted until 1815), would have gone even worse for the United States.

On June 1, 1812, when President James Madison, after months of pressure from the "War Hawks" in Congress, finally asked Congress to consider the possibility of war, he singled out two major grievances against the British: interference with America's neutral rights at sea and the impressment of American seamen ("manstealing") into the British navy. For westerners, though, there was an additional grievance (which Madison mentioned only in passing): the British in Canada supplied the Indians in the West with arms and ammunition to use against American settlers there. Some Westerners talked of taking over Canada during the war, and some Southerners had their eyes on East and West Florida, then controlled by Spain, Britain's ally. But maritime grievances, not territorial expansion, were the primary factors motivating the "War Hawks"; there was also the conviction that the young republic should stand up for its rights against the British or earn the contempt of the world. "Before we relinquish the conflict," Kentucky's Richard M. Johnson told the House of Representatives a few months before the war declaration, "I wish to see Great Britain renounce the piratical system of paper blockade; to liberate our captured seamen on board her ships of war; relinquish the practice of impressment on board our merchant vessels . . . and cease, in every other respect, to violate our neutral rights; to treat us as an independent people." He went on to suggest "the occupation of the Canadas, and the other British possessions upon our borders, where our laws are violated, the Indians stimulated to murder our citizens, and where there is a British monopoly of the peltry and fur trade. I should not wish to extend the boundary of the United States by war if Great Britain would leave us to the quiet enjoyment of independence," he added, "but, considering her deadly and implacable enmity, her continued hostility, I shall never die contented until I see her expulsion from North America, and her territories incorporated into the United States."[1]

When Congress came to consider the war resolution, a majority of the Republicans (Madison's party) cast their ballots for war, but the Federalists (who thought the United States should side with Britain against Napoleonic France) voted solidly against it. In the House, the vote on June 4 was 79 for war and 49 opposed; in the Senate on June 18, the vote was 18 to 13. There was a great deal of enthusiasm for the war at first, but plenty of opposition too. Vietnam wasn't the only war that produced vociferous opposition. The War of 1812 was enormously unpopular with many Americans (especially in New England), but so was the Mexican War, the Spanish-American War, and even World War I. Only World War II (the "Good War") produced negligible antiwar sentiment. Most Americans wanted to stay out of the Second World War when it began in 1939, but with the U.S. entry into the conflict after the attack on Pearl Harbor in 1941, they gave it their wholehearted support.

When the United States took on Britain in 1812, some of the "War Hawks" thought it would be a quick and easy war. "On to Canada," they cried. The "militia of Kentucky alone," bragged Henry Clay, leading Hawk, "are competent to place Montreal and Upper Canada at your feet." In four weeks, announced John C. Calhoun, another Hawk in Congress, "the whole of Upper, and a part of Lower, Canada will be in our possession."[2] But it was not to be. The United States entered the war poorly prepared, and the effort to conquer Canada failed miserably. Instead of concentrating on Montreal (whose capture would have cut British communications along the St. Lawrence River and the Great Lakes), U.S. forces attempted to invade Canada at three separate points and failed each time. First, General William Hull marched an army from Detroit toward the British garrison at Malden, then changed his mind and returned to Detroit, only to be surrounded by the British and forced to surrender without firing a shot. A second invasion across the Niagara River also ended in failure when New York militiamen, who were quarreling with officers in the regular army, refused to enter Canada to reinforce their countrymen there. And a third attempt—General Henry Dearborn led an advance along Lake Champlain toward Montreal—also fizzled out when Dearborn's militiamen refused to cross the border into Canada, and he was forced to return to Plattsburg. About all the United States accomplished in 1812 was to unite the Canadian people in their determination to stick with the British.

The year 1813 brought some victories. On September 10, Captain Oliver Hazard Perry ("We have met the enemy and they are ours") defeated a British fleet on Lake Erie (making the British position in Detroit hopeless), and on October 5, General William Henry Harrison beat British forces in the Battle of the Thames (in which the great Shawnee chief Tecumseh was killed), thus ending the war in the West. But there were no more cries of "On to Canada!" In 1814, in fact, the United States found itself very much on the defensive, for the British, having defeated Napoleon temporarily, gave priority to the American war for the first time and sent some of their best troops across the Atlantic to harass cities on the Atlantic coast with amphibious operations and to launch some invasions of their own.

In August 1814, a British fleet sailed into Chesapeake Bay, landed a large army, and, as Madison and other government officials fled, entered Washington and set fire to the President's house, the Capitol, and several other public buildings before withdrawing. "Few thought of going to bed," one Washingtonian wrote her sister afterward. "They spent the night in gazing on the fires and lamenting the disgrace of the city." The *New York Post* could hardly believe the news of the disaster. "Certain it is," wrote the editors, "that when General Ross' official account of the battle and the capture and destruction of our CAPITOL is published in England, it will hardly be credited by the Englishmen. Even here it is still considered a dream." But it was all too true. "Yes, Fellow Citizens," exclaimed the *Spectator* in New York City, "we have to record the humiliating, disgraceful fact, that, in the third year of the war, the City of Washington, the SEAT OF OUR GOVERNMENT, situated 300 miles from the ocean, and in the very heart of this great and extensive country, has been captured and its public buildings destroyed, by a paltry force of 5,000 men."[3]

Elsewhere, however, British invasion plans were less successful— at Niagara, Lake Champlain, and of course, New Orleans—partly because the United States had by this time found some vigorous young officers (like Andrew Jackson) who knew how to make use of militiamen as well as army regulars and succeeded in inspiring confidence and loyalty in their men. On the high seas, moreover, the little American navy won some stunning victories in single-ship engagements that astonished the British public and boosted the American morale. But victories like these had no serious strategic significance and presented no real challenge to British naval supremacy. By 1814 the proud British navy had succeeded in imposing a blockade on the Atlantic coast which practically killed America's carrying trade and kept American men-of-war bottled up in their home ports. "Our harbors were blockaded," wrote Francis Wayland; "communications coastwise between our ports were cut off; our ships were rotting in every creek and cove where they could find a place of security; our immense annual products were mouldering in our warehouses; the sources of profitable labor were dried up."[4] If the war on land was a stalemate by this time, the war on the high seas was practically a British victory.

Meanwhile disaffection, particularly in New England, where the pro-British Federalists were strong, mounted steadily. Some New Englanders called the war an "unholy, unrighteous, wicked, abominable and unnatural" conflict. "This war," declaimed Massachusetts Congressman Josiah Quincy, "the measures which preceded it, and the mode of carrying it on, are all undeniably southern and western policy, not the policy of the commercial states."[5] In New England antiwar activists discouraged voluntary enlistments, boycotted government loans, and resisted tax measures to pay for the war. Federalist governors, moreover, resisted calls by the federal government on the state militia, and in September 1814 Massachusetts defiantly withdrew her well-drilled and well-equipped militia from the federal service and placed it under a state commander. Some New Englanders continued to trade with Canada during the war and even furnished supplies to the British fleet. And a few extremists talked of seceding from the Union. But in Virginia the *Richmond Enquirer* set them straight. Secession, announced the *Enquirer*, was "treason to all intents and purposes."[6]

New England did not of course secede from the Union. In October 1814, however, the Massachusetts legislature issued a call to the other New England states to send delegates to a convention in Hartford, Connecticut, to decide what to do about a war ("Mr. Madison's War") which had wreaked havoc with New England's commercial enterprises. Twenty-six delegates from Massachusetts, Connecticut, Vermont, and Rhode Island met in secrecy for three weeks and finally came up with a report listing the evils the country had suffered under the "withering influence" of the Republicans and recommending several amendments to the Constitution designed to prevent the South and the West from controlling Congress, make it harder for Congress to declare war, and curtail the power of the President.[7] The Hartford Convention sent a committee of three to Washington to present its demands, but when the delegates reached the capital they found the people there celebrating Jackson's victory at New Orleans as well as the news that a peace treaty had been signed at Ghent. The delegates quietly left town.

The Treaty of Ghent, concluded on December 24, 1814, was far different from the one the War Hawks had looked forward to at the beginning of the war. There were no territorial acquisitions for the United States and no real twisting of the proud British lion's tail in the settlement reached at Ghent. The treaty provided for ending hostilities and releasing of prisoners of war, but said nothing about impressment, blockades, the right of search, or neutral rights. Henry Clay, one of the peace commissioners, called it a "damned bad treaty," and John Quincy Adams, another negotiator, said frankly: "Nothing was adjusted, nothing was settled—nothing in substance but an indefinite suspension of hostilities was agreed to."[8] Still, Perry's victory on Lake Erie, Harrison's in the West, and, above all, Jackson's at New Orleans, gave many Americans the impression that they had won the war after all. They put the disastrous Canadian campaign out of their minds, as well as the sacking of Washington and the humiliating British blockade, and soon found themselves looking back on the "Second War of Independence" (as they called it) with bursting pride and patriotic fervor over having whipped the British for a second time. President Madison knew better, but with the end of the war people saw him smile again for the first time since the burning of Washington.[9]

The Vietnam War was of course far different from the War of 1812–15. When it ended in 1974 there was absolutely no way the American people could pretend that it had been a victory. Perhaps the United States should have done years earlier what Vermont's Republican Senator George Aiken suggested in 1966: announce that she had won the war and then promptly withdraw from Vietnam lock, stock, and barrel.

CHAPTER 16

President Fillmore's Bathtub

Millard Fillmore installed the first bathtub in the White House. No, he didn't.

The Fillmore bathtub was the product of H. L. Mencken's lively imagination. In a facetious column, entitled "A Neglected Anniversary," for the *New York Evening Mail* on December 28, 1917, Mencken wrote that Adam Thompson, an Ohio businessman, built the first modern bathroom for his Cincinnati house in 1842 and then persuaded several other wealthy Cincinnatians to do the same. There was considerable medical opposition to bathtubs at first; the *Western Medical Depository*, according to Mencken, warned that the tub was dangerous to health and produced "phthistic, rheumatic fevers, inflammation of the lungs and the whole category of zymotic diseases." But the new invention gradually won acceptance, he said, particularly after Millard Fillmore took a bath in a tub while visiting Cincinnati in 1850 and then early in 1851 arranged for the installation of a spanking new bathtub in the White House, thus giving it "recognition and respectability in the United States."[1]

Mencken expected his readers to chortle over his spoof; instead they thought he was serious. Though he subsequently made it clear he had been kidding, his leg-pull fooled historians as well as newspaper readers and soon found its way into encyclopedias and into books and articles listing the achievements of the Fillmore presidency. In 1926, Mencken wrote an article about his prank, "The American Public Will Swallow Anything," which appeared in thirty newspapers across the country, but it failed to clear up the misunderstanding. The *Boston Herald,* for one, featured Mencken's exposé of his practical joke, and then, three weeks later, to his surprise and chagrin, reprinted the ten-year-old *Mail* column as if it were news. In *Adventures in Error,* an examination of fabricated history, published in 1936, Arctic explorer Vilhjalmar Stefansson made a long list of newspapers and magazines, including the *New York Times,* that continued to take the Fillmore tale seriously even after HLM came clean about it in 1926.[2] The Baltimore satirist himself concluded that "there is something in the human mind that turns instinctively to fiction, and that even the most gifted journalists succumb to it."[3]

The fact is that Andrew Jackson deserves the credit that HLM impishly gave to Millard Fillmore. It was Jackson, not Fillmore, who first installed running water (conveyed through iron pipes from a nearby reservoir) in the White House, thus making it possible to construct in the east wing a bathroom containing a hot bath, a cold bath, and a shower bath. And it was Franklin Pierce who, twenty years later, extended that plumbing and added another bathroom, in the dressing room off the President's bedroom on the second floor. Fillmore himself presumably used the bathtub Jackson had installed. But if he wanted to take a bath on the second floor, he had to do what all the Presidents did until Franklin Pierce: arrange to have warm water from the east-wing bathroom hauled up in kettles and poured into a portable tin bathtub lined with soft linen bathcloths to protect his body from the hot tin. The wonder is that Fillmore didn't actually do what Pierce did and deserve at least some of the credit HLM was to bestow on him.[4]

CHAPTER 17

William T. Seward and
the Higher Law

In 1850, when William T. Seward declared that there was a "higher law" than the Constitution, he revealed himself to be as radical an abolitionist as William Lloyd Garrison was.

No, he didn't. He used the phrase "higher law," to be sure, but he was by no means a radical.

William Seward, a Whig and Senator from New York from 1848 until he became Abraham Lincoln's Secretary of State in 1861, was no William Lloyd Garrison. Garrison was a radical; Seward, a moderate. Garrison demanded the "immediate and complete emancipation" of slaves, while Seward favored the gradual emancipation with compensation to the slave-owners. Garrison was a disunionist who called on the free states of the North to secede from a Union that contained slave states; Seward remained a staunch Unionist, and a sincere opponent of slavery. In January 1843, Garrison persuaded the Massachusetts branch of the American Anti-slavery Society to pass a resolution denouncing the U.S. Constitution as "a covenant with death and an agreement with hell" which "should be annulled." On Independence Day, 1854, moreover, he burned the Constitution at a public abolitionist meeting in Framingham, Massachusetts, and, as the document went up in flames, exclaimed triumphantly: "So perish all compromises with tyranny!" Seward never dreamed of breaking the law or repudiating the Constitution.[1]

Unlike Garrison, Seward simply did not have the agitator's temperament. Still, as an antislavery Whig, he opposed the expansion of slavery into the territories acquired from Mexico after the Mexican-American War (1846–48); he also refused to support a fugitive slave law requiring Northerners to return runaway slaves to the South. Henry Clay's famous Compromise of 1850—a series of measures Clay hoped would be acceptable to both the northern and the southern states—contained both a fugitive slave law and a provision letting the people of New Mexico and Utah decide whether they wanted slavery or not, and for that reason Seward absolutely refused to support it. In a long speech made in the Senate on March 11, 1850, he explained at one point the basic reason for his opposition to Clay's compromise measures. The Preamble to the Constitution, he reminded his colleagues, singled out union, justice, defense, welfare, and liberty as the objectives of the federal government, and, he went on to say, it was these objectives, and not slavery, that should prevail in all the territories acquired by the United States. "But," he added, "there is a higher law than the Constitution, which regulates our authority over the domain, and devotes it to the same noble purposes."[2]

Seward's reference to a "higher law than the Constitution" was widely misunderstood. His southern colleagues charged he was disparaging the Constitution and virtually calling on people to take the law into their own hands. Some Senators even recommended his expulsion from the Senate for his inflammatory remarks. But Seward was no firebrand. He was not advocating anarchy, or even civil disobedience; he was simply stating what he regarded as obvious: that basic moral principles ("higher law") dictated the "same noble purposes" that the Preamble to the Constitution enumerated. For some reason, he never adequately explained what he meant, and, amid the torrent of criticism that followed his speech, he won the reputation of being a radical, even though he was actually a moderate who, unlike Garrison, was willing to let slavery alone in the states where it already existed.

The great black abolitionist Frederick Douglass began as a Garrisonian and then moved toward Seward's view of the Constitution. Instead of burning the document, Douglass decided to "abolitionize" it. The word "slave," he noted, appeared nowhere in the Constitution, and if the document were to fall from the sky onto a land unfamiliar with slavery, the people there would never dream there was anything in it sanctioning human bondage. He also pointed out that there were numerous phrases in the Constitution which were clearly incompatible with slavery. The Preamble to the Constitution, for one thing, began with the words "We the People"—not white people, not rich people, not privileged people, but all the people, white and black, rich and poor, great and small, who lived in the United States. For another, the basic purposes of the Union announced in the Preamble (defense, welfare, tranquillity, justice, and liberty) were all obviously inconsistent with slavery and favorable to freedom. In the main body of the Constitution, moreover, there were a number of provisions which Douglass thought categorically ruled out slavery: the clause prohibiting bills of attainder, the clause guaranteeing every person the right to a trial by jury; the clause ensuring every person the writ of habeas corpus; the clause stating that no person shall be deprived of life, liberty, and property without "due process of the law"; the clause specifying that "the right of the people to be secure in their persons shall not be violated"; and, finally, the clause asserting that "the United States shall guarantee to every State in the Union a republican form of government." All of these clauses, Douglass maintained, made slavery unconstitutional and imposed a duty on Congress to abolish it everywhere in the land. The Constitution, in short, was a charter of freedom, not a slaveholder's document. And as such it was entirely compatible with the "higher law" that Seward talked about in 1850.[3] Still, Douglass (and Seward, too) expressed great pleasure when the Thirteenth Amendment, freeing the slaves, was added to the Constitution in 1865, making all this quite explicit, once for all.

CHAPTER 18

Uncle Tom as
a Black Hero

In Harriet Beecher Stowe's *Uncle Tom's Cabin* (1852) Uncle Tom, the main character, was depicted as a meek, submissive, obsequious old slave.

Not so.

Stowe's Uncle Tom was no "Uncle Tom." He was the real hero of her novel, and she did not regard obsequiousness as a heroic virtue. "Cringing subserviency," she wrote, was "one of the most baleful effects of slavery," and she was obviously unsympathetic to characters in the novel (like Simon Legree's slaves, Sambo and Quimbo) who truckled to their master and cheerfully did his wicked bidding. Popular dramatizations of *Uncle Tom's Cabin* after the Civil War (some of them bordering on farce) tended to present Tom as a meek, shuffling, white-haired old man, but the Tom portrayed by Stowe was as far as could be from the traditional stage-and-film Tom.[1]

Stowe's Tom was young and vigorous: "a large, broad-chested, powerfully made man," with "an expression of grace and steady good sense, united with much kindness and benevolence."[2] He had to be strong and healthy, indeed, to endure the physical abuse he undergoes in the novel. But it was his religion—his profound Christian faith—that chiefly enables him to cope with the pain, sorrow, and suffering he experiences as a slave and, in the end, to triumph over his oppressors. Converted at a camp meeting, Tom has, Stowe tells us, a "natural genius for religion." He reads the Bible, prays, sings hymns, holds little services at times for other slaves and acts as their spiritual adviser, and eventually comes to be called Father Tom. "I'm in the Lord's hands," he tells his wife, Aunt Chloe; "nothin' can go no furder than He lets it. . . ."[3]

Tom's trust in the Lord gives a Stoic tinge to his religious outlook. When the going gets tough, he does not wail or whine or bemoan his fate; he continues to do the best he can and to strive for peace of mind even in the worst of situations. "He saw enough of abuse and misery to make him sick and weary," Stowe recounts, "but he determined to toil on, with religious patience, committing himself to Him that judgeth righteously, not without hope that some way of escape might yet be opened to him."[4] When one of his masters, Shelby, who has promised him eventual freedom, is forced by his debts to separate Tom from his wife and children and sell him to a slavetrader named Haley, Tom is at first devastated. "I felt as if there warn't nothin' left," he confessed, "and, then," he added, "the good Lord, He stood by me and He says, 'Fear not, Tom,' and He brings light and joy into a poor feller's soul,—makes all peace; and I's so happy, and loves everybody, and feels willin' jest to be the Lord's and have the Lord's will done, and be put jest where the Lord wants to put me."[5]

But Tom's religion is by no means quietistic. No predestinarian, he believed that putting forth one's own efforts to do God's will made a difference in his own and other people's lives. For Tom, the essence of Christianity was love—love of God and one's neighbors— and he thought that striving for righteousness required acts of kindness and generosity to others, particularly the suffering and downtrodden. "We does for the Lord," he says, "when we does for his critturs." Whenever he can, Tom consoles the despairing and lifts the spirits of the dejected, but he also lends a practical helping hand to the weary and heavy-laden. He gives his tattered blanket to women field-workers shivering in the cold and grinds corn for them when they are ill. Laboring in the fields, he also risks his brutal master Simon Legree's wrath by sneaking some of the cotton he picks into the baskets of the weaker slaves so they can meet their quotas and escape punishment. He was reconciled to being separated from his family at the beginning of the novel when he realized it would be better for his wife and children that way. "If I must be sold," he tells Aunt Chloe, "of all the people on the place, and everything go to rack, why, let me be sold." There is the hope, too, of course, that if and when Shelby gets out of debt he will buy Tom back and in due course give him his freedom.[6]

Several of the characters in *Uncle Tom's Cabin* succeed in escaping to freedom in Canada. Uncle Tom approves and even helps two of them make good their escape, but he never tries to get away himself. Why not? Partly because two of his masters—Shelby and St. Clare—treat him decently and promise eventual manumission, and partly because when he falls into the hands of the sadistic Simon Legree he is convinced that it is God's will that he remain on the plantation to help the other suffering slaves rather than join Cassy and Emmeline, the two slaves who decide to make a getaway. Pressed to join them, he refuses. "No," he explained, "time was when I would; but the Lord's given me a work among these yer poor souls, and I'll stay with 'em and bear my cross with 'em till the end."[7]

But Tom is never reconciled to slavery, even when his situation, as with St. Clare, is a pleasant one. St. Clare, a Southerner who detests the "peculiar institution," is, in fact, a bit hurt at the joy Tom expresses when he learns that St. Clare has begun legal proceedings for his emancipation. "You haven't had such very bad times here, that you need to be in such a rapture," murmurs St. Clare, somewhat taken aback. "No, no Mas'r!" cried Tom, "'tan't that—it's bein' a *free man!* that's what I'm joyin' for." "Why, Tom," says St. Clare reproachfully, "don't you think, for your own part, you've been better off than to be free?" "*No, indeed,* Mas'r St. Clare," persists Tom, "No, indeed!" "Why, Tom," says St. Clare, "you couldn't possibly have earned, by your work, such clothes and such living as I have given you." "Knows all that, Mas'r St. Clare," admits Tom; "Mas'r's been too good; but, Mas'r," he goes on, "I'd rather have poor clothes, poor house, poor everything, and have 'em *mine,* than have the best, and have 'em any man's else,—I had *so,* Mas'r; I think it's natur, Mas'r." After St. Clare leaves, Tom dreams of what it will be like when he is a free man: "He thought how he should work to buy his wife and boys. He felt the muscles of his brawny arms with a sort of joy, as he thought they would soon belong to himself, and how much they could do to work out the freedom of his family."[8]

But Tom's dream is soon shattered. St. Clare is accidentally killed and his wife reneges on the promise of freedom, and Tom eventually ends up on the plantation of the cruel and despotic Simon Legree. It is the nadir of Tom's existence. Overwork, abuse, degradation, hatred, and malice are the order of the day under Legree, and Tom no longer has time even to read his Bible for consolation. He does, though, have a chance to improve things for himself if he agrees to do things Legree's way. From the outset, Legree is impressed with Tom's strength and vitality and toys with the idea of making him his overseer. First, though, he must find out if Tom is tough enough for the position. "I mean to promote ye," he tells Tom one evening, "and make a driver of ye; and to-night ye may jest as well begin to get yer hand in." He then hands him a whip and orders him to flog one of the slaves he charges with having failed to produce her quota of cotton that day.[9]

Tom's refusal to flog the woman is absolute. "I beg Mas'r's pardon," he says mildly; "hopes Mas'r won't set me at that. It's what I ain't used to,—never did—and can't do no way possible." "Ye'll larn a pretty smart chance of things yer never did before, before I've done with ye!" explodes Legree, taking up a cowhide and showering him with blows. "There!" he cries, stopping to rest, "now, will ye tell me ye can't do it?" "Yes, Mas'r," says Tom, wiping blood from his face, "I'm willin' to work, night and day, and work while there's life and breath in me; but this yer thing I can't feel it right to do;—and, Mas'r, I never shall do it,—Never!" "Ain't I yer master?" thunders Legree. "Didn't I pay down twelve hundred dollars cash for all there is inside yer old cussed black shell? An't you mine, now, body and soul?" "No! no! no! my soul an't yours, Masir," Tom exclaims. "You haven't bought it,—ye can't buy it! It's been bought and paid for, by One that is able to keep it;—no matter, no matter, you can't harm me!" "I can't!" sneers Legree; "we'll see—we'll see." And he orders Sambo and Quimbo, two gigantic slaves, who have learned to become almost as depraved as he is, to thrash Tom within an inch of his life. Afterward, as Tom lies groaning and bleeding, he wonders if he can really hold out. "O, good Lord!" he implores. "*Do* look down,—give me the victory! give me the victory over all!" One of the slaves he has befriended urges him to yield to Legree, reminding him that "the miserable low dogs" in the fields whom he is trying to help would "turn against you" the first time they got a chance. "Poor critturs!" sighs Tom, "what makes 'em so cruel?—and, if I give out, I shall get used to 't, and grow, little by little, just like 'em!—I've lost everything in *this* world, and it's clean gone, forever,—and

69

now I *can't* lose Heaven, too; no, I can't get to be wicked, besides all!"[10]

Tom's quiet resistance almost drives Legree mad, and he is more than ever determined to break the will of his recalcitrant slave. The next day he seeks him out in his shabby quarters, and orders him to "get right down on yer knees and beg my pardon, for yer shines last night." Tom does not move. "Down, you dog!" screams Legree, striking him with his riding whip. "Mas'r Legree," says Tom, "I can't do it. I did only what I thought was right. I shall do just so again if ever the time comes. I never will do a cruel thing, come what may." Legree knows by now that Tom's strength of will depends largely on his deep religious faith and he does all he can to shatter Tom's reliance on his God. "You see the Lord an't going to help you," he taunts; "if He had been, He wouldn't have let *me* get ya! This yer religion is all a mess of lying trumpery, Tom. I know all about it. Ye'd better hold to me; I'm somebody, and can do something!" "No, Mas'r," returns Tom; "I'll hold on. The Lord may help me, or not help; but I'll still hold to Him, and believe Him to the last!" "The more fool you!" sneers Legree. "Never mind, I'll chase you down, yet, and bring you under—you'll see!"[11]

At times Tom wavers; he is filled with doubts, says Stowe, as the "atheistic taunts of his cruel master" sink "his dejected soul to the lowest ebb." In the end, though, the vision of Jesus, with his "majestic patience" at the time of the crucifixion, enables him to remain true to his faith, and he even turns aside the suggestion of one of the slaves that he take the axe to Legree when the latter lies in a drunken stupor in his room one night. "No! good never comes of wickedness," he tells her. "I'd sooner chop my right hand off." It is clear by now that there is only one kind of freedom that Tom can ever achieve in this life: spiritual freedom. It takes martyrdom for Tom to achieve it, but Stowe sees to it that he succeeds gloriously. Tom is her great Christian hero.[12]

Tom's martyrdom comes after his third major confrontation with Simon Legree. When two of the slaves, Cassy and Emmeline, with Tom's cooperation, manage to escape from the plantation, Legree resolves, once for all, to break Tom's will or destroy him. "Well, Tom," he cries, "do you know I've made up my mind to KILL you?" "It's very likely, Mas'r," says Tom calmly. "I have," Legree goes on, "*done—just—that—thing*, Tom, unless you'll tell me what you know about these yer gals." "I han't got nothing to tell Mas'r," says Tom firmly. "Speak!" thunders Legree, striking him. "Do you know anything?" "I know, Mas'r," says Tom frankly, "but I can't tell anything. *I can die!*" At this point Legree turns him over to his two brutal lackeys, Sambo and Quimbo, who string him up for a final beating. So valiant is Tom at the end—he even forgives Legree—that Sambo and Quimbo are overwhelmed by the enormity of what they have done, and, after Legree leaves, take Tom down, wash his wounds, put him on a rude bed of refuse cotton, and pour brandy down his throat in an effort to revive him. Tom lingers long enough to greet George Shelby (his former master's son who has come to take him back to his family) and to die in triumph: "O Mas'r George! What a thing it is to be a Christian!" (George agrees, but he also experiences exquisite pleasure—along with the reader—in knocking Legree down before lovingly preparing Tom's body for burial.)[13]

Tom's nobility seems excessive to many people, particularly in a secular age, and even improbable. Although William Lloyd Garrison, a militant abolitionist (though a nonresister), admired the character Stowe had created, Charles Dickens found the book "too celestial" and Gustav Flaubert couldn't bring himself to applaud the character. "I don't find it necessary," he wrote, "in order to sympathize with a slave who is being tortured, to have that slave be a brave man, a good husband and father, a singer of hymns, and a reader of the Bible. I don't insist that he must pardon his tormenters or that he should be sublime or exceptional."[14] Tom may have been exceptional, but one thing is unmistakable: he was obdurate, not obsequious. Stowe's Tom was, like Martin Luther King, Jr., after him, in the great tradition of Christian nonviolent resistance (Matthew V: the Sermon on the Mount).[15] Stowe regretted that so many of the churches, even in the North, defended or at least acquiesced in slavery, and she wanted to show dramatically that the slavery institution was the antithesis of the Christian love taught by Jesus. She would have been astonished by the notion that Uncle Tom was some kind of Uriah Heep. So would Simon Legree. For Legree, Tom was the "most rebellious, saucy, impudent dog" he had ever encountered.[16]

CHAPTER 19

Sexual Preferences:
Abraham Lincoln and
James Buchanan

President Lincoln was a homosexual.

Of course not.

In a book entitled *Presidential Passions,* published in 1991, California writer Michael John Sullivan presented the novel thesis that the Great Emancipator was, deep down (why is it never sideways?) where it really counts, a President with same-sex preferences. His evidence: Lincoln's awkwardness with women as a young man, his close association with friends like Joshua Speed (from whom he rented a room and with whom he shared a bed for a time) and Billy Herndon (his young law partner), and the lack of passion in his marriage to Mary Todd. Sullivan wasn't alone in his speculations about Lincoln. In *The Story the Soldiers Wouldn't Tell* (1994), a study of sex during the Civil War, psychiatrist Thomas P. Lowry somewhat more cautiously suggested that the Civil War President may have been physically attracted to men. [1]

What about Lincoln's sex life? Lincoln seems to have been a clumsy frontier lad when he was growing up, and, as Mary Owens, the woman he halfheartedly courted until she emphatically turned him down, once put it: he was "deficient in those little links which make up the chain of a woman's happiness." [2] But Lincoln was surely not the only tongue-tied suitor that ever was, and his ineptness with Mary Owens proves little except his lack of polish and self-assurance, which his marriage to Mary Todd did much to overcome. As for sharing a double bed with Joshua Speed, this was not unusual in the old days; John Adams and Benjamin Franklin slept in the same bed on one trip together during the American Revolution and spent half the night arguing about whether the window should be open or shut. As for the Lincoln marriage, it was by and large a successful one. Lincoln was moody at times and his wife short-tempered, but they had a deep affection for one another and shared the joys and sorrows of their marriage as closely knit partners. No 20th-century historian or biographer has accepted without a big grain of salt the tales Billy Herndon (who loathed Mrs. Lincoln) peddled after Lincoln's death about the miseries of his former partner as a married man.[3]

But Sullivan is insistent: "Whether or not Lincoln was ever actively homosexual will always be a subject for speculation and debate. The fact of his emotional homosexuality is an inescapable conclusion from the information available on his life."[4] But Sullivan ignored all the information available about Lincoln that renders his speculation nugatory. Psychologizing from a distance has always been a dubious enterprise, and people going in for it have almost always tended, like Sullivan, to approach their subject with parti pris. Journalist Merle Miller was wiser. Interviewing Harry Truman in the early 1960s, he observed that the former President seemed ill at ease with women and more comfortable talking to male reporters. But Miller, himself a gay, made nothing more of this fact than that Truman (who married at 35) had grown up in a male-dominated world in which easy social relations between the sexes were lacking. Lincoln lived in a similar society, as did all our Presidents until recent times, but he never condescended to his wife (and to women in general) as did, say Grover Cleveland, who had at least one fling as a young man.[5]

A far likelier candidate for presidential homosexuality was James Buchanan, Lincoln's predecessor in the White House, the only President never to marry. With Buchanan there is a great deal of information available pointing to at least latent homosexuality. Although old-time historians and biographers passed over (or never even noticed) this kind of information, it is impossible today to neglect it in any serious effort to understand what made "Old Buck" tick. Son of a hard-nosed shopkeeper and a deeply religious mother, Buchanan became deeply attached as a youth to somewhat older men like John King (popular young Presbyterian minister in his little home town in Pennsylvania) and James McCormick, one of his professors at Dickinson College. In 1819, when he was twenty-nine, he became engaged to Ann Coleman, daughter of one of the wealthiest men in the country, but his lack of warmth during the courtship led her to suspect he was only interested in her money and she finally broke off the engagement and died soon after, apparently a suicide. Buchanan's sad experience with Ann Coleman, who seems to have been unstable, became the stock explanation in later years for his reluctance to get seriously involved with another woman.[6]

As Buchanan rose in the world—Congressman, Senator, Ambassador to Russia and then to Great Britain, Secretary of State—he developed friendships with women from time to time, but always quickly terminated them when the woman became serious about him. "I feel it is not good for a man to be alone," he once wrote, "and should not be astonished to find myself married to some old maid who can nurse me when I am sick, provide good dinners for me when I am well, and not expect from me any very ardent or romantic affection."[7] But he never seriously contemplated marriage. When rumors circulated in Washington that he was engaged to President Polk's widow, Sarah Polk emphatically denied them. Old Buck was never one of Mrs. Polk's favorites. He had pushed Alabama Senator William King, not her husband, for the Democratic nomination for President in 1844, and she seems, too, to have disapproved of the close relation between King and Buchanan.

Buchanan's association with Senator King, a bachelor like himself, was something of a joke in Washington. The two met in 1821, when Buchanan first entered the House, and King, five years older, was in the Senate, and took quickly to one another, became roommates, and lived together in Washington for the next sixteen years. Buchanan amusedly noted that some people called them "the Siamese twins" and even referred to his friend King as "his wife." Once, when Buchanan and King had a little quarrel, Tennessee Congressman Aaron Brown sent a letter to Mrs. Polk (which he marked "confidential") in which he wrote: "Mr. Buchanan looks gloomy and dissatisfied & so does his *better half* until a little private flattery . . . excited hopes that getting a divorce, she might set up again in the world to some tolerable advantage. Since which *casual* events, which she had taken for neat and permanent overtures,

Aunt Fancy may now be seen every day, triggered out in her best clothes and smirking about in hopes of seeing better terms than with her former companion. . . ." Brown went on to say that some politician made a remark about the 1844 race "in the presence of Mr. Buchanan and *his wife*" that was "highly indecorous toward Mrs. B[uchanan]." What Mrs. Polk thought about Brown's report is not a matter of record.[8]

Buchanan and King were both on the fussy and fastidious side (Andrew Jackson referred to King as "Miss Nancy") and provoked mirth among hardier folk in the nation's capital. But the teasing didn't hurt them politically. President John Tyler appointed King (against his wishes) as minister to France, where he lamented his lonely life without Buchanan around, and in 1852 the Democrats picked him as Franklin Pierce's running mate in the presidential race that year. The Pierce-King ticket triumphed, but King became ill soon after election, went to Cuba to recuperate, took his oath of office there, but died soon after Pierce's inauguration.[9]

In 1856 Buchanan finally achieved a long-held ambition: the Democratic nomination for President. During the campaign there were jokes about his bachelorhood ("Who ever heard in all his life," went one campaign ditty, "Of a candidate without a wife?"), but he beat Republican candidate John C. Frémont by a comfortable margin, and entered the White House, with his niece Harriet Lane as his hostess, hoping to settle the sectional strife that was tearing the nation apart.[10] He failed, of course, but perhaps even Andrew Jackson would have failed at this point in American history. In any case, when South Carolina seceded from the Union after Abraham Lincoln's election in 1860, Buchanan's indecision in the crisis produced scorn and contempt. There were sneers about his "shrill, feminine voice, and wholly beardless cheeks," and the wife of one of his Cabinet members called him "Old Gurley." In January 1861, a man from Philadelphia wrote his Congressman to complain about the President. "I do not share in the confidence which some entertain in poor Betsy Buchanan," he wrote. "She is very weak, and I fear, very bad." He went on to lament "the shame of leaving it to her ["his" is crossed over] Cabinet whether he should or not recall his troops!" And he concluded: "Let her publicly deny (if she dare) her compact with South Carolina rebels, not to increase her force!"[11]

Like some of our other Presidents, Buchanan was a bit of a wimp.

Was he also gay? Probably not, if being gay means engaging in homosexual love-making. In Buchanan's day homosexuality was (like monogamy in advanced circles today) the "love that dare not speak its name," and Buchanan was too ambitious politically to risk losing everything by engaging in unconventional behavior in private. Whatever his inclinations (and they seem to have been unmistakably homosexual), he kept his passions under strict control. None of the taunts in Washington about him and Senator King mention sex. Nineteenth-century America was still an age of innocence, in many respects, that Americans a century later would find it difficult to comprehend. But even in the late 20th century it is extremely doubtful that a person with same-sex inclinations could be elected President. If a gay did get to the White House, the probability is that the opinion industries (newspapers, the newsweeklies, radio, television) would have such a field day with "gay-gate" that all serious public business would be suspended for the duration.

CHAPTER 20

Abraham Lincoln's Defense of His Wife

During the Civil War Abraham Lincoln appeared before a congressional committee to defend his wife against charges of treason.

No, he didn't. But there were charges of disloyalty against Mrs. Lincoln all the same.

Mary Todd Lincoln came from Kentucky, a border state, and some of her relatives (including one who lived in the White House for a time) supported the Confederacy. Mrs. Lincoln, however, was a wholehearted Unionist. She also opposed slavery and, like her husband, was an emancipationist as well as a Unionist. One of her best friends in Washington was Charles Sumner, Radical Republican Senator from Massachusetts, who continually pressed Lincoln to take stronger action to end slavery. But Mrs. Lincoln's—and Lincoln's—enemies in Washington spread rumors that not only was she pro-Confederate but that she was also secretly aiding the Confederate cause. "The President's wife," observed W. O. Stoddard, White House mail clerk, "is venomously accused of being at heart a traitor and of being in communication with the Confederate authorities."[1]

According to a dramatic tale first appearing in print in 1905, the rumors about Mrs. Lincoln's disloyalty became so insistent that finally, a congressional committee decided to look into the matter. One morning, however, according to the story, just as the hearing opened, President Lincoln suddenly appeared in the committee room unannounced, "at the foot of the table, standing solitary, his hat in hand, his tall form towering among the committee members . . . ." With his face filled with "almost unhuman sadness," the story goes, Lincoln started speaking, "slowly and with infinite sorrow" and the room became deathly still. "I, Abraham Lincoln, President of the United States," he declared, "appear of my own volition before this Committee . . . to say that I, of my own knowledge, know that it is untrue that any of my family hold treasonable communication with the enemy." Then, the story ends, he left "as silently and solitary as he came," and the committee promptly adjourned without taking any further action. It's a moving story, but unfortunately it is entirely fanciful. There is not a shred of evidence to back up a tale first told forty years after Lincoln's death.[2]

CHAPTER 21

Abraham Lincoln's
Religion

Abraham Lincoln never belonged to a church and he was essentially an unbeliever when it came to religion.

Not so.

Lincoln was never a church member, but he was by no means an unbeliever. After his death, William ("Billy") Herndon, his former law partner, asserted that Lincoln "died an unbeliever," but he was just plain wrong, for Lincoln was in fact one of America's most religious Presidents. Herndon was so anxious to disassociate the sixteenth President from the kind of religious orthodoxy that some people claimed for him after his death that he went overboard in the other direction. Lincoln, he once declared (rather confusedly), was "an infidel—a Deist . . . an atheist." He was wrong on all three counts. [1]

Pious people, it is true, tended to look on Lincoln as an "infidel" when he was growing up on the frontier in southern Indiana and in Illinois. Young Lincoln, it was clear, was amused, not edified, by the hellfire-and-brimstone preaching he encountered, and he enjoyed doing take-offs on the revivalist preachers he observed from time to time shouting and yelling and beating the air as if "they were fighting bees." He also wrote a parody of the patriarchal Biblical narratives when he was young which he called "The Chronicles of Reuben," centering on the wedding-night mix-up involving two brothers he knew who married two sisters the same day. He read Thomas Paine's deistic *Age of Reason* about this time, as well as Constantin de

Volney's agnostic *Ruins,* and got into debates with people about the Calvinistic doctrines—predestination, original sin, salvation by grace, eternal damnation—that were popular with the frontier preachers. He was repelled by the idea of endless punishment and took up for the doctrine of universal salvation, then considered a dangerous heresy by the orthodox.[2]

For a time, Lincoln later admitted, he espoused the "Doctrine of Necessity," by which he apparently meant the notion that since all human choices are necessitated, not free, people bear no moral responsibility for what they choose to do. (Benjamin Franklin similarly toyed with this idea, wrote an essay about it, and then discarded it as "having an ill tendency.") Lincoln was basically a seeker, not a skeptic, in his salad days; he felt driven to come to religious terms with the perplexing world in which he found himself. "Probably it is to be my lot to go on as a questioning doubting Thomas did," he told some friends. "But in my poor, maimed way, I bear with me as I go on a seeking spirit of desire for a faith that was with him of olden time, who, in his need, as I in mine, exclaimed, 'Help thou my unbelief.'"[3]

In 1846, when Lincoln ran for Congress as a Whig, religion became one of the issues of the campaign. His Democratic opponent, Peter Cartwright, a celebrated Methodist circuit-rider, circulated rumors that Lincoln was an infidel, and Lincoln issued a handbill strongly denying the allegation. "A charge having got into circulation . . . in substance that I am an open scoffer at Christianity," wrote Lincoln in his campaign piece, it was necessary for him to say that although "I am not a member of a Christian Church . . . I have never denied the truth of the Scripture, and I have never spoken with intentional disrespect of religion in general, or of any denomination in particular." Lincoln went on to confess he had once taken up the "Doctrine of Necessity," but insisted he had long since given it up, even though, he added (in a bow to predestination), "I have always understood this same opinion to be held by some of the Christian denominations." He concluded the handbill by saying that "I do not think I could myself, be brought to support a man for office, whom I know to be an open enemy of, and scoffer at, religion."[4]

During his campaign for Congress, Lincoln attended one of Cartwright's revival services and seems to have enjoyed the muscular preacher's vigorous presentation. But after the sermon, when Cartwright called on "All who do not wish to go to hell" to stand up, Lincoln remained seated while everyone else rose. "May I ask of you, Mr. Lincoln," cried Cartwright sarcastically, "where are you going?" "Brother Cartwright asks me directly where I am going," said Lincoln, slowly rising. "I desire to reply with equal directness. I am going to Congress." The service quickly broke up. Lincoln beat Cartwright on election day and served for a term in the Lower House.[5]

Lincoln never got over his youthful pleasure—and amusement—at seeing frontier revivalists like Cartwright in action. One of his favorite stories was about the old-line Baptist preacher who chose as his text, "I am the Christ whom I shall represent today," and then sailed into his sermon with zest and vigor. But while he was holding forth, Lincoln said, a lizard got into his pants and started up his legs and the preacher, still pouring forth a torrent of words, began to shuck his clothes—first his pants and then his shirt—in an effort to dislodge the troublesome critter. Suddenly an old lady got up in the congregation, according to Lincoln, and cried: "If you represent Christ, then I'm done with the Bible!"[6]

Lincoln's wife Mary preferred more sedate religious services. Unlike Lincoln, she was a church member—an Episcopalian and then a Presbyterian—and after his marriage Lincoln rented a pew for the family and often accompanied his wife to services in Springfield, Illinois, and then, when he became President, to the Presbyterian church in Washington to which she belonged. From time to time he attended prayer meetings too. But though pressed to join the church, he "couldn't quite see it," he said, partly because of the creeds and doctrines he couldn't bring himself to entertain. He liked to say that if he found a church with just one doctrine—"Thou shalt love the Lord thy God with all thy heart and with all thy soul and with all thy mind, and thy neighbor as thyself"—he would gladly join.[7] But the religious faith he gradually worked out for himself as he grew older was more complicated than that. It was centered on the Bible (which he read almost daily and knew thoroughly) rather than on the church, and it involved Thomas Jefferson's Declaration of Independence as well as the Scriptures.

Like Jefferson, Lincoln lived in a moral universe in which decent behavior produced fruitful results and unjust actions brought calamity in their wake. When it came to slavery (which Lincoln came close to regarding as the original sin), he liked to quote Jefferson: "I tremble for my country when I remember that God is just." But he quoted even more frequently the noble words Jefferson wrote in the Great Declaration: "We hold these truths to be self-evident: that all men are created equal; that they are endowed by their Creator with certain unalienable rights; that among them are life, liberty, and the pursuit of happiness." Lincoln was aware of the fact that the Old Testament patriarchs owned slaves, and that the New Testament itself nowhere condemned slavery. But he insisted that the whole bent of the Scriptures was against human bondage. For one thing, he noted, according to Genesis, God created man (and that meant all races) in His own image. for another, the Bible commanded, "in the sweat of thy face shalt thou eat bread," not, as Lincoln was fond of pointing out, in the sweat of someone else's face. Slavery, Lincoln reminded people, went against the Ten Commandments, for it involved stealing; it also violated the New Testament's Golden Rule of doing unto others what you wanted them to do to you. "I am naturally anti-slavery," Lincoln said firmly. "If slavery is not wrong, nothing is wrong. I cannot remember when I did not so think and feel."[8]

With the Scriptures and Jefferson's Declaration as the foundation for this thinking, Lincoln developed a providential theory of history that gave transcendent meaning and purpose to the terrible Civil War over which he presided after he entered the White House. By the time he became President, he had come to look on American history—and all history, for that matter—as a perpetual struggle between freedom and slavery in which the human race advanced steadily, despite frequent setbacks, toward the final goal of freedom for all people everywhere. Lincoln knew no Hegel, but he would undoubtedly have been charmed to know that the great 19th-century German philosopher took a somewhat similar (though more sophisticated) view of human destiny in his philosophy of history. For Hegel, history was the gradual realization (through a dialectical process) of the Absolute Spirit in historical development, with freedom as the ultimate objective. (Marx, following Hegel, used dialectic and made freedom his historical goal, too, but for him, human events were propelled by scientific laws of motion, not by Hegel's Absolute, and certainly not, as for Lincoln, by God's will.) There was something deeply predestinarian in Lincoln's way of looking at things (sometimes he called himself a "fatalist"). For him God's will supervised the movement of events, directing them unmistakably toward what he once called "a new birth of freedom."[9]

Lincoln wasn't the only 19th-century American who thought the United States had a special destiny to perform in the world. But where most Americans who talked of the nation's "Manifest Destiny" were thinking mainly of territorial expansion, Lincoln was thinking primarily of the expansion of freedom. Americans, he declared, were "an almost chosen people" whom the good Lord had selected to be freedom's special champion in the world. In practicing slavery they had grievously sinned and the Civil War had come upon them as a horrendous punishment for their betrayal of the cause. But by recognizing the error of their ways, repenting of their sins, and striving to do better, they could count on Almighty God—whom Lincoln variously called Almighty Architect, Guiding Hand, Divine Providence, Divine Will—to help them along on the road to the promised land of universal freedom. "Fellow citizens," he told Congress in December 1862, "we cannot escape history." From time to time during the Civil War he called on the American people to observe days of fasting and humiliation as well as days of thanksgiving.[10]

There is of course a paradox in Lincoln's way of looking at things (as there is in all rigidly deterministic schemes of thought): if God's will ultimately determines the course of human events, what role is there for the exercise of individual human freedom in the course of human events? Lincoln never really came to grips with this question. The most he ever said was that it was difficult to know the will of God in concrete situations and that the best one could do was to study the evidence, think it over carefully, figure out the best way to act, and then go ahead in the hope that what one chose to do accorded with the will of God. For Lincoln, there was never any absolute certainty that the choices one made were the right ones; one could only hope and pray that they were. "I suppose I am not to expect a direct revelation," he told a group of Chicago clergymen who came to the White House to tell him what he should do. "I must study the plain physical facts of the case, ascertain what is possible and learn what appears to be wise and right." To another clerical delegation that lectured him severely on his moral duties, he responded dryly that "it is not often that one is favored with a delegation *direct* from the Almighty." Lincoln often spoke of himself as being an instrument of the Almighty at a crucial moment in history, but the thought humbled him, for the responsibility was awesome. "It is a momentous thing," he said, "to be the instrument, under Providence, of the liberation of a race." He wasn't sure he always measured up to his grave responsibilities. "I am very sure," he told a friend, "that if I do not go away from here a wiser man, I shall go away a better man, for having learned here what a very poor sort of man I am."[11]

Lincoln's faith produced neither dogmatism nor intolerance. He never regarded his judgments as final or beyond criticism and he carefully refrained from identifying them with the will of God. He had an extraordinary ability to rise above the fierce hatreds that accompanied the Civil War and to view the bloody conflict *sub specie aeternitatis.* "What I have to do here," he once remarked, "is too vast for malicious dealing." In September 1862, after the Second Battle of Bull Run, he jotted down some reflections on the Divine Will that were discovered and published after his death. "The will of God prevails," he wrote. "In great contests each party claims to act in accordance with the will of God. Both *may* and one *must* be wrong. God cannot be *for,* and *against,* the same thing at the same time. In the present civil war it is quite possible that God's purpose is something different from the purpose of either party. . . ." Months later, when the outcome of the war was still uncertain, he reiterated his belief that "God's purpose" transcended human purposes: "Now, at the end of three years' struggle the nation's condition is not what either party, or any man devised or expected. God alone can claim it. Whither it is tending seems plain. If God now wills the removal of a great wrong and wills also that we of the North, as well as you of the South, shall pay fairly for our complicity in that wrong, impartial history will find therein new cause to attest and revere the justice and goodness of God."[12]

When Lincoln came to give his Second Inaugural Address on March 4, 1865, the victory of the Union was assured, but he utilized the occasion for neither celebration nor self-congratulation. Instead, after reminding the American people that slavery was "somehow the cause of the war," he went on to place the conflict in the context of the providential philosophy of history that had guided him ever since the beginning of his presidency. First, he noted the irony of the situation in which both the North and the South sought divine sanction for their cause. "Both," he said, "read the same Bible and pray to the same God, and each invokes His aid against the other." But realization of this irony did not prevent Lincoln from believing that his side was right, for slavery was to be condemned even if it claimed divine approval. "It may seem strange," he observed, "that any men should dare to ask a just God's assistance in wringing their bread from the sweat of other men's faces. . . ." Still, he warned his own side against self-righteousness: "but let us judge not, that we be not judged." Perhaps the situation was more complex than either side realized. "The prayers of both could not be answered," he went on. "That of neither has been answered fully." And then came Lincoln's deepest affirmation: "The Almighty has His own purposes." He went on to quote the Scriptures—"Woe unto the world because of offenses"—and to suggest that "this terrible war" came as "the woe due to those by whom the offense of slavery came," but to affirm that the "judgments of the Lord are true and righteous altogether."[13]

Lincoln was fully aware of what he was doing when he refused to identify the cause of the North with the cause of God. He told journalist Thurlow Weed after the inauguration that he didn't think his speech would be popular. "Men are not flattered," he said, "by being shown that there has been a difference of purposes between the Almighty and them." Still, "it is a truth which I thought needed to be told; and as whatever of humiliation there is in it, falls most directly on myself, I thought others might afford for me to tell it." Without in any way relaxing his antislavery principles or doubting that God was somehow always directing humanity toward freedom, Lincoln was able to adopt an attitude of charity and magnanimity toward the defeated South. "With malice toward none," he concluded his final major public address, "with charity for all, with firmness in right, as God gives us to see the right, let us strive to finish the work we are in, to bind up the nation's wounds; to care for him who shall have borne the battle, and for his widow, and his orphan—to do all which may achieve and cherish a just and lasting peace among ourselves, and with all nations."[14]

CHAPTER 22

Senator Lodge and
the League of Nations

After World War I, Henry Cabot Lodge led the fight in the U.S. Senate against Woodrow Wilson's League of Nations primarily because he was an "isolationist" who strongly opposed U.S. involvement in foreign wars.

Not so.

Massachusetts Senator Lodge was highly critical of Wilson's League and insisted on attaching "reservations" to American membership in it, but he was in his own way just as much of an "internationalist" as Wilson was.

Like Theodore Roosevelt, Lodge favored a "Large Policy" for the United States when it came to foreign affairs. Long before World War I, he was eager for Americans to acknowledge that "we are a great nation and intend to take a nation's part in the family of nations." He favored intervention in Cuba in 1898 (as well as annexation of Hawaii), and hailed the Spanish-American War not so much because of the territorial acquisitions and expanded markets that came out of it but because it ended America's status as "a hermit nation" and enabled her to "emerge gloriously on the great world stage."[1]

For Lodge, the important thing about the Spanish-American War was that it represented "the abandonment of isolation" and the assumption of world responsibilities by the United States.[2] Throughout his Senate career, which began in 1893 and ended with his death in 1924, Lodge vigorously championed an assertive foreign policy for the United States and the kind of strong national defense program that he insisted went with it. In 1911, however, he opposed proposals by President William Howard Taft for two treaties with Britain and France because they obliged the United States to submit all disputes, including those involving the nation's "vital national interests and honor," to arbitration. Lodge doubted that the United States could live up to so sweeping a commitment. "No greater disaster could befall the cause of peace," he warned, "than to make a promise in a treaty designed to promote peace which we know when we make it will not be kept in certain contingencies." Taft dropped the idea (which he had originally planned to extend to other nations), and, years later, when President Woodrow Wilson sought another universal commitment—to the League of Nations—Senator Lodge again objected.[3]

But Lodge was neither pacifist nor isolationist. When World War I broke out in Europe in the fall of 1914, he at once sided with the Allies—Britain and France—looked upon the war as a great struggle between democracy and freedom (represented by the Allies) on the one hand, and autocracy and militarism (represented by Germany) on the other, and insisted that American values as well as its security were dependent upon an Allied victory. "If Germany conquers France, England, or Russia," he warned, "she will dominate Europe and will subsequently seek to extend that domination if she can to the rest of the world. . . . Great Britain, France and Belgium believe that they are fighting the battle of freedom and democracy against militarism and autocracy, the battle for public laws against the laws of the sword, and for the right of the small nations to exist. . . ." He was critical of President Wilson's efforts to remain neutral in the conflict as well as of his reluctance to sponsor "preparedness," that is, measures to build up the nation's defenses. And in December 1916 he was infuriated by the President's offer to act as mediator in the conflict and by his statement that "the objects, which the statesmen of the belligerents on both sides have in mind in this war, are virtually the same, as stated in general terms to their own people and to the world." Wilson's talk of "peace without victory" in January 1917 didn't help the President with Lodge either. Long before the United States entered the war on the side of the Allies, Lodge had come to despise Wilson, and Wilson, him, but principles, not personalities, were at the heart of the clash between them.[4]

When the break with Germany finally came, however, Lodge stood firmly behind Wilson. He rallied support for the President when Wilson broke off relations with Germany, backed measures giving him the power to arm American merchantmen, and warmly applauded his war message to Congress in April 1917 (though he thought it proved that Wilson's policies up to that point had been all wrong). He was one of the first, moreover, to urge that American troops be sent to France to fight alongside Allied forces. Still, Lodge continued to distrust the President. From his point of view it was essential for the Allies to win a decisive victory over Germany and take strong measures after the war to keep her from making a comeback. Wilson, he feared, would try to make the struggle a "little war" if he could and perhaps even revert to "peace without victory" if the opportunity offered itself. As did Franklin Roosevelt in World War II, Lodge favored "unconditional surrender" as an Allied war aim and "placing Germany in a position where she can never again menace the peace, liberty and civilization of the world or the independence of other nations."[5]

In January 1918, when Wilson announced his famous Fourteen Points as the basis for a peace settlement after the war, Lodge approved many of the provisions Wilson suggested (particularly returning Alsace-Lorraine to France), but he was extremely suspicious of the Fourteenth Point: a "general association of nations" to effect "mutual guarantees of political independence and territorial integrity to great and small nations alike." Senate "irreconcilables"— Wisconsin's Robert M. LaFollette on the left and Pennsylvania's Philander C. Knox on the right—opposed U.S. participation in an "association of nations" of any kind because they thought it meant involving the United States in endless overseas conflicts. But Lodge was no "irreconcilable"; he favored close ties with Britain and France after the war to keep Germany from rising again. Sometimes, even during the war, he referred to America's alliance with the Allies against Germany as as virtual "league of nations" already busily at work fighting for world peace and order.[6]

Unlike Wilson, Lodge never thought moral force was enough to restrain aggressive nations like Germany. Military force, he said time and again, was indispensable. World peace, he declared in July 1915, "can only be maintained, by the force which *united nations* are willing to put behind the peace and order of the world" (italics added). He had grave doubts about the "general association of nations" that Wilson was contemplating precisely because he thought there was something dangerously vague about the idea. In May 1916, when the two men delivered addresses at a meeting of the League to Enforce Peace (founded in 1915 by Republicans like former President Taft to compel the peaceful settlement of international disputes), the divergence in their views was unmistakable. Lodge spoke first (at Wilson's insistence) and emphasized the fact that the success of any international organization depended on military preparedness, for, he pointed out, it was necessary to "put force behind international peace." Wilson, by contrast, sidestepped the problem of enforcement. In his address, he called for "a universal association of nations" to give "a virtual guarantee of territorial integrity and political independence" to all nations, but he did not explain how this was to be done. In the original draft of his speech there were references to the use of physical force in preventing wars, but he carefully eliminated all of them before giving his speech. Lodge felt all along—both during and after the war—that Wilson shirked his responsibility to make clear to the American people the precise obligations they were undertaking if the United States joined Wilson's "general association of nations" after the war. Sometimes he wondered whether Wilson was aware of them himself.[7]

In June 1919, President Wilson presented the Treaty of Versailles, containing the Covenant of the League of Nations (which he had drafted himself in Paris), to the U.S. Senate for ratification. That he would encounter some resistance from the Republicans (who controlled the Senate after the 1918 elections) and particularly from Senator Lodge, who was majority leader as well as chairman of the Senate Foreign Relations Committee, seems not to have bothered the President. He made it clear from the outset that he expected the Senate to accept the Treaty, with the League Covenant, without any serious modifications. But Lodge—and most of the Republican Senators, including those favorable to the League—found much to criticize in Wilson's approach. They regretted that he had insisted on making the League an essential part of the Treaty; they also wondered whether League membership superseded the Monroe Doctrine and whether it gave the League power over America's tariff and immigration policies. But their objections to the

Treaty came soon to center on the commitment asked of the United States in Article X of the League Covenant.

Article X (which Wilson called the "heart of the Covenant") called for the kind of universal commitment to which Lodge had objected in President Taft's arbitration treaty proposals in 1911. "The members of the League," according to Article X, "undertake to respect and preserve as against external aggression the territorial integrity and existing political independence of all members of the League. In case of such aggression, or in case of any threat or danger of aggression, the Council shall advise upon the means by which the obligation shall be fulfilled." For Lodge, binding the United States, if it joined the League, to send U.S. troops to fight around the world whenever the League Council called for it was absolutely unthinkable. Not only did it negate the constitutional right of Congress to declare war; it also rested on the shaky assumption that the United States (and other nations belonging to the League) would in practice always honor the obligation no matter what the circumstances. "If we agree to this article," Lodge told former Secretary of State Elihu Root, "it is extremely probable that we shall be unable to keep the agreement. . . . The people of the United States certainly will not be willing ten or twenty years hence to send their young men to distant parts of the world to fight for causes in which they may not believe or in which they have little or no interest." Root, who favored membership in the League, shared Lodge's views on the sanctity of treaties. "Nothing can be worse in international affairs than to make agreements and break them," he told Wilson's adviser Colonel E. M. House. "It would be folly, therefore, for the United States in order to preserve or enforce peace . . . to enter into an agreement which the people of the United States would not regard as binding upon them."[8]

Did Article X in fact oblige the United States to "wage perpetual war for perpetual peace," as historian Charles A. Beard put it years later? Wilson equivocated on the issue. Though he regarded Article X as the "heart" and "backbone" and "kingpin" of the League Covenant, he and his supporters insisted that it imposed a "moral" rather than a "legal" obligation. "It is binding in conscience only," said Wilson, "not in law. . . ." Elsewhere, though, he admitted that armed force was "in the background" and that "if the moral force of the world will not suffice, the physical force of the world shall." At the same time, however, he said repeatedly that Congress retained its constitutional authority to determine the country's obligations under Article X. Lodge sharply rejected such reassurances. He demanded "facts, details and sharp, clear-cut definitions." It was only fair to the American people, he thought, to spell out with some precision their obligations under Article X. "I do not say," he remarked, "that the time has not come when, in the interest of future peace, the American people may not decide that we ought to guarantee the territorial integrity of the far-flung British Empire, including her self-governing dominions and colonies, of the Balkan States, of China or Japan, or of the French, Italian and Portuguese colonies in Africa, but I do suggest that it is a very grave, a very perilous promise to make, because there is but one way by which such guarantees, if ever invoked, can be maintained, and that way is the way of force—whether military or economic force, it matters not. If we guarantee any country on earth . . . that guarantee we must maintain at any cost when our word is once given, and we must be in constant possession of fleets and armies capable of enforcing these guarantees at a moment's notice. There is no need of arguing whether there is to be compulsive force behind the league. It is there in article 10 absolutely and entirely by the mere fact of these guarantees."[9]

Lodge and his supporters hammered home the point: if Congress retained its authority to declare war under Article X of the League Covenant, as Wilson insisted, why not say so openly? Not only would it reassure the American people; it would also prevent the possibility of misunderstandings after the United States joined the League. With the help of the pro-Leaguer Elihu Root, Senator Lodge drafted a "reservation" to add to the Treaty of Versailles in the interest of clarification. The Lodge "reservation," which most Senate Republicans supported, declared that the United States "assumes no obligation to preserve the territorial integrity or political independence of any other country, or to interfere in controversies between nations, whether members of the league or not, under the provisions of Article X, or to employ the military and naval forces of the United States under any article of the treaty for any purpose, unless in any particular case the Congress, which, under the Constitution, has the sole power to declare war or authorize the employment of the military and naval forces of the United States, shall, by act or joint resolution so declare."[10]

Wilson rejected the "reservation" out of hand. He flatly refused to modify the "moral obligation" contained in Article X in any way whatsoever. He refused, in fact, to accept any of the so-called reservations that Senate Republicans proposed attaching to ratification of the Versailles Treaty. The most he would agree to was a series of "interpretive reservations" contained in a Senate resolution separate from the Treaty. Allied leaders were not so implacable. Unlike Wilson, they indicated their willingness to go along with a set of "reservations" which many Senate Republicans favored. Viscount Grey (British ambassador to the United States), for one, was reported to have commented sympathetically on Lodge's handling of the Treaty. In a letter to the London *Times*, moreover, he urged British acceptance of the Lodge reservations as the best means of securing American membership in the League, for, as he put it, international co-operation was more likely to blossom if the United States entered the League "as a willing partner with limited obligations" than if "she entered as a reluctant partner who felt that her hand had been forced."[11]

Lodge thought Grey's letter "splendid." On November 6, 1919, he reported a resolution of ratification from the Senate Foreign Relations Committee which contained fourteen reservations (including the crucial one about Article X) limiting America's obligations under the League Covenant, but not, in the opinion of some historians, seriously impairing the League itself. But Wilson was uncompromising. Insisting that the Lodge resolution "does not provide for ratification but, rather, for the nullification of the treaty," he instructed Senate Democrats to vote against it. As a result, when the Treaty with reservations came to vote on November 19, a combination of Wilson Democrats and Republican "irreconcilables" succeeded in defeating the resolution. Another vote the same day on the Treaty without any reservations whatsoever also failed to pass, with only Democrats supporting it. But Wilson's League was given one more chance. On February 9, 1920, the Senate, in an unusual move (which Lodge supported), voted to reconsider the Versailles Treaty. Again Wilson made clear his opposition to the reservations, but this time around, on March 19, 1920, twenty-one Democrats deserted the President to join the Republican reservationists in voting for the Treaty. There were not enough Democratic votes, however, to supply the necessary two-thirds majority required for ratification. Even Lodge admitted there was "an element of tragedy" in the situation. But even if more Democrats had deserted Wilson in order to make the ratification possible, the President would undoubtedly have exercised his pocket veto to kill the treaty, as he had threatened to do.[12] Wilson and Lodge certainly despised each other, and personal feelings unquestionably played an important part in their struggle over the League. At the heart of the dispute, however, was a basic divergence in their outlook on world affairs.

In popular mythology Senator Lodge has been regarded as the great "isolationist" scoundrel who kept the United States out of the League and was thus somehow responsible for the renewal of war with Germany twenty years later. In fact, though, Lodge's main concern all along had been with keeping Germany down after the war. He had no objection to a "league of allies" (Britain, France, and the United States) working together to enforce the peace once Germany surrendered. "We must do our share," he said after the war, "to carry out the peace as we have done our share to win the war, of which the peace is an integral part. We must do our share in the occupation of German territory. . . . We cannot escape doing our part in aiding the peoples to whom we have helped to give freedom and independence in establishing themselves with ordered governments, for in no other way can we erect the barriers which are essential to prevent another outbreak by Germany upon the world. . . ." Lodge even favored a treaty with France after the war in which Britain and the United States would guarantee her military security against Germany. He never opposed specific international commitments; what he objected to was general commitments circumscribing the nation's freedom of action in the indefinite future. He thought it important, too, for Americans to know exactly what they were getting into if the United States became part of Wilson's League of Nations.[13]

Who knows? Perhaps Wilson, Lodge, and LaFollette were all of them right in some respects: Wilson, in his conviction that the United States should join an international organization to encourage the peaceful settlement of disputes between nations; Lodge, in his realization that it takes military force to check aggression, as well as continual military "preparedness" on the part of the aggression-checkers; and LaFollette, in his belief that the "internationalism" which Wilson and Lodge advocated meant making war a major instrument of U.S. foreign policy. But all three of them, it is safe to say, would be astonished by the globalization of American foreign policy after the second defeat of Germany in World War II and the casual bypassing of Congress thereafter in the waging of wars thousands of miles from American shores.

CHAPTER 23

President Harding's Strange Death

Mrs. Harding poisoned her husband.

Certainly not.

The story that Warren G. Harding died of poison administered by his wife first appeared in the sensational book *The Strange Death of Warren Harding*, written by Gaston B. Means, former Justice Department employee, and published in 1930, several years after both the Hardings were gone. In his book Means charged that Mrs. Harding had come to hate her husband after discovering his love affair with Nan Britton, and that she was also afraid that the revelations of corruption in his administration might lead to impeachment. So, in August 1923, she enlisted the help of the Surgeon-General, Charles Sawyer (an old Ohio friend of the Hardings), in administering poison to the ailing President in the guise of medicine, and he quickly died. There was no autopsy.[1]

Means's book became a big best-seller. Even ordinarily level-headed reviewers were for a time taken in by some of its revelations. The following year, however, Means's ghostwriter, May Dixon Thacker (sister of Thomas Dixon, author of *The Klansman*), wrote an article for *Liberty* magazine entitled, "Debunking the Strange Death of President Harding," in which she confessed "with humiliation" and "in justice to the dead" that the book was a "tremendous hoax." Means, it turned out, was a swindler, blackmailer, and perjurer, and he was serving time in the Atlanta penitentiary when he first discussed with Mrs. Thacker the possibility of doing a book about President Harding. When he got out of prison, he began meeting regularly with Mrs. Thacker and pouring out a series of sleazy stories for her to write up about the degradation of the Harding administration: the sexual infidelities, the drunken orgies, and the bribery and graft among the President's appointees. In the evening Means and his wife hooted over the tales he had made up to tell Mrs. Thacker during the day. Means had never met either of the Hardings, had never been in the White House, and he never produced the diary of Nan Britton (Harding's mistress) or Harding's letters to Nan which he promised as evidence for his tales. In her piece for *Liberty*, Mrs. Thacker said she was hoodwinked by Means and that the book they turned out was a "colossal hoax—a tissue of falsehoods from the beginning to the end."[2]

There was never anything sinister about President Harding's death in 1923. His health was wretched; he suffered from high systolic blood pressure. He was also deeply depressed by the revelations of graft and corruption that came to light in 1922 and 1923 involving friends he had appointed to high office. His wife, also ailing, was similarly depressed. Charles Sawyer, the Surgeon-General, suggested a change of scene as therapy for the two of them and they decided to take a trip to the West Coast and Alaska that summer. On June 20, 1923, they boarded a special train, together with Dr. Sawyer, a naval doctor, a trained nurse, and a couple of Cabinet members, and headed west. En route Harding made a lot of speeches (which he wrote himself) and the crowds were friendly. But he continued to feel down in the dumps. "My God, this is a hell of a job!" he exclaimed at one point. "I have no trouble with enemies. I can take care of my enemies all right. But my damn friends, my God-damn friends. . . . They're the ones that keep me walking the floor nights!" Mrs. Harding was feeling too downbeat herself to try pulling him out of the doldrums.[3]

The trip may have done Harding in. In Seattle, he became seriously ill and was rushed to San Francisco and put to bed, with local doctors as well as his own physicians in attendance. Dr. Sawyer announced that the President was suffering from ptomaine poisoning, but his diagnosis was wrong. All the other doctors agreed that he had suffered a heart attack. The end came suddenly on August 3, when Mrs. Harding was reading aloud from an article in the *Saturday Evening Post* containing some kind remarks about his policies.

"That's good," he said at one point. "Go on, read some more." Moments later he was dead as the result of a thrombosis. Mrs. Harding fell apart after his death, but finally pulled herself together and resolved, "I will not break down." The night before the funeral she went to the East Room of the White House where her husband lay in state and sat quietly there for a long time. "No one can hurt you now, Warren," she finally said and then went over, made up a little bouquet from the array of flowers sent for the funeral, and placed it on his coffin.[4]

Mrs. Harding was undoubtedly "a strange and rather difficult woman," as Elizabeth Jaffray, the White House housekeeper, reported, but she was deeply devoted to her husband despite his occasional infidelities. The night before the funeral she sent for two newspapermen whom he had praised shortly before his death and told them to go in and take a look at the President's body. "I know what some of his critics were saying," she told them. "They charged that he was weak. I want you to look at those firm lips of his and see. I look at them and know they show he was not weak. I know that he had strength and courage."[5]

CHAPTER 24

Herbert Hoover and
the Great Depression

Herbert Hoover failed as President because he did nothing to fight the Great Depression.

Not exactly.

Hoover failed, all right, but it was not from ignoring the Great Depression that hit the country early in his presidency. He was in fact the first President to try actively to do something about a major economic slump. In previous depressions, during the 1830s, 1870s, and 1890s, the nation's chief executives, Republican and Democrat, had disclaimed the responsibility of the federal government to sponsor serious measures for stimulating the economy. If the American people continued to work hard and remained patient, they insisted, conditions would gradually improve and good times return. Government intervention, they said, would only make things worse.[1]

Martin Van Buren's attitude was typical. Like Hoover, he entered the White House when conditions were good and he had pleasant things to say about the state of the Union in his inaugural address. Within a month, however, the Panic of 1837 struck the country and a major depression lasting six years ensued, with business failures, mounting unemployment, and widespread misery plaguing the nation. Van Buren's first reaction was to put the blame on the American people for their troubles; he deplored "the rapid growth, among all classes, especially in our great commercial towns, of luxurious habits founded too often on merely fancied wealth, and detrimental alike to the industry, the resources, and the morals of our people."

The federal government, he went on to say, could do little or nothing in the crisis. "All communities are apt to look to government too much," he warned. "Even in our own country, where its powers and duties are so strictly limited, we are prone to do so, especially at periods of sudden embarrassment and distress. This ought not to be. The framers of our excellent Constitution and the people who approved it with calm sagacious deliberation acted at the time on a sounder principle. They wisely judged that the less government interference with private pursuits the better for the general prosperity."[2]

For Van Buren, the federal government's "real duty" was "to enact and enforce a system of general laws commensurate with, but not exceeding, the objects of its establishment, and to leave every citizen and every interest to reap under its benign protection the rewards of virtue, industry, and prudence." A laissez-faire policy in his opinion was best. "If therefore," he concluded, "I refrain from suggesting to Congress any specific plan for regulating the exchanges of the country, relieving mercantile embarrassments, or interfering with the ordinary operations of foreign or domestic commerce, it is from a conviction that such measures are not within the institutional province of the General Government, and that their adoption would not promote the real and permanent welfare of those they might be designed to aid."[3] Both Ulysses Grant (in the depression following the Panic of 1873) and Grover Cleveland (in the depression touched off by the Panic of 1893) followed for the most part the example set by Van Buren. An anti-Cleveland joke told of a hungry citizen who started grazing on the White House lawn to dramatize his plight, only to be told by the President that the grass was better in back of the White House.

Herbert Hoover broke precedent. He was the first President to take positive action to cope with a major national economic crisis. At first, to be sure, he took the laissez-faire line, counting on "natural processes" to bring about an eventual uptick in the economy. Then, when the economy continued to deteriorate, despite rosy forecasts that prosperity was "just around the corner," he tried what might be called "voluntarism": he extracted pledges from leading businessmen to maintain existing wages, employment, and production and encouraged municipal and state governments to step up spending on public works in order to stimulate the economy. But when voluntarism failed—businessmen found they simply couldn't keep their pledges and local governments became strapped for funds—he finally turned to action on the federal level. Not only did he increase federal spending on public works to provide employment; he also endorsed legislation establishing the Reconstruction Finance Corporation (RFC) to lend money to banks, railroads, and insurance companies (and eventually to state governments) to keep them from going under. Hoover backed federal intervention grudgingly, hesitantly, and with grave reservations, and to the end he insisted that relief for the unemployed and poverty-stricken be left to local governments and private charities. Still, he backed federal action all the same and he was the first President to do so. His policies were, as historian Charles A. Beard noted at the time, "a marked departure from the renunciation of his predecessors."[4]

The measures Hoover took to fight the depression were too limited and came too late to stem the tide of disaster. In 1932, when he ran for re-election, however, he reminded voters that he had not "feared boldly to adopt unprecedented measures to meet the unprecedented violence of the storm." When the Great Crash came, he recalled, "We might have done nothing. That would have been utter ruin. Instead, we met the situation with proposals to private business and the Congress of the most gigantic programme of economic defense and counter-attack ever evolved in the history of the republic." This was true enough, but by the time he uttered these words, the economy had hit rock bottom, and his defeat by Franklin Roosevelt, offering the voters a New Deal, came as no surprise.

Roosevelt swung into action right after his inauguration on March 4, 1933, and the wide-ranging New Deal measures he sponsored shocked and horrified Hoover. But one of the major agencies FDR utilized in his program for recovery was Hoover's RFC. Writing in 1935, Walter Lippmann insisted, with some exaggeration, that most of FDR's program was an extension of President Hoover's program, which itself had set a precedent for the future. "It would seem," he wrote, "that the decision which Mr. Hoover took in the autumn of 1929 is irreversible; he committed the government to the new function of using all its powers to regulate the business cycle. With this precedent established, it is almost inconceivable that any of his successors should in another depression refuse to act." Lippmann was right. Hoover turned out to be, as historian Carl Degler noted years later, "a transitional figure in the development of the government as an active force in the economy in times of depression."[5]

CHAPTER 25

Justice Holmes and President Roosevelt

Shortly after Franklin D. Roosevelt's 1933 inauguration, Justice Oliver Wendell Holmes, Jr., remarked that the new President had "a second-class intellect but a first-class temperament."

Probably not.

Justice Holmes was referring to a Roosevelt when he made his celebrated comment, but there is good reason to believe he was thinking of Theodore Roosevelt, who appointed him to the U.S. Supreme Court in 1902, rather than of Franklin D. Roosevelt, whom he knew only slightly.

On March 8, 1933, four days after his first inauguration as President, FDR insisted on paying a courtesy call on the 92-year-old Justice, who had retired the year before, at his Washington home. He found Holmes reading, with the help of Thomas G. Corcoran, one of his former law clerks. "Why do you read Plato?" FDR asked curiously. "To improve my mind," returned Holmes.[1] When FDR asked for advice on coping with the Great Depression, Holmes, a thrice-wounded veteran of the Civil War, exclaimed: "Form your ranks—and fight!" After FDR left, Holmes turned to Corcoran and mused: "You know, his Uncle Ted appointed me to the Supreme Court." Then, after a moment or two, he added: "a second-class intellect, but a first-class temperament."[2]

Corcoran had the impression that Holmes was thinking of FDR when he made the remark and reported it that way afterward. The supposed comment on the new President was soon famous and eventually became part of the title of Geoffrey Ward's biography, *FDR: A First-Class Temperament,* published in 1989. It is quite likely, though, that Corcoran misinterpreted Holmes's comment. Holmes scarcely knew FDR, while he had known T.R. very well (he was one of the "Roosevelt Familiars," as T.R.'s intimates were called) years before. Having reminded Corcoran, after FDR left, that Theodore Roosevelt had appointed him to the Supreme Court, Justice Holmes was probably thinking of the Rough Rider when he went on to say, "second-class intellect, first-class temperament."[3]

In his biography of the Justice, *Oliver Wendell Holmes, Jr.: Soldier, Scholar, Judge* (1989), political scientist Gary J. Aiechele pointed out that Holmes had made a similar comment about T.R. a couple of years after T.R.'s death in 1919. In a letter to his friend Sir Frederick Pollack, a British judge, written on February 9, 1921, Holmes said that T.R. was "very likable, a big figure, a rather ordinary intellect, with extraordinary gifts, a shrewd and I think rather unscrupulous politician. He played all his cards—if not more. R.i.p."[4]

CHAPTER 26

Presidential
Ghostwriters

Franklin D. Roosevelt was the first President to make use of ghost-writers for his speeches.

Not so.

It was George Washington, not Franklin Roosevelt, who first sought major assistance in the drafting of important public addresses while he was President. He had extensive help on both his First Inaugural Address and on his celebrated Farewell Address.

After the electoral college unanimously elected Washington as the new nation's first President, and Congress picked April 30, 1789, as the date for his inauguration, the Hero of the Revolution went into a huddle with his friend and former aide-de-camp, David Humphreys, a minor poet, and the two of them came up with the draft of a lengthy speech, mostly written by Humphreys, for the occasion. In the end, though, Washington discarded the speech. This was possibly because it contained too many tiresome details about the difficulties accompanying the War for Independence, the economic problems facing the country after the war, and the ways in which the new Constitution, for all its shortcomings, might set the young republic on the road to peace and prosperity. There was too much of a personal note, moreover, in this first try at an inaugural address. In it, Washington protested too much. He was eager to convince Americans that he really did intend to return to private life after the Revolution, as he had promised, and that only a strong sense of public duty, not private ambition, had brought him back into the public arena. There was also an astonishingly personal passage in the Humphreys-Washington manuscript, in which Washington made the point that there was absolutely no way in which he could transform the presidency, even if he wanted to, into a hereditary monarchy: ". . . it will be recollected that the Divine Providence hath not seen fit that my blood should be transmitted or my name perpetuated by the endearing, though sometimes seducing, channel of immediate offspring. I have no child for whom I could wish to make provision—no family to build in greatness upon my country's ruins." If some of the poetic phrases in this manuscript belonged to Humphreys, surely this particular sentiment was Washington's, for he was extremely sensitive to charges of inordinate ambition. It was a clumsy passage, and it would have embarrassed his admirers if he had used it at the country's first inauguration.[1]

The Humphreys-Washington draft exists only in part today. What happened to it chills the blood of present-day historians and biographers. In 1827, years after Washington's death, Jared Sparks, Unitarian minister and editor of the *North American Review*, who was preparing to publish a collection of Washington's writings, came across the speech in Washington's handwriting, and decided to suppress it, partly because he thought some of the passages in it were a bit strange and partly because he knew it had eventually been discarded. On May 22, Sparks asked the aging James Madison's advice, and Madison, who had seen it thirty-eight years before, told him: "I concur without hesitation in your remarks on the speech of seventy-three pages and the expediency of not including it among the papers selected for the press. Nothing but extreme delicacy towards the author of the draft, who was no doubt Colonel Humphreys, can account for the respect shown to so strange a production." Sparks then blithely cut the manuscript into pieces and handed out parts of it to autograph collectors anxious to own something in Washington's handwriting. Years later scholars attempted to reassemble the fragments, but succeeded in recovering only a third to one-half of the original. The anfractuosities of what survives are probably Sparks's doing, not Washington's or Humphreys's.[2]

Washington probably wouldn't have minded the destruction of the speech. He seems to have had serious doubts about it from almost the beginning. In February 1789 he sent the manuscript to James Madison for comment, and the latter, visiting Mount Vernon later that month, persuaded Washington to put it aside. Then "little Jemmy" went to work himself and came up with a new speech which, edited by Washington, took only twenty minutes to deliver during the inaugural ceremonies on April 30. All the ideas in it were Washington's: the reluctance to accept such a difficult trust, the ardent love for his country, the country's dependence on the "Almighty Being who rules the universe," and his awareness of the momentousness of the American experiment in liberty and self-government being launched that day. Some of these ideas had appeared in the Washington-Humphreys manuscript, but none of the clumsiness of that address survived in the Madison manuscript, and when Washington finally delivered it after taking his oath of office, it deeply moved all his listeners. Madison, who was in the audience, was a member of the House of Representatives at the time, and after the inaugural ceremony he drafted for the House a reply to Washington's address, and then, at Washington's request, drafted Washington's brief response to the House's congratulatory message. He also drafted Washington's message responding to the Senate's formal acknowledgment of the inaugural address. The media today would have a field day with all these exchanges.[3]

Madison kept busy. Not only did he take a leading role in sponsoring legislation in the First Congress to put the new government on a firm foundation; he also continued to help Washington with his writing. When Washington decided to retire at the end of his first term, he turned to Madison again and asked for help in framing a valedictory message to the American people. Madison dutifully obliged and wrote a speech that Washington approved, but never got to use because his associates, particularly Alexander Hamilton and Thomas Jefferson, persuaded him to seek another term.[4]

When 1796 rolled around, however, Washington was firm in his determination to retire at the end of his second term. Upset by the party strife that developed after 1793, deeply hurt by the way Jefferson and Madison went into the opposition because of the Hamiltonian policies he had adopted, and enraged by the vituperative criticisms some of their followers were hurling at him, Washington knew he needed a quite different kind of farewell address in 1796 than the one Madison had prepared for him in 1792. His first instinct, though, was to use Madison's speech anyway, in order to show his critics that he hadn't wanted a second term in the first place and that he wasn't simply retiring under fire. He even planned to mention the fact that Madison himself had been "privy to the draft" of 1792, but then thought better of it. What he finally did was to copy passages from Madison's 1792 draft, and add some material of his own deploring party strife in the young nation, and criticizing undue attachment to foreign nations by American citizens. But as he went along, he was suddenly overcome with rage at the recent attacks on his character, and exploded into the following paragraph: "As this address, fellow citizens, will be the last I shall ever make to you, and as some of the gazettes of the United States have teemed with all the invective that disappointment, ignorance of facts, and malicious falsehoods could invent, to misrepresent my politics and affection— to wound my reputation and feelings—and to weaken, if not entirely destroy, the confidence you have been pleased to repose in me; it might be expected at the parting scene of my public life that I should take some notice of such virulent abuse. But, as heretofore, I shall pass them over in utter silence." But he found he couldn't "pass over" the assaults on him "in utter silence" after all, and he went on to write a few more paragraphs defending his integrity and finally concluded: "I leave you with undefiled hands, an uncorrupted heart, and with ardent vows to heaven for the welfare and happiness of that country in which I and my forefathers to the third or fourth progenitor drew our first breath."[5]

In April 1796, Washington showed what he had written to Hamilton and the latter offered to help him revise it. The following month Washington sent him the manuscript and suggested he delete the "egotisms" in it or even "throw the *whole* into a different form" if he thought it advisable. A few weeks later Hamilton wrote from New York that he was working on an entirely new speech and said there was no hurry since Washington should delay the announcement of his retirement as long as possible. In July, Hamilton finally sent Washington a copy of the new speech he had written and explained that he had tried to make it *"importantly and lastingly useful"* and had avoided mentioning current political controversies in it in order "to embrace such reflections and sentiments as will wear well, progress in approbation with time, and redound to future reputation."[6]

Washington liked what Hamilton had written. But he was bothered by its length. "All the columns of a large gazette would scarcely,

I conceive, contain the present draft," he wrote Hamilton. But he promised to give "Hamilton's Main Draft," as it came to be called, "the most attentive consideration." Hamilton also sent Washington his revision of the speech Washington himself had prepared. It had the advantage of being shorter than Hamilton's Main Draft, but it lacked its long-range view. "Whichever you prefer," Hamilton told Washington; he would be glad to give further help if Washington wanted it. Washington studied both speeches carefully and finally decided he preferred Hamilton's Main Draft, since, he said, it was "more copious on material points, more dignified on the whole, and with less egotism." He then did a painstaking editorial job on it, adapting the language to his own style, deleting phrases he did not like, inserting some passages he liked from the other manuscript, and adding some new ideas of his own, including the importance of education to a free nation. He also took out a sentence which Hamilton had sneaked into the manuscript containing Hamilton's Federalist belief in a high-toned government. When he finished his rewriting, the manuscript was thoroughly Washingtonian in both style and content. Hamilton was quite familiar with Washington's opinions and he had for the most part been faithful to his ideas when composing the address.[7]

The Farewell Address—with its warnings against party strife and undue attachment to foreign nations, as well as the insistence on the importance of religion and morality—soon became a classic. After it first appeared in the *Daily American Advertiser*, published in Philadelphia, on September 19, 1796, it was widely reprinted and highly praised. One of Washington's critics, it is true, dismissed the essay's comments on parties as "the loathings of a sick mind," but most newspapers hailed the address for its wisdom, and many civic organizations, as well as state legislatures, passed resolutions of gratitude for Washington's last message to the American people.[8]

But the Farewell Address soon ran into trouble. Several years after both Washington and Hamilton had passed from the scene, one of Hamilton's executors discovered a copy of the 1796 address in Hamilton's handwriting. He was shocked. He knew that Hamilton's widow had insisted her husband had written the address and here, in his hands, seemed to be unassailable proof that she was right. After thinking things over, he decided to entrust Hamilton's copy of the address, along with other relevant papers, to Rufus King (a good

Federalist like Hamilton); this way he could say he didn't have a copy of the address if anyone queried him about the authorship. But rumors leaked out about the copy in Hamilton's handwriting, and at least one of Washington's admirers regretted there was no way he could burn the pesky manuscript. Even Madison was upset; he told Jefferson he thought it would hurt the reputation of the Farewell Address immeasurably if it became associated with Hamilton's strong Federalist prejudices rather than with Washington's more nonpartisan view of the American system. Meanwhile the Hamilton family learned that Rufus King had the relevant papers and demanded their return. When King refused to hand them over, they brought suit against him and in 1826 regained the documents. By this time, though, the Hamiltons seem to have come around to Madison's view of the matter. Instead of raising a rumpus over Hamilton's part in drafting the Address and the efforts to conceal it, they simply deposited the papers relating to the Address in the Library of Congress, along with other Hamilton material. Not until 1859, when the first edition of Hamilton's papers appeared in print, did the evidence for the important part Hamilton played in writing Washington's Farewell Address become public knowledge.[9]

After Washington, most Presidents—John Adams, Thomas Jefferson, James Madison, John Quincy Adams, Abraham Lincoln, Theodore Roosevelt, Woodrow Wilson, Herbert Hoover—wrote their own speeches, sometimes, to be sure, with the advice of associates and suggestions from their wives. And even Presidents who, beginning with Franklin Roosevelt, depended heavily on speechwriters for their material, tended to go about it the way the first President had: they sketched out ideas in advance for their writers to utilize, carefully edited drafts of speeches submitted to them, and contributed phrases, sentences, and even paragraphs and pages of their own to the final product. It was FDR himself who was responsible for the dramatic first words of his war message to Congress after the attack on Pearl Harbor: "Yesterday, December 7, 1941—a date that will live in infamy. . . ." On his platform copy of the address, now deposited in the National Archives, he had scratched through the typed word, history, and inserted the word, infamy, in his own handwriting.[10]

CHAPTER 27

FDR and
Soviet Recognition

There was a general outpouring of wrath, especially among conservatives, when President Roosevelt extended diplomatic recognition to the Soviet Union in November 1933.

No, there wasn't.

Not until the 1950s did Republican Senator Joseph R. McCarthy of Wisconsin and his followers begin talking ominously about "twenty years of treason" that commenced in 1933 when FDR recognized Soviet Russia. At the time, however, Roosevelt's action met with hearty approval. In October 1933, the *Literary Digest* reported that a majority of the newspapers in the country supported his action. The American business community also liked what FDR did. There was some dissent, to be sure, but it was a minor ripple compared with the tidal wave of support for FDR's recognition policy in the fall of 1933.

Why did FDR decide to recognize the USSR in 1933? For one thing, the United States had traditionally extended diplomatic recognition to new governments which seemed stable, and the Soviet regime had been in power for sixteen years. For another, FDR thought his action might act as a deterrent to Japan, which, since conquering Manchuria in 1931, had been threatening further aggression against China. Most important, though, was the economic motive. The United States was in the depths of the Great Depression when FDR took office, and he looked upon the establishment of diplomatic relations with Soviet Russia as a possible prelude to the development of profitable trade relations between the two countries, which, he hoped, would help pull American business out of the doldrums.

Recognition did not of course mean approval. The United States had in the past maintained diplomatic relations with plenty of countries whose governments shocked American sensibilities, and it was to continue doing so for the rest of the century. To the *Dallas Morning News,* a warm supporter of President Roosevelt's action, the Soviet Union was "Just Another Customer." A *News* cartoon portrayed a Soviet woman waiting before the counter of a general store to make her purchases while Uncle Sam, the clerk, tells two protesting women (the American Federation of Labor and the Daughters of the American Revolution): "Listen! I ain't goin' to *marry* the girl!" Roosevelt, said the *News,* "returns to the older theory of recognition that a Government is entitled to recognition if it is in full possession of the Government, it is able to maintain order and protect life and property, and if its rule is acquiesced in by the people. Russia fulfills these conditions and all that now remains is to reach agreements respecting debts and pledges against propaganda. These agreements can be made in principle and details worked out through appointed commissions. Some object to recognition on the ground that Russia's system of government is communistic and in general antireligious. Internationally, however, each State in theory has the right to determine its own form of government and sphere of activity. . . . The general opinion in this country is that Russia and the United States should resume normal and diplomatic relations, since they have many common interests, especially in the Far East, and can readily develop trade relations, mutually profitable."

Twenty years later the *Dallas Morning News* completely reversed itself. A hearty supporter of Soviet recognition in 1933, the *News* was in 1953 thoroughly McCarthyite in its view of things. Recognizing Soviet Russia, it now told its readers, was a great act of betrayal. Not only did it give the rapidly disintegrating Bolshevik regime a new lease on life; it also gave the Soviets a green light for launching their program of worldwide imperialistic aggression. And who was responsible for this state of affairs? Franklin Roosevelt, of course, the New Deal President. "Russia was recognized," stated a *News* editorial, "solely because Franklin D. Roosevelt as President insisted upon it." The New Deal President, the *News* now decided, had been "soft" on Communism. The editors had nothing to say about the *News's* earlier opinions on the subject.

The *Dallas Morning News* was not alone, during the McCarthy era, in seeing a great conspiracy at the heart of FDR's treatment of the Soviet Union. Roosevelt, declared Bascom N. Timmons, a columnist for the *Dallas Times-Herald,* "took action virtually on his own, rejecting the counsel of elder statesmen who thought we should wait awhile before opening our doors to Soviet diplomats." William Bradford Huie, editor of the *American Mercury,* went farther than Timmons. He broadened criticism of FDR's action to include the Democratic party as a whole. "The gravest charge against the Democratic party," he wrote in September 1952, "is that it allowed evil and naive men within it to convert it into a vehicle which aided the growth of Soviet Russia and the extension of Soviet power." It was "a historic fact," he added, that the Democratic party first embarked on its iniquitous course "when it championed recognition of the Soviet Union in 1933." But William F. Buckley, Jr., budding young conservative in the early 1950s, went even further in his search for culprits. The American professoriate, he insisted, as well as the New Deal Democrats, bore some blame for the iniquity. In an article entitled "The Colossal Flunk" (subtitled "How Our Professors Have Betrayed the American People"), Buckley posed this question: "Now whose responsibility was it to confront Franklin Roosevelt with the available and overwhelming evidence that this capricious act was nothing more than an invitation to the Comintern to set up in the United States hemispheric headquarters for a violent revolutionary movement . . . ?" The answer was self-evident: "The responsibility sat squarely on the shoulders of the academic community." Yet, he continued sorrowfully, "a survey of the literature of the day reveals hardly a dissenting wave length originating from the nation's ivory towers. The reverse, in fact, was the case; the academic journals of the period treated compassionately and even encouragingly American Recognition, which served immeasurably to fortify Stalin's then faltering domestic position."

It is certainly possible that America's professors mostly favored recognition in 1933 (though Buckley offered no evidence for it), but if they did, they had plenty of company. The majority of the newspapers around the country (62 percent, according to one poll) applauded FDR's action. So did most members of Congress. "ROOSE-

VELT'S MOVE WINS WIDE BACKING," reported the *New York Times* in a front-page headline. "Most of the Senators and Representatives Commenting Favor the Step." Speaker of the House Henry A. Rainey, Democrat of Illinois, in a typical view, thought recognition would open an "outlet for our surplus goods."

Like members of Congress, American businessmen and bankers, according to the *New York Times*, were also eager for the development of trade relations that would follow diplomatic recognition. Many of them, according to the *Times*, felt that the "potentialities of trade with this economically youthful country were unlimited." To reassure businessmen who were wavering on the issue, officials of General Electric and RCA, both of whom "have had large dealings with the Soviets," announced that "at all times their relations with Soviet Russia have been eminently satisfactory." Reversing its previous stand, the American-Russian Chamber of Commerce, whose membership included leading business and banking houses, came out for recognition. So did the United States Board of Trade. The city of Seattle was particularly excited by the prospects: "SEATTLE SEES TRADE BOOM" was a front-page headline in the *New York Times*. "Shipping men, port authorities and other business heads" in the city forecast "the opening of a new trade era" for Seattle. Detroit was happy too; the city's Chamber of Commerce forecast a great demand in the Soviet Union for American products, following the establishment of U.S.-Soviet diplomatic relations, especially for automobiles. *Business Week* confidently predicted that "business will do much for itself in the development of trade with the Soviet Union." The American Foundation, a business organization, issued a long report urging recognition which was signed by, inter alios, James D. Mooney, president of the General Motors Export Company, Thomas W. Lamont of J. P. Morgan and Company, George M. Houston, president of Baldwin Locomotive Works. J. H. Rand, Jr., president of the Remington Rand Corporation, and Thomas A. Morgan, president of Curtis Wright. Francis T. Cole, executive vice president of the American Manufacturers Export Association, published a survey conducted among four hundred manufacturers analyzing the promising opportunities for American business expected to follow from recognition and increased trade.

On November 16, 1933, recognition became a reality. Late that night, FDR met with Maxim Litvinov, People's Commissar for Foreign Affairs, in the White House to exchange five sets of notes signalizing the start of diplomatic relations between the United States and the USSR sixteen years after the Bolsheviks came into power. "THREE CHEERS FOR ROOSEVELT," chortled William Randolph Hearst's *New York American* (one day to be an implacable foe of FDR's) in a front-page headline. "Russia Recognized at Last. She Needs Copper, Steel. Hard Blow for the Depression." Like Hearst's *American,* most newspapers across the country approved the agreement, including the formerly anti-recognitionist *New York Herald Tribune,* which announced that it could "express nothing but approval." A *Dallas Morning News* cartoon, captioned "Tea for Two," showed Uncle Sam and Uncle Joe enjoying a spot of tea together from a teapot filled with "Friendship and Trade." Roosevelt, observed the *News,* "saw the absurdity of a continued refusal to recognize a great Nation with a stable Government. . . . Russia has a people of 160,000,000, occupying a large fraction of this earth's surface. In its civilization, it is Western, not Oriental, and it is certain to become within the next twenty-five years one of the greatest in the family of nations. . . . After all, Sovietism is an experiment in a sort of democracy. . . . There will be the exchange of ideas and of political and cultural experiences, as a result of which each, it is to be hoped, may gain knowledge and wisdom from the other. The two peoples should be fast friends in the future as they were in the past." Roosevelt's recognition of the Soviet Union, the editors predicted, "will be one of the most important accomplishments of his administration when the history is written. The step will have the approval of the business world. . . ."

The *News* was right about the business world. C. W. Linscheid, president of the Export Managers' Club of New York, called recognition "a distinct step forward." Samuel M. Vauclain, chairman of the board of Baldwin Locomotive Works, agreed; so did Alfred B. Sloan, Jr., president of General Motors. The Detroit Chamber of Commerce's George Feehan forecast a boom for American trade following recognition. Some businessmen felt so pleased by the establishment of diplomatic relations with the Soviet Union that they sponsored a big party in New York to celebrate the historic event. On November 24, 1933, just before Litvinov's return to the USSR, came what the *Nation,* liberal weekly, called "the most extraordinary dinner ever given in New York City." Some 2500 people paid

$5.50 a plate for a Farewell Dinner for Litvinov (which included beluga caviar spread on thin toast, borscht, and filet of beef stroganoff) at Manhattan's Waldorf-Astoria. According to *Time* magazine, "the big warm room buzzed with the voices of General Motors' Sloan, General Electric's Gerard Swope, Ford's Sorensen, Pennsylvania's Atterbury, Baldwin Locomotive's Houston, Thomas A. Edison's son Charles, Theodore Roosevelt's son Kermit, Owen D. Young, Henry Morgenthau, Sr., and dowagers galore." Mingling with the guests could also be found S. Parker Gilbert of the firm of J. P. Morgan, Edward Eugene Loomis of the Lehigh Valley Railroad, Gordon Rentschler of the National City Bank, the publisher of the Republican *New York Herald Tribune,* and the president of the American Chamber of Commerce. The high point of that gala evening undoubtedly came when the guests stood and faced a stage behind which hung a huge American flag and the Soviet red flag with its hammer and sickle while the organ played "My Country 'Tis of Thee," and then switched into "The Internationale." The *Nation,* which had been urging recognition for years, found it all very ironic. "Not a liberal editor appeared on the dais," observed the editors, "and hardly a man or woman who battled for Russian recognition when to do so was to invite contumely, insult, and abuse."

It is part of history that the high hopes that Americans entertained generally in 1933 for the future of American-Soviet relations failed of realization. Disillusionment developed swiftly in the months following recognition, and by the middle of 1935 had become widespread within administration circles as well as in the business community. In subsequent negotiations, the Soviets failed to agree on debt payments (hanging over from World War I), and as a result the Roosevelt administration refused to extend credits through the Export-Import Bank (established in 1934 for that purpose) for Soviet purchases in the United States. And although an increase in American-Soviet trade did develop after 1933, there was nothing like the trade boom anticipated by American business interests. Nor did the Soviet leaders show any disposition to honor the pledge that Litvinov had made in his agreements with Roosevelt to refrain from interference in America's internal affairs.

In the clear light of hindsight, the failure of recognition to live up to its sponsors' great expectations seems inevitable. But it is impossible to escape the conclusion that FDR's decision to recognize the

USSR was heartily endorsed by American conservatives as well as liberals in 1933. The sound and fury that arise periodically upon occasions of major foreign policy decisions—entry into World War II, the Marshall Plan, the establishment of NATO, escalation of the Vietnam War—seem to have been notably absent while the question of Soviet recognition was being decided. The "contumely, insult, and abuse" that the *Nation* talked about did not come until the McCarthyite 1950s. And then, like all conspiracists, the McCarthyites engaged in a colossal misrepresentation of what had actually happened in the American past.[1]

CHAPTER 28

Franklin Roosevelt and
the Attack on
Pearl Harbor

President Roosevelt knew the Japanese were going to attack our naval base at Pearl Harbor, but did nothing to prevent it because he wanted to take the United States into war.

Not so.

FDR was well aware of the fact that U.S. relations with Japan had reached the breaking point by the last month of 1941, but he was still hoping to stave off war in the Pacific as long as he could and he was just as surprised as his military and naval advisers were by December 7, 1941.

The Pearl Harbor attack was a surprise; but it was FDR's Far Eastern policy, of course, that inevitably led to war with Japan. From the beginning of his presidency, Roosevelt deplored Japanese aggression in China. In 1933, when he became President, Japan had already seized Manchuria and transformed it into a puppet state, and FDR continued the non-recognition policy toward Japan's conquest that Henry Stimson, Herbert Hoover's Secretary of State, had established in 1932. When some of FDR's advisers objected, he told them his ancestors had been involved in trade with China. "I have always had the deepest sympathy for China," he said. "How could you expect me not to go along with Stimson on Japan?"[1] While Japanese proclaimed "Asia for the Asiatics," that is, for the Japanese, FDR and his Secretary of State, Cordell Hull, insisted on the "Open Door," that is, the territorial integrity of China and equal trade opportunities there for all nations. FDR was convinced that Japanese domination of Eastern Asia—like Nazi domination of Europe—posed a grave threat to America's national security.

FDR's sympathies for China—and those of most Americans, even the anti-interventionists—increased steadily during the late 1930s as Japan continued its depredations on Chinese territory. In 1937, when Japanese forces began moving into north China, FDR made a major speech in Chicago deploring "the present reign of terror and international lawlessness" and suggested that aggressors like Japan be "quarantined" by the peace-loving nations of the world.[2] In July 1937, when some trigger-happy Japanese fliers sank the gunboat *Panay* in the Yangtze River, killing three Americans and wounding many others, Roosevelt told his Cabinet that he thought the attack was deliberate and that the Japanese were trying to force all Westerners out of China. But when Claude Swanson, Secretary of the Navy, echoing the opinions of high naval officials, wanted to go to war at once, FDR exclaimed: "Claude, I am a pacifist."[3] In the end, the United States issued a strong protest, and Japan responded with profuse apologies and the payment of more than $2 million in reparations for the *Panay* incident.

But Japan's undeclared war against China continued, and it was clear that her ultimate objective was to take control of China and make her part of a "Greater East Asia Co-Prosperity Sphere" controlled by the Japanese. In 1938, the United States imposed a "moral embargo" on the sale of aircraft to Japan and arranged for a loan of $25 million to Chiang Kai-shek, Nationalist leader heading the Chinese resistance to Japanese forces in China. In July 1939, the State Department went even farther; it gave the necessary six months' notice for terminating the U.S. commercial treaty of 1911 with Japan, thus paving the way for an embargo on U.S. supplies—oil, scrap metal, copper—on which Japan depended so heavily for running its war machine. Slowly, but steadily, as Japan pushed farther into China and began moving into Indochina (after the fall of France in 1940), FDR tightened the economic noose: banned the export without license of petroleum, petroleum products, and scrap metal (July 25, 1940), restricted the sale of aviation gasoline except to nations of the Western Hemisphere (July 31, 1940), proclaimed an embargo on all iron and steel scrap except in the Western Hemisphere (September 26, 1940), and, finally, froze all Japanese assets in the United States (July 26, 1941), thus putting a complete end to

American trade with Japan. The Big Freeze came as a shock to the Japanese. For them it meant either yielding to American demands or seeking essential supplies elsewhere.

From the outset American demands were severe: the withdrawal of all Japanese forces from China and adherence to the Open Door policy. American negotiators—Secretary of State Cordell Hull and FDR himself—didn't put it that starkly at first, but there was no mistaking their intent, and negotiations with the Japanese ambassador, Kichisaburo Nomura, soon became deadlocked. But FDR was eager to keep the talks going. He was firmly convinced that America's priority was aid to Britain (and later to Russia) in the war against the Nazis in Europe and that it was important to postpone an open break with Japan (or, as he put it, "baby Japan along") as long as possible.[4] Once, when Secretary of Interior Harold Ickes urged stronger action against Japan, Roosevelt told him: "It is terribly important for the control of the Atlantic for us to keep the peace in the Pacific. I simply have not got enough Navy to go around—and every little episode in the Pacific means fewer ships in the Atlantic."[5]

The Japanese prime minister, Prince Fumimaro Konoye, seemed conciliatory. In September 1941, he offered to meet with FDR, perhaps in Honolulu, to talk things over, and for a time FDR toyed with the idea of doing so. But he finally decided to demand specific concessions from Japan in advance, and the proposed meeting died aborning. The following month the Konoye ministry resigned and a more hawkish group, headed by General Hideki Tojo ("the Razor") took over. Early in November, Tojo sent a special envoy, Saburo Kurusu, to Washington to assist Ambassador Nomura with Japan's "last proposals." When Kurusu arrived in the United States, he said he wanted to "go through the line for a touchdown," but he was not really very hopeful.[6] The final terms he brought to Washington called for the resumption of trade with the United States, U.S. abstention from interference with the undeclared war in China, and, in return, Japan's eventual withdrawal from French Indochina.

Secretary Hull expectably found Kurusu's proposals unacceptable. For a time, though, he played around with the idea of a three-month truce, or a modus vivendi, involving a partial resumption of trade with Japan in return for a withdrawal of Japanese troops from southern Indochina. But he knew the Chinese Nationalists were bitterly opposed to the truce idea and he doubted that the Japanese would agree to it, so he finally abandoned the plan. Instead, he took a hard line with Kurusu and Nomura when he met with them on November 26, to present U.S. terms. The United States, he announced, would resume trade with Japan only if she agreed to withdraw all her troops from both China and Indochina and promised to support Chiang Kai-shek's Nationalist government in China. He was under no illusions about Japan's probable response; he realized that negotiations for peace had reached a dead end with his refusal to make any concessions. "I have washed my hands of it," he told Secretary of War Stimson the following day, "and it is now in the hands of you and Knox—the Army and the Navy." The Japanese, he added, "mean to fight and you will have to watch out."[7]

By early December there was no one in the United States who followed the news in the daily press carefully—and certainly no one in the Roosevelt administration—who did not realize that war with Japan was imminent. Even without the intercepts (the United States had cracked the Japanese diplomatic code in August 1940) of secret exchanges between Tokyo and Japanese embassies around the world, U.S. officials knew that Japan was preparing to take drastic action of some kind in the near future. But the intercepts heightened the urgency of the final days before the Pearl Harbor attack. There were thousands of them, of course, and they all required translation (from classic Japanese) and evaluation, before distribution to the President and other high officials. Buried in the avalanche of messages were a few ominous ones. On November 14, a message from Tokyo to the Japanese consul in Hong Kong (translated on November 26) stated that if no agreement was reached with the United States "we will completely destroy British and American power in China. We will take over all enemy concessions and important enemy rights and interests in China." On November 15, Tokyo informed its embassy in Washington: "The following is the order and method of destroying the code machines in the event of an emergency." On November 19, Tokyo wired its Washington emissaries that the warning for breaking off diplomatic relations would come as a weather broadcast, "East winds, rain." And on November 22, Tokyo instructed Nomura that the deadline for negotiations was November 29. "This time we mean it, the deadline absolutely cannot be changed. After that things are automatically going to happen."8

What things? The intercepts (FDR saw 64 out of 1800 between November 12 and December 7) were not precise. They did not reveal that on November 25 a Japanese carrier force maintaining radio silence left its rendezvous in the Kuriles for Hawaii, prepared to strike after receiving by radio Tokyo's decision for war. Nor did they reveal that Tokyo made the decision on December 1. The Japanese fleet could have been recalled twenty-four hours before the attack on Pearl Harbor if Washington had made some last-minute concessions, but there were no concessions, though the talks went on. At a meeting with Nomura and Kurusu (who knew nothing about Tokyo's war plans), FDR expressed displeasure at Japan's occupation of Indochina, but expressed hope that "Japanese-U.S. relations will be settled peacefully."9

At a Cabinet meeting on December 5, Hull began excoriating the Japanese as "the worst people I ever saw," and Secretary of the Navy Frank Knox interposed: "Well, Mr. President, we know where the Japanese fleet is."

"I think we ought to tell everybody how ticklish the situation is," responded FDR. "We have information, as Knox just mentioned . . . well, you tell them what it is, Frank."

"We have secret information . . . ," Knox told the Cabinet, "that the Japanese fleet is out. They're out of harbor. They're out at sea."

"We haven't got any thing like perfect information as to their apparent destination," FDR admitted. "The question is, in the mind of the Navy and in my mind, whether the fleet is going south."

"Singapore?" cried several Cabinet members.

"Probably," nodded FDR. "That's the presumed objective if they go south."

"Every indication is that they are going south," affirmed Knox.

"But it's not absolutely certain that they couldn't be going north," FDR reminded Knox. "You haven't got information with regard to direction."

"That's right, we haven't," admitted Knox, "but it is unlikely they would go north."

"Well," reflected FDR, "there are the Aleutians. . . ."

"That might be," said Knox, "but it's most unlikely. . . . I must draw the conclusion that they're going south. I don't think they're out just to maneuver. We in the navy think they must be going to do something."[10]

The fleet that FDR and Knox talked about was not, as it turned out, the carrier force heading secretly for Pearl Harbor; they had in mind fleet movements off the coast of Japan about which Navy Intelligence had informed them. Even so, the idea that the Japanese would pick Pearl Harbor as a target seems never to have entered their minds. In a memo to FDR in May 1941 Army Chief of Staff George Marshall had assured the President: "The island of Oahu, due to its fortifications, its garrison and its physical characteristics, is believed to be the strongest in the world." Then, after describing its air defenses, he added: "With this force available a major attack against Oahu is considered impracticable." And in a basic summary of the situation which Army Intelligence prepared for FDR on November 27, there was no mention of Pearl Harbor. When FDR asked Chief of Naval Operations Admiral Harold R. Stark about it, Stark told him the base was in no danger and that the U.S. fleet was at sea. On the same day the War Department sent a warning to the top military and naval commanders in Hawaii, General Walter C. Short and Admiral Husband E. Kimmel, informing them that negotiations with Japan had "ceased" and that Japan was expected to make an aggressive move during the next few days, probably against the Philippines, Thai, the Kra Peninsula, or possibly Borneo. The warning did not mention Pearl Harbor because it never occurred to Washington officials that the Japanese might strike at America's mighty base on Oahu.[11]

On the night of December 6, Naval Intelligence sent Lieutenant Lester R. Schulz to the White House with intercepts of the first thirteen parts of a fourteen-part Japanese message of Nomura and Kurusu rejecting Hull's "ultimatum" of November 26. FDR looked them over, handed them to his friend and adviser Harry Hopkins and murmured, "This means war." Hopkins scanned them and then said it was too bad that the United States couldn't strike the first blow "and prevent any sort of surprise" from the Japanese. "No, we can't do that," said FDR. "We are a democracy and a peaceful people." He went on: "But we have a good record."[12] Earlier that day he had sent a last-minute appeal to the Emperor of Japan for the preservation of peace.

Shortly after dawn on December 7, the Japanese launched an attack on Pearl Harbor which succeeded in sinking or badly damaging eight battleships, three cruisers, three destroyers, and 188 planes, and killing or wounding more than 3,435 servicemen. When Gen. Lucius D. Clay first heard the news, he could hardly believe it. "The Japs would attack Guam or the Philippines," he cried, "but Pearl Harbor is impregnable. I just can't believe they would attack Pearl Harbor."[13] FDR was similarly stunned. "My God! My God! How did it happen?" he cried when he first heard the news. "How did it happen!" Extremely proud of the U.S. Navy (he had been Assistant Secretary of the Navy during World War I), it was hard for him to face the fact that Pearl Harbor was the worst naval disaster in U.S. history. When he met his Cabinet later that day, Secretary of Labor Frances Perkins observed that he found it difficult to talk about how his beloved navy had been caught off-guard. "Find out, for God's sake," he told Navy Secretary Knox twice, "why the ships were tied in rows." "That's the way they berth them," explained Knox. The following day FDR went before Congress to describe the damage the Japanese had inflicted on Pearl Harbor—"a date that will live in infamy"—and asked for recognition of the "state of war" which "has thus been thrust upon the United States." Three days later Germany and Japan declared war and the United States was finally in what FDR had tried so long to postpone: a two-ocean war.[14]

The Pearl Harbor attack was a hit-and-run raid, designed to immobilize the U.S. fleet while Japanese forces moved south, as expected, to take over the countries of Southeast Asia which had plenty of the tin, rubber, and oil that Japan needed. The Japanese were themselves surprised at catching Americans so completely off-guard at Pearl, but the admiral who conceived the operation, Isoroku Yamamoto, did no celebrating. "I fear we have only awakened a sleeping giant," he told his officers, "and his reaction will be terrible."[15] Pearl Harbor, of course, unified the country in a way it has never before nor since been unified in wartime. Even Montana Senator Burton K. Wheeler, leading antiwar foe of FDR's interventionist foreign policy, exclaimed: "The only thing now to do is to lick hell out of them."[16]

What did FDR know and when did he know it? By December 6, it is clear that he knew that Japan was going to reject Hull's "ultimatum" of November 26 and break off negotiations. He also knew that she was going to make an aggressive move in the near future, probably southward, that was likely to mean war with the United States. But the idea of an attack on Pearl Harbor was farthest from his—and his advisers'—mind. If he had had advance notice of such an attack, he almost certainly would have seen to it that every measure was taken to repel the Japanese assault. After all, a victory at Pearl Harbor would have taken the country into war just as quickly as defeat did. At an inquiry into the Pearl Harbor disaster later on, Admiral Theodore Stark Wilkinson, head of Navy Intelligence, was asked, "Was there, Admiral, during the month or so preceding December 7, 1941, any discussion in which you participated concerning the likelihood of a Japanese move toward Pearl Harbor?" Sighed Wilkinson: "Unfortunately, no."[17]

The unthinkability of a strike at Pearl Harbor rested partly on a tendency of Americans in and outside Washington to look down on the Japanese before World War II as fussy, slow-witted, buck-toothed, near-sighted, clumsy, inefficient, and unimaginative copy-cats who were perpetually bowing and scraping and muttering, "So solly, please!" (even though there is no "l" sound in Japanese). "The Japanese are not going to risk a fight with a first-class nation," Pennsylvania's Charles I. Faddis assured his colleagues in Congress in February 1941. "They are unprepared to do so and no one knows that better than they do. . . . They will not dare to get into a position where they must face the American Navy in open battle. Their Navy is not strong enough and their homeland too vulnerable."[18]

On the eve of Pearl Harbor, the American press, especially the newspapers and magazines favoring a hard-line policy, viewed Japan with a mixture of amusement and contempt. "For a time," cried New York's left-leaning daily *PM*, Japan "may bluster and retaliate, but in the end it can only whimper and capitulate." "If Japan chose war," declared the *New Republic*, a liberal weekly, "the tremendous odds against her would limit the hostilities to a relatively brief period." Reported the November issue of the *American Mercury*: "Most of Japan's 5,000 planes are obsolete. Her fliers are poor." And on December 4, *Time* carefully summed up the U.S.-Japan confrontation for its millions of readers: "Everything was ready. From Rangoon to Honolulu every man was at battle station. . . . The U.S. position had the simple clarity of a stone wall. One nervous twitch of a Japanese trigger finger, one jump in any direction, one overt act might be enough. A vast array of armies, of navies, of air fleets were stretched now in the position of track runners, in the tension of the moment before the starter's gun. With the weariness of a tired man about to be summoned to a task greater than his strength, the Japanese people waited. . . ."[19]

Soon after Pearl Harbor, the Japanese took the war to the Philippines (where General Douglas MacArthur was caught by surprise, too, though he knew about the Pearl Harbor attack), and as the struggle began, Sergeant Thomas E. Gage soon realized that after all the sneering he had heard about Japanese military incompetence, "somebody is full of bull!" "Our navy would wipe them off the ocean in one week," he recalled bitterly. "They were too small and couldn't see, couldn't shoot, couldn't fly. And their equipment was shoddy because they copy things and didn't copy them right." In fact, Sergeant Gage—and countless American servicemen elsewhere—quickly discovered that the Japanese were first-rate fighters and that their equipment was of top quality.[20] Whether a more realistic view of Japan's military capabilities would have prevented the disaster at Pearl Harbor is impossible to say.

Franklin Roosevelt's Far Eastern policy—checking Japanese aggression in China—unquestionably made war with Japan inescapable. And the Open Door policy, on which it was based, did not, in fact, triumph with Japan's defeat in August 1945. Instead, the Door was slammed tightly shut after all, when China's Communist leader, Mao Tse-tung, took over control of China three years after America's victory over Japan, and Mao replaced Tojo as America's favorite villain. Still, the question here has to do with the attack on Pearl Harbor, not on the ironic consequences of America's victory over Japan. As far as the December 7 sneak attack is concerned, it seems clear that only the Japanese themselves knew beforehand what they had planned for the United States that day. FDR was just as shocked by the attack as General Short and Admiral Kimmel, the commanders in Oahu, and every other American. It's a pity, though, that the Roosevelt administration tried afterward to shift all the blame for the Pearl Harbor disaster to Short and Kimmel, who, though warned of imminent Japanese action, shared their superiors' belief that a strike on Pearl Harbor was absolutely inconceivable and acted accordingly. Historian Thomas A. Bailey, writing in 1973, was probably right in concluding that the night before the Japanese attack, "just about every American in authority, from Roosevelt on down, was in some degree obtuse, confused, careless, bungling, inefficient, asleep, or looking the wrong way."[21]

CHAPTER 29

Eleanor Roosevelt's Love Life

Eleanor Roosevelt had at least two love affairs when she was in the White House.

Not so.

The belief that Mrs. Roosevelt carried on with Earl Miller, her bodyguard, and also had a love affair with Lorena Hickok, Associated Press reporter, is almost surely without foundation in fact. E.R. had intense friendships with both of them, but there was nothing more to it than that. She had "a genius for love," as her friend and biographer Joseph Lash put it, but not for extramarital love affairs.

In 1929, soon after Franklin D. Roosevelt became governor of New York, he arranged for Earl Miller, a former state trooper, to be his wife's bodyguard. The two got along famously and soon became pals. They went hiking and horseback riding, knocked about together, and even did some acting in a slapstick movie skit, "The Kidnapping of the First Lady," at a get-together with some of E.R.'s friends. More important, Miller confided in E.R.; he told her of his lonely childhood and sought her advice and counsel on personal problems. E.R.'s childhood had been lonely and unhappy, too, and she enjoyed trying to help him straighten out his life. She treated him like a son; she bought clothes for him, helped him move, and even made arrangements for at least one of his three weddings. FDR liked him, too, and had him dine at the family table (to FDR's haughty mother's chagrin) rather than with the servants. Miller seems to have looked on the Roosevelts as surrogate parents. "I had no home after I was twelve," he said years later. "I transferred the affection I would have felt for my parents to the Roosevelts. As I sat in back of the Packard and saw the back of FDR's head, I thought it was my dad. They gave me the first home I knew." But E.R. was his special favorite.[1]

There were whispers, of course, about the handsome young bodyguard and the middle-aged wife of New York's governor (and later President), but E.R. ignored them. After her death, Joseph Lash, another close friend and the author of several perceptive books about her, interviewed Miller and, among other things, asked about his relationship with the former First Lady. "Wouldn't Mrs. Roosevelt have married you?" he asked. "Me?" exclaimed Miller. "I never asked her or wouldn't have done so." "But might she have asked you?" persisted Lash. "You don't sleep with someone you call Mrs. Roosevelt," said Miller emphatically. "Anyway," he added, "my taste was for young and pretty things."[2]

In 1948, Miller's third wife sued him for divorce, named Mrs. Roosevelt as corespondent, and produced a batch of letters from E.R. to Miller as evidence of a liaison. E.R.'s son, Franklin D. Roosevelt, Jr., offered to act as her attorney, but told her: "Mummy, if I'm going to represent you in this action, I have to know everything." E.R. told her son that she had always loved Miller, but she made it clear: "In the sense that you mean, there was nothing." When FDR, Jr., finally got to see the letters his mother had written Miller, he found them to be effusive, but no more so than her letters to other close friends. E.R. was upset by the lawsuit, not so much for herself as for the harm it might do her sons' political careers. In the end, Mrs. Miller got her divorce and a financial settlement. Years after E.R.'s death, her son James published a quickie—a ghostwritten book about his parents—in which, to jazz things up a bit, he hinted that there may have been something to stories about a love affair between his mother and the bodyguard. Quizzed about it by Geoffrey Ward, a Roosevelt biographer, shortly before James's death, however, he retreated into vagueness. There seems no reason not to discount the latter-day guesswork and accept E.R.'s and Miller's disavowal of any real sexual involvement.[3]

What about Lorena Hickok? E.R. first met her when Hickok was covering the 1932 presidential campaign for the Associated Press and they soon became fast friends. Hick (as she was called) seems to have arrived on the scene at just the right time. Mrs. Roosevelt felt down in the dumps; she feared she would become a supernumerary if her husband won the election and became President. She had painstakingly developed a meaningful life of her own (which included writing for newspapers and magazines) while her husband was busy as governor and she was afraid she would have only ceremonial duties in the White House. On the night of her husband's election as President, her friends found her weeping, not celebrating, and when they asked her what was wrong, she sighed: "Now I'll have no identity."[4]

Hick helped Mrs. Roosevelt develop a new identity as a presidential wife. She suggested holding press conferences for women reporters (the first President's wife to do so), and the conferences were enormously successful. She also encouraged her to take an active part in the New Deal programs FDR sponsored to combat the Great Depression and build a better life for Americans. Above all, she was a lively companion, with a rollicking sense of humor, fun to be with on trips around the country, and willing to share confidences with E.R. In 1933, Hick resigned her position with AP, convinced she could no longer report the Roosevelts objectively, and took a job with the Federal Emergency Relief Administration (FERA) headed by Harry Hopkins. For FERA she traveled around the country to observe relief programs and in due course produced a report that impressed both Hopkins and FDR. She and E.R. exchanged letters and phone calls while she was away from Washington. When she returned, she accepted E.R.'s invitation to live and work in the White House.

For a time Hick's friendship was a priority for E.R. But E.R. eventually moved on. As she carefully shaped her role as the first activistic President's wife (as a journalist, as a teacher, as FDR's New Deal partner, as the champion of the underprivileged, especially the blacks), she acquired new friends, men and women, became involved in an amazing number of new activities, and had less time for Hick. Hick was for a time deeply hurt; she resented E.R.'s other friendships and even her involvement with her children. But the two remained fast friends to the end. Mrs. Roosevelt never forgot how Hick, by her love and devotion, had helped bolster her self-confidence in a difficult period of her life, and she wanted to contribute as much as she could to Hick's self-esteem and happiness.[5]

In 1978, when the correspondence between E.R. and Hick was made public by the Franklin D. Roosevelt Library in Hyde Park, New York, people were surprised by the intensity of some of the passages in the letters, particularly those exchanged during the early months of FDR's first administration. "Hick, my dearest," wrote E.R. the day after her husband's inauguration on March 4, 1933, "Hick my dearest, I cannot go to bed tonight without a word to you. I felt a little as though a part of me was leaving tonight, you have grown so much to be a part of my life that it is empty without you. . . ." The following day she wrote: "Hick, darling. Ah, how good it was to hear your voice. It was so inadequate to try and tell you what it meant. Funny was that I couldn't say je t'aime and je t'adore as I longed to do, but always remember that I am saying it, that I go to sleep thinking of you." The next night she wrote: "Hick darling, All day I've thought of you. . . . Oh! I want to put my arms around you, I ache to hold you close. Your ring is a great comfort. I look at it & think she does love me, or I wouldn't be wearing it!" Hick's letters contained passages just as high-keyed. "Dear," she wrote E.R. in December 1933, "I've been trying to bring back your face—to remember just *how* you look. Funny how even the dearest face will fade away in time. Most clearly I remember your eyes, with a kind of teasing smile in them, and the feeling of that soft spot just northeast of the corner of your mouth against my lips. I wonder what we'll do when we meet—what we'll say. Well—I'm rather proud of us, aren't you? I think we've done rather well."[6]

Do passages like these in the E.R.-Hickok exchanges indicate a lesbian relationship? Probably not. They formed only a small part of what E.R. wrote in letters to Hick. Frequently the letters contained summaries of her varied activities during the day as well as words of sympathy and reassurance when Hick was feeling lonely and depressed. E.R.'s extremely affectionate way of expressing herself, moreover, was, as her son FDR, Jr., once pointed out, not confined to her friend Hick. Years before, while on her honeymoon, she had written FDR's mother of the "kisses and cuddly times" she looked forward to when she and Franklin returned from Europe. And while Hick was for a time clearly E.R.'s favorite, she had other close friends, men and women, to whom she wrote in longhand (as she did to Hick) and sometimes used terms of endearment as intense as those in letters to Hick. "Who can tell from effusiveness?" exclaimed her grandaughter Eleanor Van Seagraves, when the E.R.-Hickok letters came to light. "She wrote all her letters with the same effusiveness. It's hard to explain to anyone under 50 that kind of style. It was more or less normal for my grandmother to reassure friends of hers."[7]

In E.R.'s time (she grew up in the last years of the 19th century) it was not unusual for American women to form strong emotional attachments to each other that were both passionate and platonic. The friendships frequently persisted after the women got married; and when they remained single the close relationship between two women was accepted routinely as a "Boston marriage." Romantic friendships between women when E.R. was growing up were largely the product of social arrangements in which middle- and upper-class men lived in a world of their own from which women were systematically excluded. In the 1970s, historian Carroll Smith-Rosenberg made a detailed study of friendships like E.R. and Hick's and found that "an abundance of manuscript evidence suggest that eighteenth- and nineteenth-century women routinely formed emotional ties with other women. Such deeply felt, same-sex friendships were casually accepted in American society. . . . Paradoxically to twentieth-century minds, their love appears to have been both sensual and platonic." E.R.'s family and friends—and FDR himself—realized that there was a special relationship between her and Hick, but they thought nothing of it.[8]

Was there a sexual relationship between E.R. and Hick? It doesn't seem likely. Hick, it is true, was undoubtedly in love with E.R. She had had a lesbian relationship some years before meeting E.R. and she was to have another after the intensity of the friendship with E.R. diminished. But it is extremely doubtful that she and E.R. ever had a physical relationship. Homosexuality, we know, was beyond the pale for Mrs. Roosevelt. When a friend lent her a copy of André Gide's *The Counterfeiters*, she was repelled by the homosexual theme. With her Victorian upbringing, she was, in fact, extremely inhibited when it came to sex. She thought Erskine Caldwell's earthy play *Tobacco Road* was "revolting," and she dismissed *A Streetcar Named Desire* as "crude and almost animal-like." In her newspaper column, "My Day," she had this to say about Tennessee Williams's play: "I felt a little soiled in my mind and quite ill. There is a certain kind of healthy vulgarity that one can endure, perhaps with some embarrassment but still with amusement. There are certain other types of artistic and emotional expression, however, that show degeneracy of the spirit, with the individual and with the nation." On the eve of her daughter Anna's first wedding, she told her that sex was "an ordeal to be borne"; she disliked its "sweaty mechanics." After she discovered her husband's affair with Lucy Mercer in 1918, she never slept with him again, and he never even went into her bedroom again. The Roosevelt marriage survived as a kind of friendly partnership, with respect and admiration on both sides. But for intimacy and emotional involvement—FDR had always been emotionally distant in any case—E.R. looked to her daughter Anna and to the small circle of close friends she gradually developed.[9]

Hick couldn't help feeling jealous of E.R.'s other friends. She even came to resent E.R.'s absorption in the affairs of her children. And as E.R. became joyously caught up in the many projects she developed as the President's wife, Hick realized she was being left behind, and her letters took on a sorrowful and reproachful tone. E.R. tried to reassure her. In an effort to explain herself, she wrote: "I know you often have a feeling for me which for one reason or another I may not return in kind, but I feel I love you just the same and so often we entirely satisfy each other that I feel there is a fundamental basis on which our relationship stands." Hick had to understand, she said, "that I love other people the same way or differently, but each one has their place and one cannot compare them."[10]

On occasion E.R. took the view that marriage might be one solution to her friend Hick's unhappiness. "I think you will remember," she wrote, "that I once told you I wished you had been happy with a man or that it might still be. I rather think that the lack of that relationship does create emotional instability but people do seem to weather it in time & who knows what the future holds." Later on she told Hick: "Of course you should have had a husband and children & it would have made you happy if you loved him & in any case it would have satisfied certain cravings & and given you someone on whom to lavish the love and devotion you have to keep down all the time. Yours is a rich nature with so much to give that the outlets always seem meagre."[11]

In the end, though, E.R. blamed herself for Hick's disappointment in the way their friendship was going. "Yes, dear, you are right," she wrote contritely after one letter of complaint. "I give everyone the feeling that you have that I've 'taken them on' & don't need anything from them & then when they naturally resent it & don't like to accept it from me, I wonder why! It is funny I know & I can't help it. Something locked me up & I can't unlock!" "Of course dear," she wrote in another letter, "I never meant to hurt you in any way but that is no excuse for having done it. It won't help you any but I'll never do to anyone else what I did to you." However much she tried, she once told Hick, she had never been able to let herself go emotionally. As a result, "I am pulling myself back in all my contacts now. I have always done it with the children, & why I didn't know I couldn't give you (or anyone else who wanted & needed what you did) any real food I can't now understand. Such cruelty & stupidity is unpardonable when you reach my age. Heaven knows I hope in some small & unimportant ways I have made life a little easier for you but that doesn't compensate."[12]

The friendship continued to the end, though as the years passed, with far fewer phone calls, letters, and get-togethers. Hick eventually took a job with the 1939 New York World's Fair, then with the Women's Division of the Democratic National Committee, and finally settled down, first on Long Island and then in Hyde Park, to write children's books as well as a book about her beloved friend: *Eleanor Roosevelt: Reluctant First Lady*, published in 1962, the year of E.R.'s death. Mrs. Roosevelt, for her part, continued her writing and public activities after FDR's death in 1945 and developed intense new friendships—with Joseph Lash, for one, and with David Gurewitsch, for another—that meant as much to her as Earl Miller's and Lorena Hickok's had. ("I want to be with you," she wrote Lash after he sent a letter expressing discouragement in his courtship of the woman he eventually married, "& put my arms around you.") Hick couldn't help feeling a bit put off by E.R.'s new enthusiasms. When she learned, after E.R.'s death, that Lash was doing research for a book about Mrs. Roosevelt, she told a friend that he certainly wasn't going to get any help from her on the project. "I'll be damned," she said, "if he's going to get his hot little hands into my papers." Shortly before her death, when she deposited her letters with the Roosevelt Library, she stipulated that they were not to be made public for ten years.[13]

In May 1978 Hick's letters became available. Soon after, Doris Faber, planning a book on E.R., came across the letters and did a book instead on Hickok herself: *The Life of Lorena Hickok: Eleanor Roosevelt's Friend* (1980). Surprised at first by the warmth of the exchanges between E.R. and Hickok in 1933 and 1934, Faber came to the conclusion that they had been intimate friends but probably not lovers. Joseph Lash reached the same conclusion. Author of several books about E.R., Lash did a new one, after examining the Hickok letters, centered on E.R.'s friendships: *Love, Eleanor: Eleanor Roosevelt and Her Friendships* (1982). "Eleanor Roosevelt loved deeply," he pointed out, "and lavished her affection on men as well as women with a force that was stronger because her husband was so little able to give her the intimate companionship she craved. Her passionate nature, which hungered for affection and appreciation, mystified some. Others it confounded, especially outsiders with neat categories about sexual roles and behaviors."[14]

Lash had a revelation of his own to make in his book on Mrs. Roosevelt's friendships. When he was in the service during World War II, Army Intelligence, he later learned, had started bugging his meetings with E.R. and reading her letters to him and had soon come to the preposterous conclusion that the two were having an affair. "Who, after the travesty of such an interpretation," he exclaimed, "can draw absolutist conclusions about the relationship between her and Hickok from the correspondence the latter deposited at the Roosevelt Library?"[15]

CHAPTER 30

FDR and
Yalta

Franklin D. Roosevelt, who was "soft" on Communism, sold out the country at Yalta.

Not so.

President Roosevelt undoubtedly lacked a sophisticated understanding of Communism, that is, Marxism-Leninism-Stalinism, but he was not, as McCarthyites charged after World War II, a great admirer of the Soviet system of government. In 1933, when he recognized the USSR, he did so simply because all the other major powers had long since done so and because he hoped the United States would develop profitable trade relations with the Soviets. The American Communists, for their part, certainly weren't "soft" on FDR at the time. They faithfully followed the "hard" line toward bourgeois liberals laid down by Stalin in 1929, dismissed the New Deal contemptuously as "social fascism," and charged that FDR was "carrying out more thoroughly and brutally than even Hoover the capitalist attack against the living standards of the masses. . . ."[1]

In the summer of 1935, however, Stalin decreed a new line for his followers everywhere: collaboration between Communists and bourgeois democratic groups against Nazism and fascism. Threatened by Nazi Germany in the West and by imperialist Japan in the East, Moscow sought allies among the capitalist democracies against Germany and Japan and instructed Communists to enter into "Popular Fronts" with non-Communists to fight fascism at home and support collective security aboard. There is no question but that with the adoption of the new "soft" line Communism began to appear less outrageous to many Americans, including FDR, than it had before. In the late 1930s American Communists worked hard to appear respectable (Communism, they declared, was "Twentieth Century Americanism") and they succeeded in becoming, for a time, a powerful force in the labor movement, in youth groups, and in American artistic and intellectual circles.

The Popular Front era was short-lived. Having failed to forge an alliance with Britain and France against Hitler, Stalin reversed himself and sought an agreement with the Nazis instead. On August 22, 1939, came a bombshell: the Nazi-Soviet Non-Aggression Pact and the signing of a commercial treaty between Nazi Germany and Stalinist Russia. Soon after, as Hitler invaded Poland in the West, touching off World War II, Stalin sent troops in to take over eastern Poland. He also absorbed the Baltic republics (Lithuania, Latvia, and Estonia) and invaded Finland. The Stalinist line toward the capitalistic democracies was again a hard one. More and more, as time passed, the American Communist Party, following Moscow's lead, took a line that was more hostile to England than it was to Germany, and the Stalinists came finally to place major blame for World War II on England. "It was not Germany who attacked England and France," declared Communist party leader William Z. Foster, quoting Stalin, "but France and England which attacked Germany, assuming responsibility for the present war." England, said the *Communist International*, had "unleashed" the war and, in so doing, British imperialism had "revealed" itself as the chief enemy of the international working class.[2]

During the Nazi-Soviet period, American Communists took an "isolationist" line toward the war in Europe and denounced FDR as in imperialistic warmonger for trying to aid Britain against Germany in all ways "short of war." President Roosevelt, declared Communist leader Earl Browder, "has studied well the Hitlerian art and bids fair to outdo the record of his teacher." In a radio address soon after the Nazi-Soviet Pact, Vito Marcantonio, fellow-traveling Congressman from New York, insisted that FDR, in one of his fireside chats to the nation, had "proclaimed the shooting and bloodshedding and dictatorship phases of the Wall Street–Downing Street Axis scheme for war, empire, and dictatorship." FDR eventually struck back at the Stalinists. In a speech to delegates of the American Youth Congress from the rear portico of the White House on February 10, 1940, he declared: "The Soviet Union, as everybody who has the courage to face the facts knows, is run by a dictatorship as absolute as any other dictatorship in the world. It has allied itself with another dictatorship, and it has invaded a neighbor [Finland] so infinitesimally small that it could do no conceivable possible harm to the Soviet Union, a neighbor which seeks only to live at peace as a democracy, and a liberal, forward-looking democracy at that." FDR was well aware of the fact that the American Youth Congress was a "fellow-traveling" (that is, pro-Soviet) group that followed the Stalinist line, and he went on to say: "It has been said that some of you are Communists. That is a very unpopular term these days. As Americans you have a legal and constitutional right to call yourselves Communists, those of you who do. You have the right peacefully and openly to advocate certain ideals of theoretical Communism; but as Americans you have not only a right but a sacred duty to confine your advocacy of changes in law to the methods prescribed by the Constitution of the United States—and you have no American right, by act or deed of any kind, to subvert the Government and the Constitution of this Nation." For his remarks, the President received boos and hisses from the delegates—a rare experience for FDR—and at a White House reception afterward his wife's secretary Malvina Thompson ("Tommy") angrily scolded them for their unruly behavior.[3]

But the Nazi-Soviet line, like the Popular Front line before it, came to an abrupt end. On June 22, 1941, Hitler double-crossed Stalin and launched an invasion of the Soviet Union. The American Communists were taken as much by surprise as everyone else at the unexpected turn of events. The leading editorial in the *Daily Worker* (New York) that morning had taken a strong anti-interventionist line, denouncing the President for his "determination to get the United States into a shooting war" and exclaiming: "The people want none of this war. They will have to state this strongly to stay the hand of the war crowd." But the editors of the *Worker* lost no time in adjusting to the new party line. The following morning they cried: "Down with the criminal war of German fascism against the Soviet Union! For full support and co-operation with the Soviet Union in its struggle against Hitlerism!" With the Japanese attack on Pearl Harbor some months later, the United States joined Britain and Russia in the war against Nazism, and after that the American Communists were among the most enthusiastic supporters of the war effort, both on the battlefield and on the home front.[4]

During the war, the Soviet Union's heroic resistance to the Nazi onslaught, at the loss of millions of lives, produced almost universal admiration in both Britain and the United States. FDR wasn't the only American to take a friendlier attitude toward Stalinist Russia during the anti-Nazi struggle. On June 11, 1942, for example, the *Chicago Tribune*, ultra-conservative daily, declared that in "Russia's fight to survive as a nation lies the great hope of the world for early peace." During the same year, at a national meeting of the DAR (Daughters of the American Revolution), Mrs. Tryphosa Duncan Bates-Batchellor announced: "Stalin is a university graduate and a man of great studies. He is a man who, when he sees a great mistake, admits it and corrects it. Today in Russia, Communism is practically nonexistent." On February 23, 1943, General Douglas MacArthur, already a hero of American conservatives, announced that "the hopes of civilization rest on the worthy banners of the courageous Russian army." The following month Henry R. Luce's *Life* said that the Russians were "one hell of a people," who "look like Americans, dress like Americans and think like Americans." Stalin's NKVD (secret police), according to *Life*, was simply "a national police similar to the FBI" with the job of "tracking traitors." In August 1943, Captain Eddie Rickenbacker, hero of two world wars, after a trip to Russia, praised the "iron discipline" in Russian industry which prevented strikes, and predicted that "Russia is likely to come out of the war the greatest democracy in the world." On September 10, 1943, the American Gold Star Mothers presented a plaque to the Soviet government to commemorate, among other things, the "common aims of the youth of Russia and of this country." On October 18, 1943, conservative columnist Raymond Moley exclaimed: "We can do business with Stalin!" In December, *Collier's* declared that the Russian system was a "modified capitalist set-up" moving toward "something resembling our own and Great Britain's democracy."[5]

Even John Rankin, the bigoted and xenophobic Congressman from Mississippi, found kind words for Josef Stalin during the war. "Stalin was educated for the priesthood," he told his colleagues in Congress. "The Bible says, teach a child the way he should go and when he is old he will not depart therefrom. It was but natural therefore that when Stalin got in power he should open the churches. . . . Stalin broke up the Comintern. . . . He restored rank and discipline in his army and introduced the incentive payment plan among the men who work in his factories." Monsignor Fulton J. Sheen also joined the chorus of praise for the Soviets. "The family is higher in Russia than in the United States," he announced in July 1945, "and God, looking from Heaven, may be more pleased with Russia than with us." And the *Dallas Morning News* (which, after the war, was to charge FDR with selling out to the Soviets at Yalta) voiced a consistent friendship for the Soviet Union during the war and for some months afterward. On September 6, 1942, the *News* declared that "the Russians have given the world a stirring example of what courage and dogged determination can do against superior forces. . . . We can ill afford to give any real grievance to an ally so valiant in battle and so valuable to the United Nations." Three days later the *News* exclaimed that "there remains an urgent need to do more than we have been doing for Russia." On October 24, 1943, the *News* warned: "Whenever anyone is heard saying that the British are outslicking us or that we dare not trust Russia much, it is well to remember that this is Nazi propaganda. No matter how honest and patriotic the American who repeats such statements, he proves himself gullible and a victim of enemy wiles."[6]

The *Dallas Morning News* reflected the views of millions of Americans, none of them Stalinist fellow-travelers, during World War II. FDR himself felt much as the editors of the *Dallas Morning News* did when he traveled to Yalta, a Black Sea resort in the Crimea, for a Big Three conference with Winston Churchill and Josef Stalin in February 1945. Like Churchill, FDR was impressed with the way the Soviets had turned the Nazis back at Stalingrad, with a tremendous loss of life, in 1943, and he was also aware of the fact that until the Allied invasion of Normandy in June 1944, the Russians had borne the major burden of fighting the Nazis in Europe. But FDR didn't go to Yalta to take part in a love-in. He went there with four major objectives in mind: to arrange for the Allied occupation of Germany after the war; to plan the organization of the United Nations as a permanent peace-keeping body; to reach agreement on Poland and the other countries of Eastern Europe then being freed by the Red Army; and to persuade Stalin to enter the war against Japan after Germany's defeat.

With Churchill's help, FDR's first two aims were achieved without much difficulty. Stalin endorsed proposals for the occupation of Germany after the war by the United States, Great Britain, the Soviet Union, and France (though he minimized France's contribution to the war effort) in four separate zones, and, after first demanding $20 billion in reparations from Germany, finally agreed to have the matter referred to a reparations commission for settlement in the future. He approved, too, plans for a United Nations conference to be held in San Francisco in April 1945 to establish a permanent international organization for collective security. He did, though, insist on three votes in the U.N.'s General Assembly, including one each for the Ukraine and White Russia. But Churchill did not object, for the British Commonwealth was to have six votes; and FDR went along with the demand, too, though reserving the right (which he never exercised) to ask for three votes for the United States, too. Stalin also insisted that the big powers represented in the U.N.'s Security Council have veto power over decisions of the U.N.'s General Assembly (in which all nations, large and small, were represented), and Churchill and Roosevelt readily agreed. It is doubtful, in fact, whether the U.S. Senate would have accepted membership in the U.N. without some such safeguard for U.S. sovereignty.

Poland—and Eastern Europe generally—posed Yalta's biggest problem. Here Stalin held all the high cards. The Red Army was already in Poland and was moving swiftly into Romania, Bulgaria, and the other countries of Eastern and Central Europe. Even before Yalta, Stalin had recognized the Lublin government (Communist-dominated) in Poland, though FDR had asked for a month's delay, and he made it clear at Yalta that he intended to have a *cordon sanitaire* of friendly states on Russia's western borders to prevent future invasions from the West. Churchill and Roosevelt understood Stalin's concern for security, but they balked at imposing the Lublin government on Poland, when the majority of Poles, thousands of whom had fought valiantly against Nazis, were non-Communists. But the most they could get out of the Soviet dictator was a vague promise to reorganize the government to include non-Communists and to allow free elections as soon as possible to determine the future government of Poland. They also won his assent to a declaration calling for free elections in all the liberated areas of Central Europe into which Soviet troops were moving. "I want the election in Poland to be beyond question," FDR told Stalin. "I did not know Caesar's wife, but she was believed to be pure." "I did not know Caesar's wife," responded Stalin, "but in fact she had certain sins." The "sins"—Stalin's violation of his pledges and his brutal takeover of Poland and the other nations of Eastern Europe—came later. But, as FDR, discussing Yalta right after he got back to Washington, told A. A. Berle: "I didn't say it was good, Adolf, I said it was the best I could do."[7]

FDR's final aim—inducing Stalin to enter the war against Japan after Germany's defeat—was easier to achieve than the agreement on Poland, but even here FDR had to approach Stalin hat in hand. At the time of Yalta, the President's military advisers were convinced that a successful invasion of Japan would take about eighteen months and cost over a million casualties, and that if Russia attacked the Japanese armies in Manchuria and Korea, it would drastically shorten the war and save the lives of countless American soldiers. But why, Stalin wanted to know, should Russia, having suffered enormous losses fighting Nazis in Europe, take on the Japanese, too? In the end he agreed to enter the Far Eastern war "two or three months" after the war in Europe ended, but on the following conditions: the continuation of Outer Mongolia, once a part of China, as a Communist satellite of the Soviet Union; the cession to Russia of the Kurile Islands (once partially Russian) and the southern half of Sakhalin Island; and the restoration to Russia of its position in Manchuria before the Russo-Japanese War of 1904–05, with the safeguarding of the Soviet interests in Dairen, Port Arthur, and the Manchurian railways. FDR was on the spot; he was being asked to dispose of property that wasn't his. He protested that he hadn't had a chance to talk to China's Chiang Kai-shek about the matter, but when Stalin remained adamant about his quid pro quo, he finally gave way and received Stalin's commitment to war against Japan. FDR's military associates at Yalta were delighted. "This makes the trip worthwhile," said Admiral Leahy, one of FDR's advisers at the conference. For the time being, the agreement was kept secret, to prevent leaks to Japan, but FDR promised to get Chiang's approval later on. Stalin agreed to recognize

Chiang as ruler of China and it was, in fact, one promise he did keep.[8]

As it turned out, Japan was nearer to the end than FDR and his advisers realized at the time of Yalta, and, in restrospect, it is clear that an agreement with Stalin about Japan was unnecessary. But even without the FDR-Stalin deal, it is entirely likely that Japan's surrender would have been the signal for Stalin to send Soviet troops into Manchuria anyway.

Was Yalta really a "sellout," as FDR's critics contended after the war? "In fact," according to Roosevelt biographer Ted Morgan, "the Americans and British left Yalta feeling that they had scored an impressive victory." They had won Stalin's promise to join the United Nations on terms they regarded as acceptable. They had gotten him to agree to their plans for the occupation of Germany (including the participation of France) and the postponement of the decision on reparations. They had persuaded him to enter the Far Eastern war despite horrendous Russian casualties in the fighting in Europe. And they had refused to accept Russian domination of Poland and other areas of Eastern Europe as a fait accompli and forced Stalin to agree to free elections and broadened government in those places. Stalin did, of course, break his promises after the war. But, as Morgan pointed out, "If Yalta was a sellout, why did he go to such lengths to violate the agreement? The post-war problems did not result from Yalta but from Stalin's violations."[9]

When the report of the Yalta conference was released on February 12, 1945, American public opinion was enthusiastic about the agreements. The *Philadelphia Record* called the conference the "greatest United Nations victory of the war"; the *New York Herald Tribune* declared that the "overriding fact" was that Yalta had "produced another great proof of Allied unity, strength and power of decision"; and *Time* pointed out that "all doubts about the Big Three's ability to co-operate in peace as well as in war seem now to have been swept away." Even former President Hoover was hopeful. "If the agreements' promises and ideals which are expressed shall be carried out," he said, "it will open a great hope in the world."[10]

Eleanor Roosevelt, for one, was disappointed with Yalta. When FDR got back to Washington, she told him she was sorry that Estonia, Latvia, and Lithuania, once independent nations, but taken over by the Soviet Union in 1939, had not been given their freedom. But FDR asked her: "How many people in the United States do you think would be willing to go to war to free Estonia, Latvia, and Lithuania?"[11]

CHAPTER 31

Harry Truman and
the Vice Presidency

Harry Truman was an obscurity when President Roosevelt picked him as his running mate in 1944.

No, he wasn't.

Truman, who was elected to the Senate in 1934 and re-elected in 1940, gradually became a national figure after 1941 when he proposed, helped organize, and then headed the Special Committee to Investigate the National Defense Program during World War II. As committee chairman, he became known for his diligence, fairness, common sense, and efficiency, and for his ability to work harmoniously with administration officials. By the end of the war the Truman Committee, as it came to be called, had saved billions of taxpayer dollars by uncovering waste, fraud, and inefficiency in war industries; it also saved countless lives by its exposure of defective weapons that were being supplied to the armed forces.[1]

On March 8, 1943, *Time* magazine featured the Missouri Senator on its cover ("Investigator Truman") and in a friendly essay about him praised his committee as "one of the most useful Government agencies of World War II" and the "closest thing yet to a domestic high command." One prominent Washingtonian, according to *Time*, exclaimed: "There's only one thing that worries me more than the present state of the war effort. That's to think what it would be like by now without Truman." In the *St. Louis Post-Dispatch* (once lukewarm to Truman) appeared a column by Washington correspondent Marquis Childs hailing the Senator as "one of the most useful and at the same time one of the most forthright and fearless" members of the U.S. Senate. A *Look* magazine poll picked Truman as one of ten men (the only member of Congress) whose services were crucial to the pursuit of the war. And in the spring of 1944 a poll of Washington reporters picked him as the man, next to President Roosevelt, who was making the biggest contribution to the war effort. It is not surprising that by the summer of 1944, Truman was being mentioned for the vice presidential nomination, particularly by Democratic party leaders who thought Vice President Henry Wallace was too starry-eyed to fill the shoes of the ailing President should he become incapacitated. Gradually they persuaded the President, seeking a fourth term, to replace Wallace with Truman.[2]

Truman wasn't interested at first. He loved the Senate and knew that the vice presidency didn't carry much clout ("about as useful as a cow's fifth teat"). "I talked it over with Bess," he told a friend, "and we've decided against it. I've got a daughter and the limelight is no place for children." When his friend Tom Evans pressed him on the issue, he told him he didn't want "to drag a lot of skeletons out of the closet." "Well, now wait a minute . . . ," cried Evans. "I didn't know you had skeletons. What are they?" "The worst thing," said Truman, "is that I've had the Boss [his wife] on the payroll in my Senate office and I'm not going to have her name dragged over the front pages of the papers and over the radio." "Well, Lord," exclaimed Evans, "that isn't anything too great," and he pointed out there were plenty of other members of Congress who had wives and relatives on the payroll and that there was nothing wrong about it so long as they all put in an honest day's work, as he knew Mrs. Truman was doing.[3]

Truman continued resistant, and when the Democrats met in Chicago in July 1944 to nominate FDR for a fourth term, he was still uncommitted. But party leaders worked hard on him, and finally FDR, who knew Truman was a loyal New Dealer, interceded. In a call to Robert Hannegan, chairman of the Democratic National Committee, from Hyde Park, Roosevelt asked: "Have you got that fellow lined up yet?" "No," said Hannegan, "he is the contrariest Missouri mule I've ever dealt with." "Well," said FDR, "you tell him, if he wants to break up the Democratic party in the middle of the war, that's his responsibility." "Now, what do you say?" Hannegan asked Truman after relaying FDR's message. "Well, if that's the situation," said Truman, "I'll have to say yes, but why the hell didn't he tell me in the first place?" Wallace received more votes than Truman on the first ballot, but on the second ballot Truman won the nomination. Some people called him "the new Missouri Compromise."[4]

Truman's style was different from FDR's but his world-view was much the same. The "Fair Deal" he sponsored after becoming President was an extension of FDR's New Deal and in some respects went even farther than the latter in its desegregation of the armed forces and proposal for national health insurance. Truman was committed, too, to the United Nations, and, like FDR, favored Universal Military Training after the war and a strong defense program in order to fulfill the nation's responsibilities to check aggression around the world. In June 1950, when the Korean War broke out, even Henry Wallace, who had been critical of Truman's foreign policy after World War II, gave his full support to the President's determination to check North Korean aggression under the aegis of the United Nations.

CHAPTER 32

Hiroshima and
the American Left

In August 1945, American rightists applauded and American leftists denounced President Truman's decision to authorize the dropping of atomic bombs on Japan.

Not so.

The majority of Americans, on both the left and the right, approved of Truman's action at the time, as a way of ending the war with Japan quickly. Some conservatives—former President Herbert Hoover and *U.S. News* editor David Lawrence—deplored the action, and some liberals—popular economist Stuart Chase and *Christian Science Monitor* correspondent Richard L. Strout—did so too. But most Americans felt as *Time, Newsweek,* the *New York Times,* and other mainstream publications did: the bombs dropped on Hiroshima and Nagasaki were horrible weapons, but they did end the war promptly, obviated the necessity of invading Japan, and thus saved countless lives, Japanese as well as American.

But were the bombs indispensable to Japan's surrender on August 15, 1945? In December 1945, the United States Strategic Bombing Survey (USSBS), after a careful study, came to the conclusion that dropping the bombs had not been essential to winning the war. "Japan would have surrendered even if the atomic bombs had not been dropped," concluded the multi-volumed USSBS report, "even if Russia had not entered the war and even if no invasion had been planned or contemplated." The USSBS report was, of course, based on hindsight; it also refrained from speculating about how much longer Japan would have held out (to strengthen its bargaining position at the peace table) had it not been for the atom bombings. But as social critic Paul Fussell pointed out in an essay, "Thank God for the Atom Bomb," published in 1980, even two more weeks of war would have produced a considerable loss of lives on both sides.[1] In any case, none of the Allied war leaders, including Franklin Roosevelt and Winston Churchill, contemplated not using the bomb if it seemed essential to victory. And Josef Stalin, when told by President Truman about "a new weapon of unusual destructive force" at the Potsdam Conference in July 1945, urged him to "make good use of it against the Japanese." (He already knew about the atom bomb from information supplied by atomic spy Klaus Fuchs.)[2]

Twenty years after Hiroshima, Americans on the left began having second thoughts about the atomic bombs. In New Leftist circles in the late 1960s, protests against U.S. involvement in Vietnam began to spill over into criticism of U.S. policies during World War II and finally came to focus on Hiroshima. In a book entitled *Atomic Diplomacy: Hiroshima and Potsdam,* published in 1965, historian Gar Alperowitz presented the thesis that Japan was thoroughly beaten by August 1945 and the use of atomic bombs was unnecessary for ending the war, and that the main reason the United States dropped the bombs was to intimidate the USSR. "Atomic diplomacy," in short, not military necessity, dictated Truman's action. Alperowitz's "revisionist" views about the atom bombs quickly took root among New Leftists and soon became conventional wisdom for many leftists in this country and abroad. "The bombing of Hiroshima," wrote political philosopher Michael Walzer, in a typical view, in 1989, "was an act of terrorism; its purpose was political, not military." By then, men and women of goodwill were in the habit of gathering in towns and cities throughout the country on August 6—Hiroshima Day—in atonement for the dropping of atomic bombs on Japan and to renew their dedication to the cause of world peace.

The charge that the United States made use of atomic bombs when it didn't need to is of course a horrendous one. It places the United States, for cold and calculated brutality, in the same category as Nazi Germany and militaristic Japan. But the charge is also a breathtakingly ex post facto one. It certainly wasn't made by American leftists (the spiritual ancestors of the New Leftists) in August

1945. No one on the left, including American Stalinists, dreamed of talking about "atomic diplomacy" against the Soviet Union in 1945. Ironically, in fact, those liberals and radicals who were friendliest to Stalinist Russia in 1945 were also the most enthusiastic about the use of atomic bombs on Japan, while those who were the most critical of the Stalinist system were also the most sharply critical of the United States for dropping the bombs on Japan.

Take, for example, the *Daily Worker*. Official organ of the American Communist Party (CP, USA), and unswervingly loyal to the policies and principles laid down by Soviet dictator Josef Stalin, the *Worker* had none of the misgivings that Herbert Hoover did about the use of atomic bombs on Hiroshima and Nagasaki. Wrote the paper's military analyst right after the Hiroshima strike: "We are lucky we have found the Thing and are able to speed the war against the Japanese *before the enemy can devise countermeasures.* Thank God for that." And he added: "So let us not greet our atomic device with a shudder, but with the elation and admiration which the genius of man deserves." The *New Masses*, the Communist Party's biweekly, published in New York, was equally gleeful about the atomic bomb. The bomb, said the editors, was a "symbol of the great potentialities that can be released once the energies of the people are fully tapped." For both the *Daily Worker* and the *New Masses*, however, the dropping of atomic bombs on Hiroshima and Nagasaki was dwarfed by the entry of the Soviet Union into the war about the time of Nagasaki. From then on they took the line that Russia's last-minute intervention in the war, not the atomic bombs, played the crucial role in forcing Japan's capitulation.

The joy which the *Daily Worker* and the *New Masses* experienced on the news of Japan's abrupt capitulation on August 14 was marred, however, by President Truman's decision to compromise with Japan at the last moment in order to hasten the surrender. Instead of hewing to the "unconditional surrender" policy proclaimed by President Roosevelt in 1943 (and warmly supported by CP, USA), the Truman administration decided to let the Japanese retain their emperor after the war instead of trying him as a war criminal. The American Communists bitterly criticized the Truman administration for scuttling the unconditional-surrender policy and letting the emperor off so easily. The fact that sticking to the unconditional-surrender policy would unquestionably have prolonged the war seems not to have bothered either the *Worker* or the *New Masses*.

If the Stalinist left stressed unconditional surrender in August 1945, approved the use of atomic bombs, and emphasized the primacy of the Soviet Union in forcing Japan's surrender, what about the non-Stalinist left? The most influential non-Communist leftist publications in 1945 were the *Nation* and the *New Republic*, liberal weeklies, and *PM*, Manhattan's liberal daily. Though following no line but their own, all three publications were extremely sympathetic to the Soviet Union and anxious to promote good relations between the United States and the Soviets during and after the war. Not only did they regard the Soviet Union as on the whole a progressive and peace-loving society; they also reminded their readers that the USSR had lost millions of people beating back the Nazi invaders during the European war. Like the Stalinist *Daily Worker* and the *New Masses*, the pro-Soviet (but non-Stalinist) *Nation*, *New Republic*, and *PM* warmly greeted the use of atomic bombs on Japan, and they also tended to see eye to eye with the Stalinists on unconditional surrender and the sacking of the Japanese emperor. They disagreed, however, with the Stalinists in thinking Russia's last-minute intervention played a crucial part in bringing about Japan's decision to surrender. For them, it was the atomic bombs that produced sudden victory and they saw no need to apologize for their use.

To say that the *Nation*, the *New Republic*, and *PM* approved of the bombing of Hiroshima and Nagasaki is to understate the matter. All three publications took for granted from the outset the necessity and desirability of the bombings. Only when some Americans expressed misgivings about the bombs did they move on to a positive defense of the bombings. "The bomb that hurried Russia into the Far Eastern war and drove Japan to surrender," wrote Freda Kirchwey, editor of the *Nation*, "has accomplished the specific job for which it was created. From the point of view of military strategy, $2,000,000,000 (the cost of the bomb and the cost of nine days of war) was never better spent. The suffering, the wholesale slaughter it entailed, have been outweighed by its spectacular success. Allied leaders can rightly claim that the loss of life on both sides would have been many times greater if the atomic bomb had not been used and Japan had gone on fighting. There is no answer to this argument."

The *New Republic* agreed with the *Nation*. Not only did the editors insist that the bombs saved countless lives by shortening the war; they also scoffed at charges by the Japanese that the bombs dropped on Hiroshima and Nagasaki had impregnated the soil with radioactivity which would be harmful to life for years to come. Pointing out that American scientists denied the allegation, the editors sarcastically proposed a way of settling the matter. "If radioactivity is present in the soil," they wrote, "such plants will be marked by an unusual number of spots and mutations. Here is the ideal job for Emperor Hirohito, an amateur geneticist, after we are through with him—which, one hopes, will be soon. Let him go to Hiroshima, sit among the ruins, and watch the mutations grow."

The editorial writers and columnists for the feisty, pro-Soviet *PM* saw things much as the liberal weeklies did. "Thank God, It's Our Atomic Bomb!" exclaimed Irving Brant in an essay by that title for *PM* right after the Hiroshima strike. "Our atomic bomb! Do we realize, can we realize, what that little possessive pronoun means? Three little letters, o-u-r, to reflect the thankfulness of all Americans and of their allies that Germany or Japan did not produce this engine of inconceivable destruction." As to the regrets by some Americans about the use of atomic bombs on Japan, *PM*'s editors pointed out that the head of Japan's leading news agency had announced that the effect of the bombs was not as "good—bad—as is claimed," and that the B-29 raids on Tokyo on March 10 had done far more damage. "The few people who thought up, made, and dropped the atomic bomb," declared Max Lerner, in the first of two lead editorials for *PM* on the subject, "did more to bring Japan to its knees than the American fleet and (despite *Isvestiya*'s recent denial) the massive Russian armies." In his second piece on the subject, Lerner conceded the horror of the atomic bombs as weapons of war, but insisted that their use was justified because "we used the atom bomb," not out of "hatred and sadism," but "to end the war quickly, and with a loathing for its needs."

Not all American liberals agreed with Lerner. America's religious liberals, for one, felt sorrow, not elation, over the atomic bombings and thought they had destroyed the nation's moral position in the world: *Commonweal*, Catholic weekly with a liberal social outlook, and the *Christian Century*, liberal Protestant weekly published in Chicago. There were secular liberals, too, writing for weekly magazines with a small circulation—*Common Sense,* published in New York, and the *Progressive,* published in Madison, Wisconsin—who also deplored the atomic bombings. The anti-Hiroshima liberals, religious and secular, criticized both the United States and the Soviet Union for ignoring Japanese peace bids earlier in the year, and they also thought the United States should have arranged a demonstration of the effectiveness of the atomic bomb in order to persuade Japan to surrender before Hiroshima. Socialist leader Norman Thomas (a staunch anti-Stalinist) shared their views. "I shall be told that it was the bomb which ended the war," he declared. "As things were that is probably true, but I shall always believe that the war might have been ended before the first atomic bomb was dropped on Hiroshima bringing death to at least a hundred thousand men, women, and children." Like the anti-Hiroshima religious and secular liberals who denounced the atomic bombings, Thomas had been a pre-Pearl Harbor dove (unlike the pro-Hiroshima leftists who took a hawkish position long before Pearl Harbor) and also extremely critical of what Nikita Khrushchev years later called "the crimes of Stalin."[3]

There is something ironic in the New Left's charge, years later, that the United States was trying to intimidate the Soviet Union when it dropped atomic bombs on Japan in August 1945. It was, after all, American Stalinists (the *Daily Worker,* the *New Masses*) and the non-Stalinist but pro-Soviet liberals (the *Nation,* the *New Republic,* and *PM*) and, presumably, their readers who were the most fervent supporters of the unconditional-surrender policy toward Japan and the atom bombs that went with it. And it was the anti-Stalinist liberals, religious and secular, who were the most condemnatory of both the unconditional-surrender policy and the atomic bombings. If President Truman was engaging in "atomic diplomacy" against Russia in 1945, as the New Left came to believe in the late 1960s, he had his strongest support from the militant Old Left that was friendliest to Stalinist Russia.

It was a Brit, not an American, who seems to have been the first to propose atomic intimidation of the Soviet Union. In June 1946, the United States offered to surrender its monopoly of atomic power to an International Atomic Development Authority "to which should be entrusted all phases of the development and use of atomic energy." British philosopher Bertrand Russell hailed the proposal as a magnanimous act of statesmanship, and, when all the members of the United Nations except the Soviet Union and its satellites accepted the proposal, he urged that if the Kremlin continued its intransigence, the atomic bomb be dropped on Russia. President Truman wisely refrained from such reckless action.[4]

CHAPTER 33

Losing China

After World War II the United States "lost China" because the U.S. policymakers at the highest levels were "soft on Communism." Not so.

China, a proud and ancient civilization, was not America's to lose, in the first place, and, in the second, the United States sided with Nationalist leader Chiang Kai-shek during the civil war with the Chinese Communists and did everything it could short of military intervention to help him triumph in the struggle.

Unlike Winston Churchill, President Franklin Roosevelt took Chiang Kai-shek seriously. After Pearl Harbor, when the United States went to war to punish Japanese aggression, FDR had high hopes for Nationalist China. He regarded the Nationalists as invaluable allies who would tie down millions of Japanese forces on the mainland while U.S. forces advanced against Japan in the Pacific. He also expected Nationalist China to emerge from the war as a major power worthy to stand beside the United States, Britain, and the Soviet Union as one of the "Four Policemen" upholding peace and order in the world. Chiang, for his part, was gleeful when he heard about Pearl Harbor, for he was convinced that U.S. entry into the war solved his problem. While the United States took on Japan, he decided, he could devote his energies to building up strength to put down the Chinese Communists who—concentrated as they were in north China, with their capital at Yenan—challenged his rule.

The stage was set for misunderstanding and frustration. FDR expected Chiang to help whip the Japanese, but Chiang was primarily interested in licking the Communists. When FDR sent General Joseph W. ("Vinegar Joe") Stilwell to China to help Chiang organize his forces to fight the Japanese, clashes were inevitable. Stilwell, who spoke Chinese, served as commander of U.S. forces in China and as military adviser to Chiang, but he quickly learned that Chiang did not welcome advice. Stilwell wanted to reorganize, train, and arm the Chinese with American equipment to take on the Japanese, but Chiang dragged his heels. His major objective was to conserve his men and materials as much as he could in preparation to take on the Communists when the war ended.

Stilwell was appalled by the corruption and inefficiency of Chiang's regime as well as by its unwillingness to do any serious fighting. Like other American observers, he was also shocked by the arbitrary way Nationalist military officials roamed the countryside conscripting peasants into the army and thereafter kept their pay for themselves, fed and clothed them miserably, and, in general, treated them with contempt and cruelty. Stilwell went to China in April 1942 with high hopes; two and a half years later he left (at Chiang's request) discouraged and disillusioned. "The cure for China's trouble," he concluded, "is the elimination of Chiang Kai-shek."[1] FDR's faith in Generalissimo Chiang wavered during these years and from time to time he put pressure on the Generalissimo to make peace with the Communists and do some fighting, but basically he stuck by the "G-mo" (as Stilwell called him) to the end. Ironically, if Chiang had followed Stilwell's advice and developed Chinese armies high in morale and experienced in fighting the Japanese, he might have had a chance of success in the civil war that erupted right after the surrender of Japan in August 1945.

The Chinese Communists, led by Mao Tse-tung, were in a far better position at the war's end to win the support of the masses than the Nationalists were. While the Nationalists "traded space for time" (that is, let Japan take over more and more of China while they waited for an American victory), the Chinese Communists moved into the countryside behind Japanese lines and organized a peasant guerrilla army to fight the Japanese (and later the Nationalists). In wooing the peasants, the Communists played down class struggle and radical land reform and emphasized patriotism and the struggle against foreign domination. But they also lowered rents, redressed grievances, and, in general, treated the peasants, long exploited by landlords and money lenders, as human beings. When a Communist unit entered a village, according to a U.S. Military Intelligence report, "its retinue of propagandists, social and economic workers and school teachers . . . immediately started organizing and training the peasants for resistance through guerrilla warfare. The central idea in all these efforts was that the social and economic level of the peasants had to be improved in order to maintain morale and to instill among the people a will to resist Japan and support their own armies."[2]

During the war, American journalists, foreign service officers, and military officials like Stilwell—none of them Communists—couldn't help contrasting Nationalist ineptness with Communist shrewdness. Stilwell once summed it all up: the Nationalists—"corruption, neglect, chaos . . . trading with the enemy" and "a terrible waste of life, callous disregard for all the rights of men"—and the Communists—"reduce taxes, rents, interest. Practice what they preach."[3] Journalist Theodore White, who covered China for *Time* during the war, thought the reason for Communist success was obvious. "If you take a peasant," he wrote, "who has been swindled, beaten, and kicked about for all his waking days and whose father transmitted to him an emotion of bitterness reaching back for generations—if you take such a peasant, treat him like a man, ask his opinion, let him vote for a local government, let him organize his own police and gendarmes, decide on his own taxes, and vote himself a reduction in rent and interest—if you do all that, the peasant becomes a man who has something to fight for, and he will fight to preserve it against any enemy, Japanese or Chinese."[4] In 1937, the Communists controlled only a few thousand square miles in north China, a million people, and an army of about 80,000; eight years later, when Japan surrendered, they had almost a million troops, occupied a quarter of China, and governed 100 million people.

The United States of course continued to back Chiang after the war. Upon Japan's surrender, President Harry Truman ordered all Japanese and puppet forces in China to surrender their positions as well as their arms and equipment to Chiang and his representatives. To help Chiang extend his rule, moreover, U.S. authorities rushed almost 60,000 Marines from the Pacific to China so they could take over important rail centers, ports, and airfields from Japanese forces and hold them until the arrival of the Nationalists. The U.S. Navy and the Air Force helped too; they transported hundreds of thousands of Nationalist soldiers from the south to north China. Military aid to Chiang under the wartime Lend-Lease program continued, and eventually additional aid on a large scale—amounting to about $2 billion after 1945—was forthcoming.

But the Chinese Communists steadily expanded their holdings as Chiang's armies moved north. While the Nationalists seized urban centers in north China, Communist guerrilla forces increased their control of the countryside and in time they succeeded in isolating Nationalist positions. They had some help from the USSR; when Soviet forces departed from Manchuria in March 1946 they left tons of Japanese equipment there for the Chinese Communists to take over. But the Soviet Union signed a treaty of friendship with Nationalist China in August 1945 and for the most part refrained from giving the Chinese Communists any real help. The United States on the other hand remained heavily involved with Chiang. And when Nationalist forces, plagued by corruption, inept leadership, and lack of morale, continued to lose ground to the Communists despite American aid, President Truman decided reluctantly to intervene. In December 1945 he sent George C. Marshall, former Army Chief of Staff, to China to try to bring about some kind of settlement that would save Chiang's neck.

Marshall made some progress at first. He succeeded in arranging a cease-fire in the disputed areas of China and in initiating talks between the Nationalists and the Communists directed toward creating some kind of national coalition government. But the talks soon broke down. The Communists demanded real power in the coalition as well as the right to maintain their separate armies, while the Nationalists insisted on disarming the Communists and giving them a subordinate role in the new government. As discussions, presided over by Marshall, became deadlocked, the cease-fire he had arranged began breaking down, and by the end of 1946 the civil war was raging again. And though Nationalist armies were larger and better equipped, they were in continual retreat before the battle-trained and more energetic Communist forces. In January 1947, a discouraged Marshall returned to Washington to become Secretary of State, thoroughly pessimistic about America's ability to help Chiang maintain his rule in war-torn China. In a closed session before the House and Senate committees, he said frankly that to destroy the Communists, the United States would have to "underwrite the Chinese Government's military effort, on a wide and probably constantly increasing scale, as well as the Chinese economy. The United States would have to be prepared virtually to take over the Chinese Government and administer its economic, military, and governmental efforts. . . . It would be impossible to estimate the final cost of such a course of action of this magnitude. It certainly would be a continuing operation for a long time to come. . . . [I]t would be practically impossible to withdraw."[5] A fact-finding tour, headed by General Albert Wedemeyer, a staunch supporter of Chiang, was not much more optimistic. In a report to President Truman in September 1947, Wedemeyer recommended continued aid to Chiang, but acknowledged that "until drastic political and economic reforms are undertaken, United States aid cannot accomplish its purpose."[6]

As Chiang's position continued to deteriorate in 1947 and 1948, there were cries in Congress, especially among Republicans, for more vigorous action to help the Nationalists, but even President Truman's harshest critics were no more willing than he was to send U.S. combat troops to China to take on Chiang's foes. One day, after Maine Republican Senator Owen Brewster had delivered one of his many blasts at Truman's China policy, Texas Senator Tom Connally, chairman of the Senate Foreign Relations, exclaimed: "But let me ask the Senator from Maine if he would have wanted to send his son to China to take part in a fight between Chinese rival armies. The Senator from Texas does not have such a desire." Brewster at first called this "a red herring," but when Connally pressed him, he finally admitted, "I had already made it very clear to the Senator from Texas that I had never proposed to send an American Army to China. . . ." Even California Senator William F. Knowland, one of Chiang's strongest champions in the Senate, told Connally: "Will not the Senator agree that there has never been a proposal on the part of those who are critical of the policy [they] have pursued in the Far East to send an Army to China?" The most that either the Truman administration or Chiang's friends in Congress would do at this point was to sponsor more military and financial aid to his regime.[7]

By the end of 1948, Chiang's armies were in full retreat and

Nationalist troops were defecting to the Communists en masse. In February 1949, fifty Senators asked the administration to approve a $1.5 billion loan to Chiang's collapsing regime, but when they learned that American weapons were being captured by the Communists almost as soon as they reached China, they reduced the request to $75 million. By this time the Nationalists had abandoned Peking and Tientsin; and soon Shanghai fell to the Communists, and then Canton. In a White Paper released by the State Department in August 1949—a massive review of U.S. Chinese relations for the past decade—the Truman administration defended its China policy, insisted that the United States had done everything within its power to save the Chinese Nationalists, but that decadence, corruption, and downright incompetence had led to their defeat. "The unfortunate but inescapable fact," declared the report, "is that the ominous result of the civil war in China was beyond the control of the United States."[8]

In December 1949, Chiang and the Nationalists fled from the Chinese mainland and established themselves in Formosa (Taiwan), still claiming to be the legitimate government of China. But, for the first time since the 1930s, U.S. policy, formulated by Dean Acheson, General Marshall's successor as Secretary of State, centered on remaining aloof from Chiang's regime and "letting the dust settle" in Eastern Asia. There was no more aid to Chiang, military or economic, but no friendly gestures to the new Communist government of China either. Where Britain, France, and the other major powers extended diplomatic recognition to the People's Republic of China, proclaimed by Mao in October 1949, the United States followed a policy of non-recognition. In the United Nations, moreover, the chief U.S. delegate utilized the veto power to prevent the replacement of Nationalist China by the People's Republic of China in the Security Council.

But the outbreak of the Korean War in June 1950 led the United States back to Chiang. Soon the United States was sending military and financial aid again to Chiang's Nationalists on Taiwan; it also deployed naval vessels between the Chinese mainland and Taiwan to prevent the Communists from launching an assault on the island. But President Truman's decision to start aiding Chiang again scarcely helped him with his critics inside and outside of Congress. During the 1950s, disgruntled demagogues, led by Senator Joseph R.

McCarthy of Wisconsin, charged that FDR, Truman, Marshall, Acheson, and their underlings in the State Department had by their "softness on Communism" betrayed Chiang (as well as the United States) and delivered him into the hands of his enemies. The charge was, of course, preposterous; no one who knew anything about China took it seriously. Even General Wedemeyer explained his friend Chiang's defeat—as had the White Paper—by "lack of spirit, primarily lack of spirit" on the part of the Nationalists. "It was not lack of equipment," he acknowledged. "In my judgment they could have defended the Yangtze with broomsticks if they had the will to do it."[9]

CHAPTER 34

McCarthy and
the Commies

Wisconsin Senator Joseph R. McCarthy's methods were crude, but he did succeed in uncovering Communists who had been in high places in Washington and had influenced U.S. foreign policy during and after World War II.

Not so.

McCarthy was a reckless rabble-rouser who succeeded only in stirring up fears and hatreds in the 1950s and encouraging witch hunts, book banning, and character assassination. His legacy was McCarthyism: irresponsible name-calling and the reckless identification of heresy with conspiracy. McCarthy "has netted no spies," wrote Walter Lippmann in March 1954, "but only a few minnows at the cost of the terrible injustice or enormous injury to the good name of America, and the filling of our air with poison and stink."[1]

McCarthy was in a way a kind of anti-Commie-come-lately. It was several years after entering the Senate in 1947 before he began exploiting anti-Communism in a big way for personal advancement. As a freshman Senator he didn't push the Communist issue particularly; he left that to reactionary Republicans like Indiana's William Jenner, who raved on the Senate floor about FDR's "sell-out" to Stalin at Yalta and Truman's "loss of China" to Mao in 1949. He distinguished himself largely at first by his coarse behavior and crude attacks on his colleagues, soon alienating prominent Senators in both parties and leading the Washington press corps to pick him as the "worst Senator" on Capitol Hill. In February 1950, when

Republican party officials chose speakers for Lincoln's Birthday rallies around the country, they gave McCarthy a minor assignment: a speech to a Woman's Republican Club in Wheeling, West Virginia.[2]

McCarthy's Wheeling appearance started him on the road to national—and international—fame. In his Lincoln Birthday speech, he talked about "Communist victories and American defeats in the Cold War" for a time, and then suddenly held up a piece of paper (reportedly a laundry list) and cried: "I have here in my hand a list of 205 who were known to the Secretary of State as being members of the Communist Party and who, nevertheless, are still working and shaping policy in the State Department." In Salt Lake City, however, where he spoke again a little later, he talked about 57 "card-carrying Communists" in the State Department. A few days later, as headlines mounted, he again revised his figures; there were 108 infiltrators, he told the Senate, in a lengthy bumbling speech that went on until midnight. But a Senate committee, headed by conservative Democrat Millard E. Tydings of Maryland, found it almost impossible to get any precise information out of the Wisconsin Senator, and when McCarthy finally did name a few names, he turned out to be completely wrong in every instance. After extensive hearings, the Tydings committee concluded that there was no evidence to support any of McCarthy's allegations ("a fraud and a hoax"), but this didn't faze the freewheeling Red-hunter a bit. Sneered he: "The most loyal stooges of the Kremlin could not have done a better job in giving a clean bill of health to Stalin's fifth column in this country." That fall he helped get Tydings defeated for re-election—the campaign featured a fake picture of Tydings hobnobbing with former Communist leader Earl Browder—and took credit, too, for the defeat of Democratic Majority Leader Scott Lucas of Illinois. He had already done what he could to discredit Maine Senator Margaret Chase Smith, who in June 1950 had presented the Senate with a "Declaration of Conscience," signed by six other liberal Republicans, warning the Republicans against "riding to political victory on the four horsemen of calumny—fear, ignorance, bigotry, and smear."[3]

As McCarthy's fame rose, however, his associates in the Senate, even Senator Smith, became increasingly reluctant to tangle with him. In July 1951, when he went after General George C. Marshall—he charged that Marshall, as Truman's Secretary of State, was part of an immense "conspiracy of infamy" to ensure the triumph of Communism in China—only a few Democrats came to Marshall's defense in the Senate. One Democrat who blasted McCarthy for his meanness and mendacity—Connecticut's William E. Benton—lost his bid for re-election in 1952, and, again, McCarthy took credit. Even Dwight D. Eisenhower, running for President in 1952, seemed intimidated. During the campaign he planned to pay a personal tribute to General Marshall, his superior in the army during World War II, in a speech in Milwaukee, but when McCarthy heard about it, he raised such a rumpus that Ike agreed to omit the remarks he had planned in defense of his old friend.[4]

With Eisenhower's victory in 1952, the Republicans took over Congress and McCarthy became chairman of both the Senate Committee on Government Operations and its investigative arm, the Permanent Subcommittee on Investigations. If he had made life miserable for Democrats when Truman was President, he made it even tougher for Eisenhower Republicans. He harassed the Voice of America, the State Department's foreign-broadcast station; sent two young men—chief counsel Roy Cohn and consultant G. David Schine—to Europe to make a fuss about some of the books in State Department libraries there; and, by his smear attacks, forced leading experts on East Asia out of the State Department. In none of his rambunctious activities did he produce anything but headlines, yet he attracted a devoted following and inspired hysterical inquisitions on the state and local level throughout the country. He even intimidated McCarthy-haters on the left; some of them were afraid to criticize the crimes of Stalin lest they be thought "soft on McCarthyism." Not surprisingly, some Americans became a bit confused. "If McCarthy is a Communist," whined a woman in the Midwest, "why don't they kick him out of the State Department?" In New York City, when a policeman pushed a demonstrator at a political rally and the latter yelled, "Look, I'm an anti-Communist," the cop barked: "I don't care what kind of a Communist you are. Get back on the sidewalk!"[5]

In 1954, McCarthy took on the U.S. Army. Learning that a left-wing dentist had done a tour of duty at Camp Kilmer, N.J., and then been honorably discharged, he hauled both the dentist and the Camp Kilmer commandant, General Ralph Zwicker, before his committee for grilling. The dentist (probably a Soviet sympathizer) refused to discuss his political views, and General Zwicker, for his part, explained that he was only following orders in issuing the discharge. But McCarthy subjected Zwicker, a war hero, to such outrageous abuse that Eisenhower's Secretary of the Army, Robert T. Stevens, assured Zwicker he did not need to make any more appearances before McCarthy and announced his own determination to protect other army officers from harassment. He also revealed that McCarthy and his chief counsel, Roy Cohn, had been pulling strings for months to get special treatment for Cohn's young friend, David Schine, who had recently been drafted into the army. Furious, McCarthy charged that Stevens was using Schine as a "hostage" to force him to call off his investigation of Communism in the armed forces.[6]

The Army-McCarthy hearings growing out of these charges and countercharges opened in the Senate Caucus Room on April 22, 1954, went on for five weeks, held millions of televiewers enthralled day after day, and astonished America's friends and allies around the world. From the outset, McCarthy took the offensive: interrupted proceedings with cries of "point of order, Mr. Chairman, point of order," got off on rambling irrelevancies, badgered witnesses, and doggedly refused to answer questions about his own use of a doctored photograph and a stolen classified letter to support his side of the controversy. At length, however, he went too far. Goaded into fury by Army special counsel Joseph N. Welch's skillful (and at times satiric) cross-examination, he suddenly charged that a junior member of Welch's Boston law firm had once belonged to an organization which the House Un-American Activities Committee (HUAC) had labeled a "Red front." Welch was stunned; he had never dreamed that McCarthy, for all his unscrupulousness, would drag the name of his young partner, absolutely irrelevant to the proceedings, into the case. "Until this moment, Senator," he exclaimed, tears appearing on his cheeks, "I think I never really gauged your cruelty or recklessness." Then, as McCarthy busied himself with some papers, Welch went on to explain that his young associate had for a time belonged to the Lawyers Guild as a law student, was now active in the Republican party, and, unless McCarthy succeeded in destroying him, had a brilliant future ahead of him. "Little did I dream," Welch told McCarthy, "that you could be so reckless and so cruel as to do an injury to that lad." Then, as McCarthy tried to interrupt, he exclaimed: "Have you no sense of decency, sir? At long last, have you left no sense of decency?" There was a moment of stunned silence when Welch finished talking, and then most of the people in the Caucus Room—Senators, lawyers, spectators, reporters, and cameramen—started applauding. "What did I do wrong?" muttered McCarthy afterwards, as people began filing out of the room, pointedly ignoring him, when the subcommittee chairman declared a recess.[7]

The Army-McCarthy hearings ended McCarthy's career as a Not-So-Grand Inquisitor. On June 11, 1954, Republican Senator Ralph Flanders of Vermont introduced a resolution in the Senate calling for McCarthy's censure; on November 25, a special committee headed by conservative Republican Senator Arthur Watkins of Utah recommended censure, after extensive hearings, on two counts; and on December 1, the Senate voted 67 to 22 that the Wisconsin Senator's conduct was "contrary to Senatorial traditions" and "tended to bring the Senate into dishonor and disrepute, to obstruct the constitutional processes of the Senate, and to impair its dignity, and such conduct is hereby condemned." Afterward, Senator McCarthy, a rabble-rouser with no deep convictions about Communism or anything else (except perhaps a resentment against people he believed thought themselves better than he was), seemed genuinely bewildered. "I wouldn't exactly call it a vote of confidence," he said after the Senate vote, "but I don't feel that I've been lynched." He spent his remaining years in the Senate largely ignored by his colleagues. But McCarthyism continued on the American scene long after his death in 1957, though not in as flamboyant a form.[8]

McCarthy wasn't the only member of Congress to go in for witch-hunting in the 1950s. Indiana Senator William Jenner was almost as unscrupulous as McCarthy in hurling charges of treason against Democrats; and even Senator Richard Nixon, soon to become Eisenhower's Vice President, charged that "Mr. Truman, Dean Acheson [Truman's Secretary of State] and other administration officials covered up the Communist conspiracy for political reasons." McCarthy himself may have sincerely believed the Reds were taking over the country, but most of his supporters in the Senate went along with him for partisan political reasons. "There may conceivably be as many as three Republicans in the Senate who sincerely believe that there is substance behind the McCarthy charges," wrote *Christian Science Monitor* columnist Joseph C. Harsch in July 1950, "but I doubt it. I would not know where to find one, other than McCarthy himself, who would seriously contend in private and between friends that he believed the charges." The FBI, not McCarthy, uncovered some espionage in the 1950s, and several other federal agencies discovered a number of people with Soviet sympathies (partly because the Soviets had fought the Nazis so heroically during World War II) and fired them, but none of them had had any influence whatsoever on the policies of the agencies that employed them. "For all the thunder in Congress and the White House about disloyalty," wrote Thomas C. Reeves, in his 1982 study of McCarthyism, "all the hearings and loyalty-security programs were unsuccessful in obtaining a single conviction for substantial acts against the United States."[9]

H. L. Mencken, who enjoyed belittling the intelligence of the American people, once cracked that Americans were dumb, but not dumb enough to be Communists. He was right: McCarthyism was the dumbness of their choice in the 1950s.

CHAPTER 35

JFK and
Vietnam

President Kennedy was planning to withdraw from Vietnam just before his assassination on November 22, 1963.

Not really.

JFK took seriously the Communist threat to South Vietnam. He regarded Ho Chi Minh's efforts to unify North and South Vietnam under Communist control as a clear and present danger to both the United States and to the non-Communist world in general. While he was President he steadily increased America's military presence in South Vietnam and never wavered in his belief that the United States must stand firm in its responsibility to prevent a Communist takeover in Southeast Asia. "I don't agree with those who say we should withdraw," he told Walter Cronkite in a television interview on September 2, 1963. "That would be a great mistake." Queried about French President Charles de Gaulle's call in August for peace talks directed toward neutralizing the area, he responded somewhat impatiently that "we are glad to get counsel, but we would like a little more assistance, real assistance. But we are going to meet our responsibility anyway. It doesn't do any good to say, 'Well, why don't we all just go home and leave the world to those who are our enemies.'" In private discussions with his chief advisers, civil and military, he expressed the same determination to stay the course in Vietnam.[1]

Like Dwight D. Eisenhower, Kennedy believed in the "domino theory," the theory that one country after another would go Communist in Southeast Asia if South Vietnam fell into Communist hands. "It is apparent . . . ," he wrote in December 1962, "that the Communist attempt to take over Vietnam is only part of a larger plan for bringing the entire area of Southeast Asia under their domination." When TV interviewer David Brinkley asked him point-blank on September 9, 1963, whether he had any doubts about the domino theory, he replied: "No, I believe it. I think that the struggle is close enough. China is so large, looms so high just beyond the frontiers, that if South Vietnam went, it would not only give them an improved geographic position for a guerilla assault on Malaya, but would also give the impression that the wave of the future in Southeast Asia was China and the Communists. So I believe it." And he went on to say: "We must be patient, we must persist. What I am concerned about is that Americans will get impatient and say because they don't like events in Southeast Asia or they don't like the government in Saigon, that we should withdraw. . . . I think we should stay."[2]

If JFK had seriously intended to withdraw from Vietnam before blunting the Communist drive, he had a splended opportunity to do so in the spring and summer of 1963. The American people were lukewarm about the Vietnam venture and there were doubts about it in both Congress and in the news media. In addition, prominent military men—Generals Douglas MacArthur, Matthew Ridgway, and J. Lawton Collins, as well as Marine Commandant David Shoup—strongly advised against U.S. military involvement in Vietnam. In South Vietnam itself there was no great enthusiasm for the increase in U.S. forces, some of them engaged in combat operations, after Kennedy became President. South Vietnam President Ngo Dinh Diem and his brother-in-law Ngo Dinh Nhu (who was considered the power behind the throne) complained about U.S. infringements on Vietnamese sovereignty and began calling for a reduction in the number of U.S. personnel in the country. In an interview with the *Washington Post* on May 12, 1963, Nhu announced that "South Vietnam would like to see half of the 12,000 to 13,000 American military stationed here leave the country." But not only did Diem and Nhu call for troop withdrawals; they also began toying with the idea of entering into negotiations with North Vietnam for a peaceful settlement of the conflict.[3]

But JFK did not seize the opportunity for disengagement. Instead, he stepped up pressure on Diem to continue and intensify the fight against the Communists and, when that failed, encouraged the replacement of Diem and Nhu by leaders who were willing to fight the good fight the way the United States wished. When a military coup finally occurred on November 1, 1963, with a group of generals led by Duong Van Minh, committed to victory against the Communists, replacing Diem and Nhu (who were assassinated), Kennedy was delighted; he called the coup an achievement "of the greatest importance." With the generals in power, he told Henry Cabot Lodge, ambassador to South Vietnam, it was now possible to confront "the real problems of winning the contest against the Communists and holding the confidence of its own people."[4]

While seeking a military victory in Vietnam, President Kennedy did, it is true, from time to time, reassure the American public by noting that the task of defeating the Communists was primarily South Vietnam's, not America's, responsibility. "In the final analysis," he announced in September 1963, "it is their war. They have to win it or lose it." But permitting South Vietnam to "lose it" was never a real option for JFK. He always made it clear in discussions with Secretary of Defense Robert McNamara and his other advisers on Vietnam that "our fundamental objective" in Vietnam "is victory." His public statements reflected his private sentiments. "I think we should stay," he said in an NBC interview on September 9, 1963. "What helps to win the war, we support," he announced on September 12, "what interferes with the war effort we oppose. . . . [W]e have a very simple policy in that area. . . . we want the war to be won, the Communists to be contained, and the Americans to go home." (These remarks, the State Department's Roger Hilsman noted in 1967, became "a policy guideline" for Kennedy's advisers.) After the overthrow of Diem, Kennedy told the press that there was "a new situation here" and "we hope, an increased effort in the war" (November 14). In Fort Worth, a few hours before his assassination, in his last statement about Vietnam, he declared: "Without the United States, South Vietnam would collapse." And in the speech he planned to give in Dallas that day, he reminded Americans of the military build-up he had undertaken in order to check the "ambitions of international Communism" and he insisted that the United States, as the "watchman on the walls of the world freedom," had to undertake tasks that were "painful, risky and costly, as is true in Southeast Asia today. But we dare not weary of the task."[5]

What about the plan to withdraw 1000 U.S. troops from Vietnam by the end of 1963? This was first proposed by Kennedy's advisers in the spring of 1963 and was based on optimistic forecasts of the outcome of the struggle against Communism in Vietnam and on the belief that it was important to show the American people (who continued to be unenthusiastic about involvement in Vietnam) that the President's Vietnam policy was working admirably. With Kennedy's escalation of the war in Vietnam in 1961 and 1962, the future did indeed look bright for a time, and some of Kennedy's advisers even thought that victory over Communism in Vietnam was in sight. "The spearpoint of aggression," Kennedy told Congress in his State of the Union message in January 1963, "has been blunted in Vietnam."[6]

On May 6, 1963, Secretary of Defense Robert McNamara requested a plan for the withdrawal of "1,000 or so personnel late this year if the situation allows." Secretary of State Dean Rusk approved the idea and so did Chairman of the Joint Chiefs of Staff Maxwell Taylor, Kennedy's chief military adviser. In September, Kennedy sent McNamara and Taylor to Saigon to appraise "the military and paramilitary effort to defeat the Viet Cong," and when they returned they reported that "the military campaign has made great progress and continues to progress." Their recommendations to Kennedy on October 2 centered on stepping up the war effort in Vietnam and training the South Vietnamese to take over the tasks handled by U.S. military personnel by the end of 1965 so that "it should be possible to withdraw the bulk of U.S. personnel by that time." They also recommended that the Defense Department announce plans to withdraw 1000 U.S. military personnel by the end of 1963. "This action," they added, "should be explained in low key as an initial step in a long-term program to replace U.S. personnel with trained Vietnamese without impairment of the war effort."[7]

Kennedy approved the report, but, noting that "the major problem was with U.S. public opinion," balked at a commitment to withdraw some forces in 1963 because "if we were not able to take this action by the end of this year, we would be accused of being over optimistic." McNamara argued that announcing some withdrawals in 1963 would help counter "the view of Senator Fulbright and others that we are bogged down forever in Vietnam," but Kennedy refused to associate his name with the 1000-man withdrawal statement. In the end, the White House issued a press release reporting the McNamara-Taylor belief that "the major part of the U.S. military task can be completed by the end of 1963," and that the program for training the South Vietnamese "should have progressed to the point" where 1000 American military personnel could be withdrawn from Vietnam by the end of 1963. "As you know," said Kennedy in a news conference on October 31, 1963, "when Secretary McNamara and General Taylor came back, they announced that we would expect to withdraw 1,000 men from South Vietnam before the end of the year. . . . If we are able to do that, that will be our schedule." At a news conference on November 15, he talked of withdrawing "several hundred" instead of 1000, and emphasized the need "to intensify the struggle."[8]

President Kennedy's caution turned out to have been justified. The hopes of his advisers turned to disappointment as Diem and Nhu dragged their heels despite U.S. pressure, and even their replacement by a military junta on November 1 didn't seem to help much. What JFK would have done had he lived is impossible to say. Journalist Joseph Alsop (a Vietnam hawk), for one, thought he would have "stayed the course" had he lived, and Kennedy's advisers, most of whom stayed in their posts after his assassination, had nothing but praise for the way Lyndon Johnson handled the Vietnam issue after he became President. None of them—even the most dovish—advised withdrawal from Vietnam without victory. "The stakes are high," McNamara told LBJ in March 1964. "Unless we can achieve [our] objectives in South Vietnam, almost all of Southest Asia will probably fall under Communist domination." Robert F. Kennedy, JFK's brother, who stayed on as Attorney General for a time, agreed with McNamara (who also remained in the Cabinet). He did not like LBJ at all, but he regarded the new President's Vietnam policy as a continuation of his brother's. In May 1965, RFK condemned the idea of withdrawal from Vietnam without victory as "a repudiation of commitment undertaken and confirmed by three administrations" which would "gravely—perhaps irreparably—weaken the democratic position in Asia."[9]

RFK eventually changed his mind, and in February 1966 he called for a negotiated settlement in Vietnam. Several other former Kennedy advisers followed his lead, especially after North Vietnam's Tet offensive in early 1968 showed the futility of LBJ's massive escalation of U.S. military involvement in Vietnam. The time came when some of JFK's former advisers even revised their memories of his—and their—hawkish approaches to Vietnam in the early 1960s. But there was only one real dove back in the early days of the Kennedy presidency: Assistant Secretary of State George Ball. In November 1961, when JFK decided to commit U.S. forces to South Vietnam, Ball told him it would be a tragic error. "Within five years," he warned, "we'll have three hundred thousand men in the paddies and jungles and never find them again. That was the French experience. Vietnam is the worst possible terrain from both a physical and political point of view." "George," exclaimed JFK, "I always thought you were one of the brightest guys in town, but you're just crazier than hell."[10]

Ball was, so far as the record shows, the lonesome dove in Camelot. In his exhaustive study of JFK's Vietnam policy, *Rethinking Camelot* (1993), MIT linguist (and zealous critic of U.S. policies) Noam Chomsky made this almost irrefutably clear. In time, most of President Kennedy's advisers came to realize, with Ball, that America's vital national interests were not involved in Vietnam and that military intervention there was a tragic error and, as Robert Kennedy later put it, "doomed from the start." Years afterward, at a news conference in April 1991, a *London Observer* correspondent asked former Secretary of Defense Robert McNamara, one of the major architects of JFK's Vietnam policy, how he could explain his support of the Vietnam War back in the Kennedy days. "I got it wrong," said McNamara simply. Pressed to say more, he exclaimed: "My God, I said it was wrong."[11]

CHAPTER 36

The Kennedy Assassination

It is preposterous to think that Lee Harvey Oswald was the lone assassin who murdered President John F. Kennedy when he was visiting Texas in 1963.

Not at all so.

Lee Harvey Oswald had the motive, the means, and the opportunity to do in JFK on November 22, 1963, and there is far more hard evidence to prove that he did the deed by himself than there is to bolster any of the dozen or so alternative explanations centering on a Grand Conspiracy involving scores of other people.

Oswald proclaimed himself a radical—an ultra-leftist—and there seems to be no reason not to take him at his word. From an early age he despised the American capitalistic system as one of oppression and exploitation, and he came to look to the Soviet Union and then to Castro's Cuba as his beau ideal. When he was only fifteen he became interested in Marxism and, a self-assured autodidact, he began reading books on the subject and soon came to think of himself as an expert on socialist doctrine. He liked to show off the copy of Marx's *Capital* he had on the bookshelf, but it is doubtful that he read much (if any) of it, for it is a lengthy and difficult book.[1]

It is impossible to take Oswald's Marxism seriously. To judge from his pontifications on the subject and from scattered scribblings, his grasp of Marx was pretty primitive, on the level of that of, say, J. Edgar Hoover or Joseph R. McCarthy. Michael Paine, an Irving,

Texas, acquaintance with some sophistication, talked politics with him on occasion, but was not impressed. At seventeen, Oswald, already calling himself a Marxist, went into the Marine Corps to get away from his domineering mother; at nineteen, he went to the Soviet Union to get away from capitalistic America. He wanted to defect, but the KGB (secret police) didn't take him seriously, and it took a suicide attempt on his part to induce the Soviet authorities to let him stay in Russia. They sent him to Minsk, four hundred miles southwest of Moscow, where he worked in a radio and television factory, met and married Marina Prusakova, a young pharmacology student, joined a hunting club, and continued the study of the Russian language which he had begun as a Marine.

But two and a half years in the Soviet Union left Oswald unhappy and disillusioned, partly because of his stifling obscurity. When he returned to the United States in 1961 with his wife and baby girl, he was almost as contemptuous of socialist Russia as he was of capitalistic America. This was good Trotskyist doctrine ("a plague on both your houses"), but though he subscribed to the *Militant* (organ of the Trotskyist Socialist Workers Party) and had a letter he wrote featured in one of its issues, he also had a subscription to the *Worker* (oldline Stalinist organ of the American Communist Party) and corresponded some with Arnold Johnson, Communist Party leader. By this time, though, his heart was deep in Cuba. As a Castroite radical, he engaged for a time in what political anarchists used to call "propaganda of the word," that is, peaceful persuasion, in an effort to win sympathy for the Cuban revolution. In New Orleans, he organized a chapter of the Fair Play for Cuba Committee, tried to infiltrate anti-Castro groups, distributed pro-Castro leaflets, and defended the Castroite cause in radio interviews. But the fruits of his activities were negligible. He won no fame (something he desperately sought) and recruited no members for his Fair Play for Cuba Committee chapter. Nor did his efforts have any impact on U.S. policy toward Cuba. In an interview with an Associated Press correspondent on September 7, 1963, Fidel Castro took note of U.S. attempts on his life (sponsored by the CIA), blasted President Kennedy as a "cretin" who was "the Batista of his times," and denounced U.S. plots against Cuba. "We are prepared to fight them and answer in kind," he warned. "U.S. leaders should think that if they are aiding terrorist plans to eliminate Cuban leaders, they themselves will not be safe." The *New Orleans Times-Picayune* featured Castro's belligerent remarks, and Oswald, who read newspapers every day, undoubtedly knew all about Castro's threat.[2]

The vast majority of American radicals, including American Stalinists, have confined their activities to "propaganda of the word," but in the late 19th century a few dedicated anarchists, here and in Europe, espoused "propaganda of the deed," that is, violence, terrorism, and the assassination of prominent people, as a means of undermining the capitalistic system and paving the way to a better world. Anarchist Emma Goldman, at the turn of the century, concentrated on propaganda of the word, but Leon F. Czolgosz, inflamed by her words, went from word to deed and ended by assassinating President William McKinley when McKinley attended the Pan-American Exposition in Buffalo in September 1901. There is no evidence that Oswald—whose ignorance of history was as profound as his conceit—ever heard of either Goldman or Czolgosz, or, for that matter, knew anything about the anarchist philosophy they espoused, but he did have one thing in common with anarchist Czolgosz: he was emotionally unstable and he was not at all averse to violence. He was a loner, too, like Czolgosz, and anxious to leave his mark on the world.[3]

Not all radicals are unbalanced, of course, any more than all reactionaries are, but in Oswald's case, everyone who encountered him came soon to believe there was a screw loose. His mental instability—fellow marines called him "Bugs" and his wife said he was "crazy"—undoubtedly grew out of his wretched childhood. His widowed mother (whose bed he shared until he was almost eleven) went unhappily from job to job and from town to town, and by the time Oswald was fifteen, they had moved twenty-one times and he had attended more than a dozen schools, doing poorly in all of them. In the Bronx, where they lived for a time, a judge sent him to a Youth House for truancy, and a staff psychiatrist, after three weeks of observation, concluded that he had "a potential for explosive, aggressive, assaultive acting out" as well as a "vivid fantasy life, turning around the topics of omnipotence and power." Asked whether he preferred the company of boys or girls, young Oswald exclaimed: "I dislike everybody."[4]

When Oswald was older, he admitted that he had "a far mean streak of indepence (*sic*) brought on by negleck [*sic*]." The "mean streak" found its outlet in continual confrontation with other people. He abused his mother (though she frequently assured him he was brighter than other people), quarreled with schoolmates, fellow marines, and coworkers at the jobs he held after leaving the Marines, and, after getting married, he lambasted, slapped, punched, and pushed his wife around, and on occasion threatened to kill her. "I think he had a sick imagination," said Marina of their early years together. "I already considered him to be not quite normal." He was explosive about politics, too. Even as a youngster he denounced President Eisenhower as an oppressor of the workers and said he would kill him if he got the chance. From Russia he wrote his brother Robert: "I fight for *communism,*" and then warned him: "In the event of war I would kill *any* american who put a uniform in defense of the american government—any american." Later on, back in this country, he made it clear that if the United States invaded Cuba he would fight for Cuba.[5]

In April 1963, Oswald moved, like Czolgosz, from word to deed. His target: General Edwin Walker, right-wing agitator who, relieved of his post in 1961 for distributing propaganda to his troops, left the army and settled in Dallas to become active in anti-Communist, anti-integrationist, and anti-Castro causes. In February 1963, after reading a front-page newspaper story about Walker's anti-Communist activities, Oswald went to work. He began studying Dallas maps and bus routes, visiting Walker's neighborhood to take pictures of his house, while checking the post office frequently for the arrival of two weapons he had ordered under the name "Hidell" (not Fidel)—a Smith & Wesson .38 special revolver, ordered in January, and a 6.5 mm Mannlicher-Carcano, complete with four-power (4 ×) scope, ordered in February. The weapons came on the same day, March 20, and he was ready to act. By this time he had carefully put together a blue loose-leaf folder containing pictures and maps, "a complete record," he later told Marina, "so that all the details would be in it." He also wrote out an explanation of the action he was planning against Walker, whom he regarded as "the leader of a fascist organization," and he presented, too, his fond hope, as a "radical futurist," that "after the military debacle of the United States," the U.S. government would be replaced by a "separate, democratic, pure communist society."[6]

Oswald struck at Walker on the night of April 10, but, as he told

Marina dejectedly afterward, "I missed." The bullet went through the window where Walker was sitting, but was deflected by the wooden frame across the middle of the double window and passed through Walker's hair instead of his skull. A few days later Oswald returned to get the rifle he had stashed near Walker's house; he also destroyed the operations book. Disappointed by his near miss, but pleased with himself for having tried, he moved soon after to New Orleans with his wife and child, engaged in pro-Castro activities for a time, and then, humiliated by his lack of accomplishments, decided to return to Texas and seek work. To his wife's consternation, however, he began talking of hijacking a plane to Cuba—he would confront the pilots with his rifle, while Marina held the passengers at bay with his revolver—but to her immense relief he finally dropped the idea. [7]

In the end, Marina went back to Texas to stay with her friend, Ruth Paine, in Irving while Oswald took the bus to Mexico City in what turned out to be a fruitless effort to get a visa to Havana as soon as possible. Despite his insistence that he was a diligent and dedicated radical, with much to offer the Communist cause, both the Cuban and Soviet embassies there instructed him to follow the normal procedures, which took several weeks, for obtaining a visa. Oswald was furious at what he took to be bureaucratic stupidity, but his devotion to Communism—especially his adoration of "Uncle Fidel"—remained undimmed. At the Cuban consulate he even offered to kill JFK in order to stop the CIA plots against the Cuban dictator. Soon after he got back to Texas, he had a long political argument with Michael Paine, a pacifist, in which he defended his radical views and insisted that "change was necessary," but that "it would only come through violence." Afterward, he told Marina gleefully: "If only Michael knew what I wanted to do to Walker! Wouldn't he be scared!" [8]

Oswald had spent two months planning the Walker hit. With JFK it was perforce a last-minute decision. It wasn't until November 19, three days before the assassination, that the Dallas newspapers announced the motorcade route of President Kennedy's visit to Dallas: along Main Street onto Dealey Plaza, the public square on which the Texas State Book Depository bordered, and then onto Houston Street and left along Elm Street before reaching Stemmons Freeway and heading for Kennedy's luncheon speech at the Trade Mart. In the weeks before the President's visit, moreover, Oswald's life, like that of all human beings, was strewn with fortuities. If he had obtained a visa to Havana in September, one can't help thinking, he probably wouldn't have been in Dallas in November. If, moreover, he had received any of the four jobs for which he applied when he returned from New Orleans to Texas in September, he wouldn't have been in the Texas Depository on November 22. And if a neighbor hadn't told Ruth Paine, Marina's friend, of a possible opening at the Depository, and if Ruth hadn't called Roy Truly, the man in charge there, and if Truly, who had two openings, hadn't assigned Oswald to the Dealey Plaza location instead of the other one, American history would have been quite different. Oswald began working as a clerk at the Depository on October 16, rented a room in a boarding house in Dallas in which to stay during the week, and arranged to hitch a ride with Wesley Frazier, a young coworker, to Irving every Friday after work, to spend weekends with Marina, who was living there with Ruth Paine.

On Thursday, November 21, Oswald changed his routine. He asked Frazier for a ride a day early so he could "get some curtain rods" for his room (as it turned out, the place didn't need any). Marina was surprised to see him that day; their marriage had been strained for a long time and she wasn't exactly pleased by his unexpected appearance. When he told her he was lonely, wanted to make up with her, and take her back to Dallas to live, she turned him down. Whether Oswald would have behaved differently the following day had Marina responded favorably to his request (as some psychiatrists have conjectured) is an open question. Later that evening first Marina and then Ruth Paine mentioned the President's visit the following day, but Oswald lapsed into silence. "It was quite unusual that he did not want to talk about President Kennedy being in Dallas," Marina said later, aware of his interest in politics. "That was quite peculiar. . . . I asked him . . . if he knew which route President Kennedy will take . . . and he said he doesn't know anything about it." Oswald went to bed two hours earlier than usual that night and before retiring he told his wife: "I won't be out this weekend." "Why not?" she asked. "It's too often," he said. "I was here today." The next morning, after Oswald left the house to seek out Wesley Frazier for the ride to Dallas, carrying a brown paper bag which he told Frazier contained curtain rods, Marina discovered that he had left $170 (almost all their savings) on the top of the bureau. She didn't notice at the time that he had also left his wedding ring (which he had never taken off before) in a cup on the bureau.[9]

No one knows exactly when Oswald took the paper parcel containing his Carcano rifle to the sixth floor of the Book Depository. He was there, however, late in the morning, when some men were laying a plywood floor, and after they left for lunch, just before noon, he had plenty of time to assemble the rifle, move boxes of books together to form a sniper's nest, and then await the arrival of the presidential motorcade. "He was just staring out the window," said Robert Fischer, a county auditor in the festive crowd below, who happened to glance up before the President came by. "Everyone else was in a good mood with the President coming, but he seemed different, and that's why I stared at him and remembered him later." Another onlooker, Howard Brennan, a construction worker who happened to be far-sighted, saw even more than Fischer. As he stood across from the Depository awaiting the President, he noticed a man he later identified as Oswald in the window in the southeast corner of the sixth floor. "As I looked at the man," he said later, "it struck me how unsmiling and calm he was. He didn't seem to feel one bit of excitement. His face was expressionless. . . . He seemed preoccupied." When the first shot came, Brennan, like many others in the crowd in Dealey Plaza, thought it was a backfire. "I looked up then at the Texas State Book Depository building," he recalled. "What I saw made my blood run cold. Poised in the corner of the sixth floor was the same young man I had noticed several times before the motorcade arrived. There was one difference—this time he held a rifle in his hands, pointing toward the Presidential car. He steadied the rifle against the cornice and while he moved quickly, he didn't seem to be in any kind of panic. All this happened in the matter of a second or two. Then came the sickening sound of a second shot. . . . I wanted to cry, I wanted to scream, but I couldn't utter a sound." As Brennan watched, horror-stricken, the man in the window steadied his rifle for the third shot. "He was aiming again," recalled Brennan, "and I wanted to pray, to beg God to somehow make him miss the target. . . . [W]hat I was seeing, the sight became so fixed in my mind that I'll never forget it for as long as I live. . . . Then another shot rang out." Brennan hit the ground at this point, and as the President's car began speeding away, he looked up at the window again. "To my amazement," he said, "the man still stood there in the window. He didn't appear to be rushed. There was no particular emotion visible on his face except for a slight smirk. It was a look of satisfaction, as if he had accomplished what he set out to do. . . . [Then] he simply moved away from the window until he disappeared from my line of vision."[10]

Oswald's "propaganda of the deed" on November 22, 1963, as Brennan observed, took three shots to accomplish. Gerald Posner's superb study, *Case Closed* (1993), utilizing the latest computer techniques, has established convincingly that the first shot missed, the second hit JFK in the back of the neck and then passed through Texas Governor John Connally, seated next to him, inflicting serious wounds, and the third shot blew JFK's brain apart.[11] Then, as panic hit the crowd in Dealey Plaza, Oswald dropped his rifle into the midst of some boxes and made his escape down the stairs and out of the front of the Depository, which had not yet been secured. First by bus and then by taxi (his first taxi ride), he made it back to his rooming house in Oak Cliff, picked up his revolver, and then went out looking for a bus, that would take him, presumably, to Monterrey, Mexico. At this point the fortuities turned obtrusive. Stopped by Dallas patrolman J. D. Tippit (who had heard a broadcast describing JFK's assassin, based on Brennan's observation), he pulled out his revolver, shot and killed Tippit, took to his heels, and eventually sought refuge in an Oak Cliff movie house. Alerted by the ticket seller, policemen arrived soon after, found Oswald sitting near the back of the theater, and ordered him to get on his feet. "Well, it is all over now," he said as he got up; then he struck one of the policemen and reached for his revolver. After a scuffle in which the policemen got the revolver away from him, they arrested him, put him in a patrol wagon, and took him to the city jail for questioning.

Two days later Oswald encountered violence himself. As the police brought him out of his cell to transfer him to the county jail, he was shot and killed by Jack Ruby, a somewhat sleazy Dallas nightclub owner whose fury at Oswald's murder of his beloved President rivaled Oswald's anger at the Kennedy administration's attempts on the life of his beloved Fidel Castro. As with Oswald, a series of coincidences made Ruby's deed possible, and, like Oswald, when the opportunity came, he struck. "You killed my President, you rat!" Ruby shouted as he shot Oswald. Asked after his arrest why he fired, Ruby exclaimed: "Well, you guys couldn't do it. Someone had to do it. The son of a bitch killed my President." Ruby—like Oswald—regarded his action as heroic. Sentenced to death, he deteriorated rapidly, both physically and mentally, while in prison, and in 1967 died of a blood clot.[12]

When the Warren Commission, appointed by JFK's successor, Lyndon B. Johnson, to investigate the assassination, issued its report in August 1964, citing Lee Harvey Oswald as the lone assassin, the majority of the American people accepted its findings. In the years that followed, however, confidence in the Commission's conclusions declined rapidly. This was in great measure because gradually, as new material relating to the assassination became available, it became clear that both the FBI and the CIA had withheld relevant information about the assassination from the Warren Commission investigators. The FBI, it turned out, had concealed evidence of its surveillance of Oswald from 1959 onward, fearing it would be criticized as delinquent for dismissing him as a harmless "weirdo" on the eve of the assassination. The CIA, for its part, kept quiet about its efforts, actively encouraged by President Kennedy, and especially by his brother Robert, the Attorney General, to eliminate Fidel Castro, with or without the aid of the Mafia. Curiously enough, as the shortcomings of the Warren Report became apparent, some left-wing critics came to rival the ultra-rightist John Birch Society ("Impeach Earl Warren!") in their scorn and contempt for Supreme Court Chief Justice Earl Warren who had headed the commission investigating the assassination and endorsed its conclusions.

But the Warren Commission, in fact, had it right: Oswald did the deed. There is no evidence that would hold up in a court of law that the Soviet Union or Castro Cuba or the Mafia or the FBI or the CIA or LBJ or the Joint Chiefs of Staff or a group of New Orleans homosexuals—or most of the above, as Oliver Stone's *JFK* suggested in 1991—had anything to do with either Oswald or the assassination itself. (Stone's conspiracist movie was overlong, heavy-handed, and boring; Senator Joseph McCarthy did this kind of thing with far more verve and imagination back in the 1950s.) But Oswald was not simply "a wretched waif," as writer William Manchester called him, who acted like a madman when he killed a young President who was enormously popular with the majority of Americans in 1963. Oswald was a sociopath, to be sure, like Leon Czolgosz, and perhaps even a psychopath, but he did have a political motive: to avenge Fidel Castro for the Kennedy administration's plots on his life. And the plots against Castro, as Alexander Cockburn pointed out in his column for the *Nation* on November 29, 1993, did eventually come to an end after the killing in Dallas.[13]

Following the terrible event of November 22 there was a great deal of mind-, heart-, and soul-searching in the United States. Was Dallas itself, a center of right-wing rancor in 1963, somehow to blame? Was America itself a seriously "sick society" and in some way responsible? Or was the assassination another instance of history's irrationality? Amid all the efforts to place the tragedy in some kind of meaningful context, perhaps the most perceptive comments came from I. F. Stone, that skeptical dissenter on the left who since the 1950s had published a lively newsletter analyzing American policies at home and abroad. "Let us ask ourselves honest questions," he wrote in the first issue of *I. F. Stone's Bi-Weekly* to appear after the assassination. "How many Americans have not assumed—with approval—that the CIA was probably trying to find ways to assassinate Castro? How many would not applaud if the CIA succeeded? . . . Have we not become conditioned to the notion that we should have a secret agency of the government—the CIA—with secret funds, to wield the dagger beneath the cloak against leaders we dislike? Even some of our best young liberal intellectuals can see nothing wrong in this picture except that the 'operational' functions of the CIA should be kept separate from its intelligence evaluations! . . . Where the right to kill is so universally accepted, we should not be surprised if our young President was slain."[14]

CHAPTER 37

Richard Nixon's Domestic Policies

Richard Nixon had an innovative foreign policy, but his domestic policies were essentially conservative, even reactionary.

Not so.

Except for Vietnam, where he kept the United States involved for four more bloody years after promising withdrawal during the 1968 campaign, President Nixon pursued a creative foreign policy (opening relations with China and pursuing détente with Russia), but his domestic policies were in some ways just as innovative. In retrospect, it is hard not to be impressed with how much he accomplished on the home front before resigning office in 1974 in the wake of the Watergate scandal. Writing soon after Nixon's death in April 1994, conservative columnist George Will pronounced Nixon's administration as more liberal than any other President's, except for Lyndon Johnson's, since World War II. And in *Nixon Reconsidered*, a study of Nixon's policies appearing in the spring of 1994, Joan Hoff insisted that Nixon "exceeded the accomplishments of the New Deal and the Great Society in the areas of civil rights, social welfare spending, domestic and international economic restructuring, urban parks, government reorganization, revenue sharing, draft reform, pension reform, and spending for the arts and humanities." Privately, it is true, Nixon liked to belittle the reforms he sponsored in public, but, as historian Hoff demonstrated, he was something of a liberal activist all the same.[1]

Nixon's major interest was admittedly foreign affairs. "This country could run itself domestically without a President," he told journalist Theodore White just before his election in 1968. "All you need is a competent Cabinet to run the country at home. You need a President for foreign policy."[2] Once he became President, though, he seems to have forgotten his famous dictum, for he soon became actively involved in the domestic problems facing the nation. His approach was a moderate, not reactionary one, for he was basically a centrist, moving somewhat to the left and sometimes to the right, as circumstances (and political expediency) dictated. When it came to environmental issues, Indian affairs, and welfare, he sponsored surprisingly progressive measures. And though he was never a warm supporter of civil rights the way Lyndon Johnson was, it is a fact that desegregation of the public schools proceeded steadily (if quietly) while he was in the White House.

Nixon wasn't exactly an "Environment President," but he did respond positively to the demands for protecting the environment that had been gathering momentum since the early 1960s: cutting down on smog and water pollution, eliminating the use of dangerous pesticides, protecting endangered species, and preserving the country's natural beauty. In February 1970, he sent a message to Congress centering on environmental problems in which he made 36 recommendations, including a proposal for a ten million-dollar clean water act and suggestions for air-pollution regulations. "Clean air, clean water, open spaces," he told Congress, "—these should once again be the birthright of every American."[3] Following the observance of Earth Day on April 22, 1970, by schools, colleges, and communities throughout the land, he proposed (and Congress established) the Environmental Protection Agency (EPA), with real power to deal seriously with environmental problems. The following year he proclaimed the period of April 18–24 as Earth Week.

Nixon did, to be sure, drag his heels at times. Sometimes he impounded funds because he thought Congress was voting too much money on environmental concerns. Sometimes, too, he sided with industry when the latter complained of the EPA's tough standards and strict deadlines. His was essentially a middle-of-the-road policy which pleased neither industry nor the environmentalists. Still, under his administration the nation took a big step forward in coming to grips with the environmental crisis. Nixon "was there when it began," observed David Sive, member of the National Resources

Defense Council, "he signed all the basic legislation, he appointed some absolutely wonderful people."[4]

Nixon's record when it came to Indian affairs was also not half bad. The concern of American Indians did not, to be sure, occupy a high place on his domestic agenda, but he did, when alerted by presidential aide John Ehrlichman, respond sympathetically whenever Indian rights were being threatened. In 1971, when the Taos Pueblo protested the U.S. Forest Service's decision to give white ranchers grazing rights in the vicinity of Blue Lake in New Mexico (regarded as sacred ground), Nixon backed legislation blocking Forest Service action. He also supported the Alaska Native Claims Act later that year, thus honoring the 100-year-old claims of Eskimos, Aleuts, and Indians to land ownership in the region. Nixon, declared Bruce Willkie, executive director of the National Congress of American Indians, was the only President since George Washington to commit his administration to honoring the nation's obligations to the tribes. While he was President, Nixon also proclaimed a new federal policy recognizing the sovereignty of the tribes, increased the budget for the Bureau of Indian Affairs, and expanded federal funds for Indian health care.

It was in the field of welfare, however, that Nixon's policy was the most innovative. In August 1969, he proposed replacing all existing welfare programs with a Family Assistance Plan (FAP) which, by direct payments to the poor, would place "a foundation under the income of every American family." His proposal, he said, was "simple but revolutionary." It was not particularly simple, for it contained "no work, no welfare" provisions for the able-bodied heads of families that would have been hard to implement. But it was certainly revolutionary; it contemplated a guaranteed annual income (though Nixon shunned the phrase) of $1600 (later raised to $2500) for a family of four, something that seemed almost unthinkable to most American conservatives.[5]

Nixon's hope was that FAP would eliminate the unpopular welfare bureaucracy, ease the burdens of welfare on the states, and, by improving the purchasing power of the poor, act as a stimulus to the national economy. The *New Republic*, liberal weekly, called FAP "the most substantial welfare reform proposal in the nation's history," but most liberals disagreed. They insisted the cash payments were too low to eliminate poverty, and called the program "racist" (though it would have been a big help to impoverished blacks in the South) because of its work requirements. In Congress, the liberals teamed up with the conservatives (who looked on FAP as a way of coddling the lazy and improvident) to defeat the President's proposal. FAP, Nixon concluded, was "an idea ahead of its time." So apparently was his proposal in a message to Congress in February 1971 for a National Standards Act (requiring employers to provide basic health insurance for their employees). Congressional liberals rejected it, as they had FAP, because they thought it didn't go far enough.[6]

With desegregation, Nixon seemed behind, not ahead of the times. Though he accepted the Supreme Court's decision in *Brown v. Board of Education of Topeka, Kansas* (1954) ordering the desegregation of the public schools, he made it clear he opposed busing to achieve "racial balance" in the schools, sought delays in the federal courts for desegregation deadlines, and, by his Supreme Court appointments, showed his sympathy for the southern whites who were critical of the Brown decision. As usual, he took a middle-of-the-road position on the issue. "There are those who want instant integration," he said, "and those who want segregation forever. I believe that we need to have a middle course between these extremes." In October 1969, the Supreme Court flatly rejected the Nixon administration's request for delay in desegregation in Mississippi and declared that the obligation of every school district was "to terminate dual school systems *at once* and to operate now and hereafter only unitary schools." Asked afterward at a news conference what his policy would be, Nixon told reporters: "To carry out what the Supreme Court has laid down. I believe in carrying out the law even though I may have disagreed as I did in this instance with the decree that the Supreme Court eventually came down with. But we will carry out the law."[7]

Nixon was as good as his word. In Feburary 1970, he appointed a Cabinet Committee on Education, headed by George Shultz, Secretary of Labor, to carry out the Supreme Court's directive, and he worked closely with Shultz thereafter in planning the committee's work. In March, at his suggestion, the Cabinet committee began setting up advisory committees of local citizens, black and white, first in Mississippi, and then in all the other southern states, to arrange for the desegregation of the schools by the fall of 1970. To encourage the local participants, Nixon addressed a meeting in New Orleans of representatives from all the southern state advisory committees to offer words of praise and encouragement for their diligence and dedication. ("It will be politically harmful," he told aides before delivering his speech, "but it will help the schools so let's do it."[8])

Nixon's method—working quietly and sympathetically with Southerners at the local level—was surprisingly successful. In 1969, when he became President, fifteen years after the Brown decision, only 5.2 percent of black children were in desegregated schools. By the time he left the White House, more than 90 percent of black children in the South were enrolled in unitary school systems. "There's no doubt about it," wrote Tom Wicker, liberal columnist of the *New York Times*, in 1991, "the Nixon administration accomplished more in 1970 to desegregate Southern school systems than had been done in the sixteen previous years or probably since." And he added: "There's no doubt either that it was Richard Nixon personally who conceived, orchestrated and led the administration's desegregation effort. Halting and uncertain before he finally asserted strong control, that effort resulted in probably the outstanding achievement of his administration."[9]

Why have Nixon's achievements in desegregation received so little recognition? Partly because of his "Southern strategy" (courting the votes of southern whites in the 1968 campaign and afterward) and partly because he insisted on carrying out his desegregation policy without fanfare and with as little publicity as possible. He refused, moreover, to use the "bully pulpit" of the presidency (as Theodore Roosevelt called it) to speak out against racism and thus made his views suspect. But he got the job done, as one Nixon official pointed out, "without tensions, bayonets and bullets." In a detailed study of the Nixon administration, *One of Us: Richard Nixon and the American Dream* (1991), Tom Wicker concluded that Nixon had "overseen—indeed planned and carried out—more school desegregation than any other president," and that he deserved credit "for putting an end, at last, to dual systems in the South."[10]

CHAPTER 38

Watergate

Watergate was a "third-rate burglary" blown all out of proportion by President Nixon's enemies.

Not so.

The break-in of Democratic headquarters in the Watergate complex in Washington, D.C., on the night of June 17, 1972, was not an isolated event. It was simply the latest in a series of clandestine and illegal activities sponsored by the Nixon administration, and it touched off an amazing cover-up by the President and his associates involving fraud, extortion, obstruction of justice, misleading and mendacious public statements, and subornation of perjury. When Sam Dash, chief counsel of the Senate committee investigating Watergate, first talked to John Dean, White House aide who decided to come clean after Nixon fired him, Dean warned against getting bogged down in the Watergate burglary. "Sam, that is not the beginning," he expostulated. "You are making the mistake of concentrating on the break-in of the Democratic National Committee headquarters. Frankly, that was not very significant when viewed in its total context. You cannot understand the Watergate burglary without knowing its background."[1]

What was the background? Watergate, it gradually became clear, took place in the context of what *Time* called the "siege mentality" of the White House. Richard Nixon, who was gracious in defeat, after losing the presidential race to JFK in 1960, turned mean and vindictive in victory, after beating Hubert Humphrey in the 1968 election. When John Dean became Nixon's counsel in July 1970, he found "a climate of excessive concern with leaks, an insatiable appetite for political intelligence, all coupled with a do-it-yourself White House staff, regardless of law." One day Nixon told Dean: "I want the most comprehensive notes on all those who have tried to do us in. Because they didn't have to do it." He went on to say that his administration had never used the FBI or the Justice Department against its enemies, "but things are going to change now. And they *are* going to change, and they are going to get it, right?"[2]

No change was needed. The White House was already utilizing federal agencies to get at its critics: bugging homes and offices, auditing tax returns, and combing through FBI files in an effort to find material to use against them. Just to be sure no one was overlooked, members of the White House staff compiled an "enemies list" of more than two hundred prominent Americans—journalists, movie stars, educators—with whom the administration hoped to get even when the chance arose. One aide came up with an ambitious program (the "Huston Plan") calling for wiretapping, electronic surveillance, burglaries, and break-ins that appealed mightily to Nixon. "The President loves this stuff," Attorney General John Mitchell told Dean. When FBI Director J. Edgar Hoover's opposition killed the program (Hoover didn't welcome intruders on his turf), the White House created a special investigative unit known as the "plumbers" to do the job. Directed by J. Gordon Liddy, former FBI agent, and E. Howard Hunt, onetime CIA worker, the plumbers' mission was, among other things, to plug leaks and discredit anyone who kept the press informed of activities the White House wanted to keep secret. In 1971, when Daniel Ellsberg, former Defense Department official, gave the *New York Times* a copy of what came to be known as the *Pentagon Papers* (a classified report dealing with the Vietnam War), Liddy and Hunt went into action. They illegally tapped the telephone of Ellsberg's psychiatrist in Los Angeles and broke into his office in search of material to use against Ellsberg. But about all that the two "plumbers" accomplished was to derail the government's prosecution of Ellsberg for conspiracy and misappropriation of government property. When news of the Hunt-Liddy break-in came to light, the judge declared a mistrial.[3]

Watergate was another Liddy-Hunt job. It was part of a "dirty tricks" enterprise undertaken by Nixon's campaign workers in 1972 to harass the Democrats and ensure the President's election in November to a second term. Sponsored by the Committee to Re-Elect the President (CREP, or, as it came to be called, CREEP), Liddy and Hunt employed James McCord, CREP official, and four other men to break into the Democratic headquarters in Watergate to locate material damaging to Lawrence O'Brien, chairman of the Democratic National Committee, and to the Democrats generally. There were two break-ins. The first, on May 20, bore some fruit: the burglars tapped the phones in O'Brien's office and photographed some documents. The second, on June 17, an effort to get more documents, ended in disaster. While the burglars were at work, a security guard discovered them with their equipment and turned them over to the police. Soon afterward, when the burglary was reported in the newspapers, Ron Ziegler, the President's press secretary, airily dismissed it as a "third-rate alleged burglary attempt," but it was far more than that. The five burglars were not acting on their own; nor were Hunt and Liddy simply engaged in some kind of rogue operation they had dreamed up by themselves. The Watergate Seven, who soon went to trial, were acting under the highest authority. CREP officials like John Mitchell (who had resigned as Nixon's Attorney General to head the campaign organization) had approved the break-in. So had the President's major advisers in the White House. With the President's approval, they went on to offer the Watergate Seven substantial bribes to keep quiet during the trial and to avoid implicating higher officials in the break-ins.[4]

President Nixon seems not to have had any foreknowledge of the Watergate break-ins. Six days after the arrest of the Watergate burglars, however, he discussed the episode with H. R. Haldeman, White House Chief of Staff, and proposed using the CIA to head off the FBI in the latter's investigation of the Watergate burglary. It was a fatal decision, for the cover-up he launched of activities involving so many people in his administration was almost bound to unravel at some point. First James McCord broke ranks and agreed to talk; then John Dean, White House Counsel, about to be made a scapegoat, decided to give inside information to the Senate committee investigating Watergate and to Judge John Sirica, the federal district judge presiding over the trial of the Watergate Seven. Meanwhile, Carl Bernstein and Bob Woodward, *Washington Post* reporters, were diligently unearthing unsavory details about what John Mitchell himself called the "White House horrors," and keeping the public informed. As the ramifications of the break-in gradually surfaced during 1973 and 1974, Nixon was forced to call for the resignations of his highest advisers and to take an increasingly defensive position himself.[5]

Repeatedly President Nixon assured the American people that he had nothing to do with the cover-up. In his first public comment on the break-in, on June 22, 1972, he announced: "The White House has had no involvement whatever in this particular incident." On August 29, he declared that "no one on the White House staff, no one in this administration, presently employed, was involved in this very bizarre incident. This kind of activity, as I have often indicated, has no place whatsoever in our political process." On April 17, 1973, responding to public pressure, he announced that he had ordered "intensive new inquiries" into Watergate and that no one in his administration would be given immunity from prosecution. He also indicated that it was not until March 21, 1973, that he first learned of attempts to cover up the scandal. A week later he went on television to announce his determination to bring the guilty to justice and "maintain the integrity of the White House." He also announced the resignation of his key advisers, H. R. Haldeman and John Ehrlichman, and his legal counsel John Dean. The following month, as criticism mounted, he said he had never had any "intent" or "wish" to impede an investigation of Watergate and had not tried to use the CIA for that purpose. On August 15, 1973, he appeared on TV again to say he accepted "full responsibility" for the actions of his subordinates who were involved in the cover-up, but to assert: "Not only was I unaware of any cover-up. I was unaware there was anything to cover up." Touring the South in November 1973, he exclaimed: "People have got to know whether or not their President is a crook. Well, I'm no crook."[6]

Nixon's protestations of innocence produced wry amusement in John Dean, for he knew better. Not only had he discussed the cover-up with the President from time to time; he had also raised the question with him of getting money to the Watergate Seven to purchase their silence about the involvement of higher-ups in their activities. But it was, after all, only Dean's word against the President's, and after Dean had testified before the Senate investigating committee headed by North Carolina's Sam Ervin, the White House did all it could to destroy his credibility. In the end, it was tape recordings of the President's conversations with members of his staff that corroborated Dean's testimony and implicated the President in the cover-up beyond all shadow of doubt.

The existence of the President's tapes came to light in July 1973, when Alexander Butterfield, White House aide, revealed to the Ervin committee that Nixon had arranged for the installation of secret recording devices in the Oval Office and elsewhere in the spring of 1971. Butterfield's revelation touched off immediate demands for the release of tapes that might shed light on the Watergate episode. Nixon at first "stonewalled" (his word) the various investigators—Judge Sirica, the Ervin committee, the special prosecutor appointed to look into Watergate, and, later, the House Judiciary Committee contemplating impeachment—citing executive privilege. He even told Judge Sirica that a President's authority was, for four years, as absolute as that of King Louis XIV. Faced with subpoenas (as well as with an increasingly hostile public mood), he at first released some tapes with gaps on them (one contained an erasure amounting to eighteen and a half minutes), and then 1,250 pages of edited transcripts of selected tapes. Confronted, finally, in July 1974, with a unanimous Supreme Court decision ruling that executive privilege could not be invoked to withhold evidence for a criminal trial, he yielded and agreed to turn over all the tapes requested by the investigators. On August 6, he released a batch of tapes which, he acknowledged, were "at variance with certain of my previous statements." One of them contained the "smoking pistol"; a recording of his conversation with Haldeman on June 23, 1972, launching the cover-up. It was the end of the road for Nixon. [7]

Why didn't Nixon destroy the tapes when the Watergate investigations commenced? "Well, I think he *loved* the tapes at first. . . ," suggested Dean, when asked this question. "He thought he could use them selectively to prove his case. And by the time he couldn't, he would have been impeached if he'd destroyed them. And a lot of people would have had to go to jail to let him do it." As it was, a lot of people did go to jail—25 including Mitchell, Haldeman, Ehrlichman, and Dean—for the part they played in the cover-up and the obstruction of justice, and Nixon found himself facing impeachment. By the time he bowed to the Supreme Court order regarding the tapes, the House Judiciary Committee had voted for three articles of impeachment, charging the President with obstruction of justice in the Watergate case, misuse of federal agencies to violate the rights of American citizens, and defiance of subpoenas issued by the House committee. Told by Republican leaders that he could count on scant support in the Senate if there was an impeachment trial, Nixon decided to throw in the towel. On August 9, 1974, he went on television to resign his office—the first President to do so. Even at this point, he refused to admit more than errors of judgment.[8]

The American people overwhelmingly approved of President Nixon's decision to resign. It wasn't only the Watergate cover-up that gradually disillusioned them with a President whom they had returned to office in 1972 with huge popular and electoral majorities. There were other revelations, having nothing to do with Watergate, that came to light in 1973 and 1974 and helped turn people against the President: illegal corporation contributions to CREP, the use of federal funds to improve his Florida and California estates, and, above all, his attempt to evade income tax payments by falsifying the date of his gift of vice-presidential papers to the federal archives. It didn't help him any, moreover, when the public learned that the President, now a millionaire, had paid less than $1000 in income taxes in 1970 and 1971.

Why didn't Nixon refrain from authorizing a cover-up in the first place? Partly, no doubt, because he regarded the Watergate break-in as a minor incident, simply one of the "dirty tricks" that political parties commonly engage in during presidential contests. Later on, he doubtless realized that if it came out during the trial of the Watergate Seven that White House officials had approved their criminal activities (and other illegalities), it would tarnish his reputation as a law-and-order President and provide the Democrats with rich fodder to use in the 1972 campaign. As far as we know, however, Nixon seems never to have regarded admitting the truth as a viable option, even after Dean solemnly warned him: "We have a cancer—within—close to the Presidency, that's growing." He was obsessed by secrecy, for one thing, and, for another, he felt that the President was justified in stretching things a little, here and there, in pursuit of what he regarded as the country's national interest. Patrick Buchanan, one of his speechwriters, caught the Nixon spirit perfectly in a memo he wrote outlining strategy for the 1972 campaign. "We ought to go down to the kennels and turn all the dogs loose . . . ," he advised. "The President is the only one who should stand alone, while everybody else gets chewed up. The rest of us are expendable commodities, but if the President goes, we all go, and maybe the country with us." For Nixon, as for Buchanan, the nation's security depended on his re-election in 1972 and his right to govern pretty much as he pleased.[9]

Were President Nixon's transgressions unexceptionable? Was he unfairly singled out by his enemies for victimization? The House Judiciary Committee didn't think so; even Nixon's supporters on the Committee reversed their positions and voted for impeachment when the President's flouting of the law became unmistakable. Nor did leading Republicans, like Arizona Senator Barry Goldwater, think Nixon was being crucified. Exclaimed the Arizona conservative: "There are only so many lies you can take and now there has been one too many. Nixon should get his ass out of the White House—today!" And most Americans—four to one, according to the polls—approved the resignation.

Sam Dash, chief counsel for the Ervin committee, denied that Nixon's behavior was the rule, not the exception, among America's Presidents. "Although abuses of power occurred on numerous occasions during the earlier administrations," he wrote in a book about Watergate appearing in 1976, "there is nothing in these revelations that approximates the dominance of the Nixon White House in police-state activities and the pervasive role in illegal conduct played by the President of the United States and his advisors." Dash pointed out that presidential involvement in illegal action in the past had "occurred on an ad hoc basis with the Presidents fully aware that they had no authority to permit such conduct. Richard Nixon carried this practice to the extreme. What had been ad hoc became systematic and pervasive. The essential difference was that Nixon believed he was a sovereign who had the authority to act above the law and approve or authorize illegal acts." As Nixon himself told interviewer David Frost in May 1977, "When the President does it, that means it is not illegal." In a postmortem on Nixon for *Esquire* in July 1994, Garry Wills, a perceptive Nixon-observer, concluded: "There can be no Nixon without Watergate. Watergate *was* Nixon."[10]

CHAPTER 39

The Pledge of
Allegiance

The Pledge of Allegiance is an ancient and honorable document in U.S. history like the Declaration of Independence and the U.S. Constitution.

No, it isn't. But it was presented that way during the presidential campaign of 1988.

During the 1988 campaign the Republicans learned that in 1977 Massachusetts Governor Michael Dukakis, the Democratic candidate, had vetoed a bill requiring the recitation of the Pledge of Allegiance in the classroom every morning, and they decided to make an issue of it. Referring to the Pledge in one of his speeches, Vice President George Bush, the Republican candidate, pointed out that the Massachusetts legislature had overridden Dukakis's veto, and he exclaimed: "I believe that is right and I am glad that those teachers say the Pledge of Allegiance to the flag of the United States of America. I am glad that the veto is not in effect." Curiously enough, though, when he quoted the Pledge in another speech, he garbled the words. He wasn't the only American to make mincemeat of it. For years, schoolchildren, dutifully reciting the words in unison, had a way of turning "the republic for which it stands" into "the republic for Richard Stands," "one nation indivisible" into "one naked individual," and "one nation under God" (added to the pledge in 1954) into "one nation under guard."[1]

The Pledge soon became a major campaign issue. But, as reporters delved into the matter, they came up with some surprising—even disconcerting—facts about the sacred mantra. It was a devout socialist, Francis Bellamy, vice president of the Society of Christian Socialists, who wrote the Pledge; he did so in 1892 to commemorate the 400th anniversary of Columbus's discovery of America. The Pledge was in part a paean to big government ("one nation indivisible") and a resolute rejection of the state's rights view of the Union that persisted even after the Civil War. It also summed up his socialist faith: "with liberty and justice for all." Bellamy, a Unitarian minister, gave many speeches on the evils of capitalism and one of them was entitled "Jesus the Socialist."[2]

The original instructions for reciting the Pledge called for the right hand to be removed from the heart at the mention of the word "flag" and extended outward toward the flag, but this practice ended during World War II because it looked too much like a Nazi salute. Some fundamentalists, notably the Jehovah's Witnesses, regarded the Pledge as blasphemous and refused to let their children make it. But they received a great deal of abuse for their intransigence. In 1940, in Kennebunkport, Maine, near the Bush family summer home, a mob of 2500 irate citizens attacked and burned down a Witness church to show their contempt and hatred for the nonconforming fundamentalists. In 1943, however, the Supreme Court ruled that students couldn't be forced to recite the Pledge. "A Bill of Rights which guards the individual's right to speak his own mind," declared Justice Robert Jackson, speaking for the majority, does not permit "public authorities to compel him to utter what is not on his mind."[3]

Governor Dukakis was familiar with the Supreme Court's 1943 ruling and he decided to veto the mandatory Pledge bill in his state because he thought it was unconstitutional. First, though, he sought the advice of the Massachusetts Supreme Judicial Court. The court backed him up; by a vote of 5 to 2 (with three Republicans voting with the majority), the court held the law to be both unconstitutional and unenforceable. Still, Dukakis's constitutional scruples in 1977 hardly impressed his critics in 1988. Vice President Bush, for one, continued the attack. "Should public school teachers be required to lead children in the Pledge of Allegiance?" he cried. "My opponent says no and I say yes." Actually the issue was by then long since dead. Though the Massachusetts legislature overrode Dukakis's veto, there was no attempt to enforce the Pledge in the public schools of the commonwealth.[4]

Still, soon after the Pledge became a campaign issue, Congress decided to start reciting it every morning before opening its sessions. When Texas Congressman Henry B. Gonzalez strenuously objected to the practice (he compared it to the Nazi incantation, *"Sieg Heil, Sieg Heil"*), Georgia's Newt Gingrich fired off a letter to House Speaker Tom Foley demanding that the feisty Texan be reprimanded. Foley responded by saying he didn't agree with Gonzalez but that he doubted the latter had violated House rules. Gonzalez himself was unmoved by the criticism hurled at him for his stance. "Some people think the pledge comes with the Declaration of Independence," he told the House. "That downgrades Thomas Jefferson," for the great Virginian would never have "concocted that kind of banal recital!"[5]

CHAPTER 40

Presidential
Salutes

The President of the United States is obliged to return military salutes in kind.

No, he isn't. But most Americans don't seem to realize this.

Soon after Bill Clinton became President in January 1993, reporters began twitting him for not seeming to know that as civilian Commander-in-Chief of U.S. armed forces he was not only entitled to receive salutes from military officials but also expected to salute them in return. The reporters were only partly right. The President receives salutes all right; but there is no rule in or outside of the Constitution requiring him to respond to the courtesy with salutes of his own.

This omission troubled Ronald Reagan. Soon after entering the White House, he learned that it was customary for men and women in the armed forces to greet Presidents with a salute, but that because the President was a civilian and not wearing a uniform he did not salute in return. "I think there ought to be a regulation that the president could return a salute," he told a Marine commandant, "inasmuch as he is commander in chief and civilian clothes are his uniform." "Well," said the commandant amiably, "if you did return a salute, I don't think anyone would say anything about it."[1]

The exchange with the Marine officer emboldened the former Hollywoodian. From that moment he began returning salutes with the precision and dash of a professional, and, upon leaving the White House, he encouraged his successor to do the same. George

Bush happily obliged. In January 1989, when the two men parted after Bush's inaugural ceremony, they exchanged brisk military salutes that looked awesome on television. (Apparently an ex-President may salute, too, if he wants to, in his capacity as ex-Commander-in-Chief.)

In the old days, though, George Washington and Thomas Jefferson seem to have gotten along nicely without saluting when they held the office of President. So did John Adams, for all his love of ceremony. James Madison ventured into the field when he was President during the War of 1812 (and was almost captured by the British), but he did no saluting, so far as the record shows, while inspecting the troops. Neither did Abraham Lincoln when he visited one of the forts defending Washington during the Civil War (and almost got himself killed). Woodrow Wilson did no saluting, so far as we know, during World War I; nor did Franklin D. Roosevelt during World War II. Harry Truman did plenty of saluting when he was in the army during World War I, but he did so only occasionally when he was President. Surprisingly enough, Calvin Coolidge, about as unmilitary a man as the voters ever sent to the White House, did some saluting while reviewing the fleet one day from the deck of the *Mayflower*, the presidential yacht, wearing a yachting cap, in Virginia Capes. For half an hour, according to Wilson Brown, his naval aide, "Silent Cal" stood queasily (there was a heavy ground swell), "looking sternly through the long signal glass, pointing to each ship as she came abeam, returning salutes endlessly while trying to stand at attention and steady himself against the roll with the unengaged hand." When all the battleships had passed, he sank out of sight into a sofa, where a photographer sneaked over and got a snapshot of the President "seated disconsolately on the sofa, grim-lipped, clearly dreaming only of terra firma and an end to his malaise."[2] He is not known to have repeated the experience.

Among 20th-century Presidents, only Dwight D. Eisenhower (a West Pointer) and Jimmy Carter (an Annapolis man) are known always to have returned military salutes in kind the way Reagan did. John F. Kennedy deliberately refrained from saluting while President, according to his friend David Powers, in order to emphasize his civilian status as Commander-in-Chief of the Army and Navy. Lyndon B. Johnson also avoided hand salutes, and he placed his hand or his hat over his heart instead of saluting the colors. Gerald R. Ford responded to salutes, like most other Presidents, with a smile, a nod of the head, wave of the hand, or a friendly "Hello."[3]

When Clinton became President he continued to behave as a civilian at first. Then, possibly because some of the journalists covering the White House chided him for not saluting, he decided to follow in Reagan's footsteps after all. But his performances had none of the striking show-biz panache that Reagan brought to the act. "Oxford University isn't the best place to learn military habits," teased *Time* magazine. "Word is that President Clinton's sloppy salute is drawing winces from the Pentagon. Aides are subtly suggesting that he work on it." A week or two later, when Clinton essayed a salute upon boarding USS *Theodore Roosevelt,* he received a gentle back-of-the-hand from *Newsweek:* "Goes for saluting practice on carrier cruise to nowhere. Pray for peace." The sailors aboard the vessel were unimpressed. "I don't care about all that spit-and-polish stuff," murmured a young Navy Seal from Utah. "Who cares if he can salute?"[4]

In June 1994, when Clinton flew to Europe for the 50th anniversary celebration of D-Day, he was welcomed at an American cemetery in Italy by a 73-year-old former army nurse who greeted him "with a saucy smile," according to Maureen Dowd, the *New York Times* White House correspondent, "and the crisp salute of a professional." Clinton, observed Dowd, returned her salute slowly, tentatively, and with a "self-conscious gesture." And after he made a speech honoring American veterans of the Italian campaign, the 68-year-old Jerry Halpern, a veteran of the 45th Infantry Division from Little Rock, Arkansas, remarked with a smile that he hoped the President's military advisers would teach him "how to salute."[5]

Two days later, when Clinton was in Portsmouth, England, he seems to have done better. As he joined the administration flotilla headed across the Channel to re-create the invasion of Normandy in June 1944, he wore a USS *George Washington* cap with "Commander-in-Chief" and gold-braid "scrambled eggs" on the edge, and swore in a group of re-enlisting seamen on the deck of the nuclear-powered aircraft carrier (the largest ship in the world). "Always a fast learner," reported Dowd, "Mr. Clinton had much improved his salute by today, finally giving it the stiff-wristed snap at the end that puts it nearly on a par with the one Ronald Reagan polished as a celluloid warrior." While Clinton was perfecting his military greeting, however, some of his advisers seem to have discovered that the presidential salutes were not at all de rigueur and they began to think he shouldn't be saluting at all. By this time, though, Clinton seemed to be enjoying the military gesture. One of his aides, according to Dowd, "speculated that he might feel, if he stopped right now, that it would seem as though he was guilty about not having served in the military. It may not be so easy to get him to stop. With the sailors, the President was clearly relishing his new panache, having so much fun with that greeting that he followed it up with a second: a firm handshake."[6]

It was a pity, in a way, that pressure from the opinion industries (whose toilers in the field reported the Arkansas President's daily, even hourly, doings in loving—even erotic—detail) succeeded in inducing Clinton to adopt Ronald Reagan's practice of executing full salutes whenever he encountered military personnel. The President is, to be sure, Commander-in-Chief of U.S. armed forces, as the Constitution provides, but he remains a civilian all the same and an important symbol of a basic principle established by the Founding Fathers: the supremacy of the civilian branch of government over the military. "While a purposeful and occasional salute can be an appropriate gesture of respect toward the men and women in the armed services," wrote columnist Christopher Matthews when Clinton first began experimenting with salutes, "the ritualized salute inaugurated in the Reagan reign fuzzes the line between the country's civilian leader, the president, and the armed forces whose duty lies in serving him. . . . We have had some extremely patriotic presidents—I can think of Franklin Roosevelt, John F. Kennedy, Lyndon Johnson—who managed to lead the country without greeting sailors, soldiers and Marines as if our elected president was one other officer in uniform. He's not. The president of the United States does not wear a uniform, and for a reason. He did not rise through the military ranks, nor does he, in any imaginable way, owe his office as commander-in-chief to the military forces. He represents a republican form of government dependent on regular election by the people. He is a civilian and he should act like one. He no more need adopt the military form of greeting than the military form of dress."[7]

Columnist Matthews was surely right. Clinton would have done better to follow the example of JFK, his boyhood hero, than the instructions of the journalist-advocates covering his activities. In so doing, he might have succeeded in making it clear to an apparently confused public that the elected Commander-in-Chief, no matter who he is, outranks every man and woman in uniform including the Chairman of the Joint Chiefs of Staff.

More mischievous, though, than the insistence on presidential salutes, was the myth, which developed in the 1980s, that "the President of the United States is our Commander-in-Chief." During debates in Congress on President Bush's decision to use U.S. forces to repel Iraq's invasion of Kuwait in the fall of 1991, some members of Congress announced that it was their duty to support their Commander-in-Chief. There may have been reasons for U.S. intervention in the Middle East, but "supporting our Commander-in-Chief" could not have been one of them. The President, according to the Constitution, is "commander in chief of the army and navy of the United States, and of the militia of the States, when called into the actual service of the United States." If American citizens—including members of Congress—want the President to be "their Commander-in-Chief," they need to enlist in the armed forces. That way they get to salute him too.

In the 1990s came a new myth: that our best Presidents were those who, like George Washington, had military experience before achieving the highest office in the land. Washington was unquestionably a great President, but the fact is that sixteen of the nation's forty-one Presidents, from Washington to Clinton, had no military experience whatever before becoming President and that four of them occupied the presidency during wartime: James Madison (War of 1812), James K. Polk (Mexican War), Woodrow Wilson (World War I), and Franklin D. Roosevelt (World War II). Such notables as John Adams, Thomas Jefferson, John Quincy Adams, and William Howard Taft never wore a uniform, but no one complained. Grover Cleveland was twice elected President even though he paid $150 for a substitute during the Civil War so he could stay home and take care of his family.

Abraham Lincoln, the Civil War President, is a special case. During the Black Hawk War of 1832, he served for three months in the Illinois militia, but the only action he saw, he said later, consisted of "a good many bloody struggles with mosquitoes." Soon after he enlisted, the men of his company elected him captain, but by his own admission he was no great shakes as a company commander. Once he was marching in front of his company during a drill, with his men lined up forty abreast, and when they came upon a narrow gate, Lincoln, not knowing what to do, simply shouted: "Halt! This company will break ranks for two minutes and form again, on the other side of the gate." Twice, subsequently, he was reprimanded by his commanding officers for not having proper control over his men and for disobeying a general order.[8]

In 1848, when the Democrats ran General Lewis Cass for President and tried to build him up as a military hero in the Mexican War, Lincoln, then in Congress, made a hilarious speech in the Lower House ridiculing Cass's—and his own—military experience. Lincoln himself was opposed to the Mexican War. So was Ulysses Grant (a West Pointer), though he saw action in the war. In his memoirs, written years after he had achieved fame as the "Hero of Appomattox" and served two terms as President, Grant declared that "to this day" he regarded the Mexican War "as one of the most unjust ever waged by a stronger against a weaker nation. It was an instance of a republic following the bad example of European monarchies in not considering justice in their desire to acquire additional territory."[9] Bill Clinton wasn't the only President who in his younger days opposed one of his country's wars.

CHAPTER 41

Presidential
Campaigns

Presidential campaigns are a lot dirtier these days than they used to be.

Not so.

Presidential campaigns in recent years have certainly had their sleazy moments, but they never approached the viciousness of campaigns for the presidency in the "good old days."

The plain fact is that America's quadrennial confrontations used to be far nastier than they are today. In days of yore the invective at election time was exuberant, the character assassination spectacular, and the mudslinging unrestrained. What respectable person today would think of announcing that one of the candidates for the highest office in the land was a "carbuncled-faced old drunkard"? Or a "mutton-headed cucumber"? Or a "howling atheist"? Or a fool, drunkard, lecher, syphilitic, gorilla, crook, spy, thief, pickpocket, traitor, anarchist, revolutionary, madman, degenerate, murderer? Yet such charges were freely bandied about in American presidential contests in the 19th century; and high-toned people as well as low-brows indulged in the vilification. Outright lies were unexceptionable; vicious slanders were commonplace.

In 1800, Abigail Adams lamented that the contest between her husband John and Thomas Jefferson that year had exuded enough venom to "ruin and corrupt the minds and morals of the best people in the world." In 1864, *Harper's Weekly* published a depressingly long list of nasty epithets hurled at Abraham Lincoln in his bid for re-election. In 1872, the *Nation* moaned that the contest between Ulysses S. Grant and Horace Greeley had become "a shower of mud to a far greater extent than any other campaign within our re-membrance. Everybody," the editors noted, "is a liar, a traitor, a thief, a drunkard, a cotton thief, a Tammany thief, a common thief, obscene in hotel offices, a defaulter, a fool . . . , a libeler, a swindler, an unconverted Know-Nothing, a gift-taker, a nepotist, personally filthy, a dishonor to our profession, a corrupter of morals, a butcher, a rebel, a Tammany Republican, a political bummer, a blaspheming atheist, or something else." And in 1888, Lord Bryce, sojourning in the New World, was astonished to find that Grover Cleveland–James G. Blaine match that year had come to center on the "copulative habits" of one candidate and the "prevaricative habits" of the other. Bryce was shocked by the "tempest of invective and calumny which hurtles around the head of a presidential candi-date." He told Britishers they could get some feeling for its vehe-mence only if they imagined that "all the accusations brought against all the 670 seats in the English Parliament" were concen-trated on one man. But an American journal, the *Lakeside Monthly*, had explained it all some years before: "A presidential campaign is a discussion with sticks; nobody reasons, everybody lies as hard as ever he can, and the forces are in the nature of clubs."[1]

The clubs and sticks (and stones and bricks) first entered the picture in 1796. By that time the estimable George Washington (chosen President by the Electoral College in 1789 and 1792) had bowed out after two terms, and the fledgling political parties were sponsoring candidates for the first time. In 1796 came the first real presidential campaign—with the Federalists backing John Adams, and the Republicans supporting Thomas Jefferson—and it turned out to be astonishingly scurrilous. On both sides handbills, pam-phlets, and articles in party newspapers denounced, disparaged, damned, deprecated, decried, denigrated, and declaimed. In the end Adams won the shouting match and faced four years of what he called "squibs, scoffs, and sarcasms." But 1796 was a mere dress rehearsal for 1800. The turn-of-the-century campaign, in which Adams and Jefferson faced each other again, was one of the dirtiest campaigns in American history. After it was over Federalist Con-gressman Fisher Ames decided that "the pig sty and politics" were "two scurvy subjects that should be coupled together." He blamed the vituperative Jeffersonian press for the low level of the campaign (and for Adams's defeat). But he overlooked the scurrilous attacks of his fellow Federalists on Jefferson during the contest.[2]

In 1800 the Federalists charged that Jefferson had cheated his creditors, robbed an old widow of her pension, and, as governor of Virginia, behaved like a coward when the British invaded the state during the American Revolution. Worse still, he was "a howling atheist"! If he became President, they said, he would confiscate all the Bibles in the land and have them burned, then see to it that all the churches were torn down, and finally dissolve the marriage institution and throw all the women of the country into houses of prostitution. In Hartford the *Connecticut Courant* warned that if Jefferson became Chief Magistrate, "murder, robbery, rape, adultery, and incest will all be openly taught and practiced. The air will be filled with the cries of the distressed, the soil will be soaked with blood, and the nation black with crimes." In sheer desperation, toward the end of the campaign, the Federalists even set afloat a rumor that Jefferson had died and that it would be a waste of time to cast a vote for him.[3]

But Jefferson's followers slung a great deal of mud of their own in 1800. They called President Adams a fool, a hypocrite, a criminal, and a tyrant. He was, said one Jeffersonian, "old, querulous, bald, blind, crippled, toothless." His real aim, the Jeffersonians warned, was to become King of America. His plan, they said, was to marry one of his sons to one of King George III's daughters and then found an Anglo-American dynasty with himself as King John I. According to the Jeffersonians, only the intervention of the aging and ailing George Washington—who threatened to run Adams through with a sword—induced him to abandon his scheme. But Adams, they said, was not only a monarchist at heart; he was also a dirty old man. Hadn't he sent his running mate, General Thomas Pinckney, to Europe to procure four lovely European lasses, two for Adams and two for Pinckney? "I do declare," chuckled Adams, when he heard the charge. "If this be true, Pinckney has kept them all for himself, and cheated me out of my two!" In the end, Jefferson defeated Adams (in a complicated outcome that threw the contest into the House of Representatives) and in his inaugural address offered the Federalists the olive branch. But the Federalists and the Jeffersonians never really came to trust each other in the years that followed. "It was a pleasure to live in those good old days," mused a New York Congressman years later, "when a Federalist could knock a Republican down in the streets and not be questioned about it."[4]

Even more scurrilous than the 1800 contest was the campaign of 1828, in which Andrew Jackson challenged John Quincy Adams, who was trying (like his father in 1800) for a second term. It was hard for the Jacksonians to dig up much dirt about JQA—hardworking, conscientious, principled, strait-laced, and fiercely patriotic—but they did their best. They portrayed him to the voters as a reckless spendthrift who lived in "kingly pomp and splendor" in his "presidential palace," despised the common people, and aspired to be King John the Second. He also installed "gambling tables and furniture" in the White House at public expense, they charged, traveled on Sunday when he should have been in church, and even had had premarital relations with his wife Louisa. And when he was minister to Russia some years before, they announced, he had acted as pimp for the Czar and procured a beautiful young American woman for Alexander I. There was of course not a modicum of truth in any of the charges.[5]

But the Adamsites rolled around in the gutter too. They pulled out all the stops in their assaults on Jackson during the 1828 campaign. They accused him of adultery, gambling, cock-fighting, bigamy, drunkenness, theft, lying, and murder. They also circulated a thick pamphlet entitled *Reminiscences; Or, an Extract from the Catalogue of General Jackson's Youthful Indiscretions, between the Ages of Twenty-three and Sixty*, which listed fourteen fights, duels, brawls, and shooting and cutting affairs, in which Old Hickory "killed, slashed and clawed various American citizens." But they went after Jackson's family too. They reduced him to tears when they reported in party newspapers that "General Jackson's mother was a *common prostitute*," brought to this country by the British during the American Revolution to service the troops. And they infuriated him with their attacks on his beloved wife Rachel, whose divorce from her first husband hadn't come through until after she married Jackson in 1791. "Ought a convicted adulteress and her paramour husband be placed in the highest office of this free and Christian land?" cried the Adamsites. Jackson's supporters went to great lengths to explain the unintended irregularities in Mrs. Jackson's divorce and remarriage, but in vain. To the end of the campaign, the Adamsites made the supposed immorality of Andy and his wife Rachel the center of their campaign strategy. Jackson won the election anyway, but victory brought no great joy. Soon after the election his wife died of a heart attack, brought on, Jackson was convinced, by the slander of his political foes. "May God Almighty forgive her murderers," he exclaimed at her funeral, "as I know she forgives them. I never can."[6]

Jackson was to remain bitter to the end of his life, but Abraham Lincoln took a resigned attitude toward campaign slander, even though he received more of it than Old Hickory did. The 1864 campaign, in which he sought a second term, with the Democrats running General George B. McClellan against him, probably exceeded both the 1800 and the 1828 campaigns in sheer viciousness. Soon after the Republicans renominated Lincoln and teamed him up with Tennessee's military governor, Andrew Johnson, who had been a tailor, the *New York World* sneered: "The age of statesmen is gone; the age of rail splitters and tailors, of buffoons, boors and fanatics has succeeded. . . . In a crisis of the most appalling magnitude requiring statesmanship of the highest order, the country is asked to consider the claims of two ignorant, boorish, third-rate backwoods lawyers for the highest stations in the Government." The *New York Herald* was even more scornful than the *World*. Lincoln's renomination, declared the editors, "was a very sorry joke. The idea that such a man should be President of such a country as this is a very ridiculous joke. His debut in Washington was a joke. . . . His inaugural address was a joke. . . . His cabinet is and always has been a standing joke. All his state papers are jokes. His letters to our generals, beginning with those to General McClellan, are very cruel jokes. . . . His emancipation proclamation was a solemn joke. . . . His conversation is full of jokes. His title of 'Honest' is a satirical joke. His intrigues to secure a renomination and the hopes he appears to entertain of re-election are however, the most laughable jokes of all."[7]

But there was a dearth of mirth in 1864. The campaign was noisy and abusive. The Republicans harped on cowardice, defeatism, lack of patriotism, and even treason among the Democrats, and they held General McClellan's war record up to ridicule. But their attacks on McClellan, though cruel, paled beside Democratic assaults on Lincoln. By late September hatred for the President had reached such a high point that *Harper's Weekly*, friendly to Lincoln, listed with sorrow some of the names that partisans of McClellan were hurling at Lincoln: Filthy Story-Teller, Despot, Liar, Thief, Braggart, Buffoon, Usurper, Monster, Ignoramus Abe, Old Scoundrel, Perjurer, Robber, Swindler, Tyrant, Fiend, Butcher. Lincoln himself couldn't help being saddened by the contempt and contumely he encountered. "It is a little singular that I, who am not a vindictive man," he mused, "should have always been before the people for election in canvasses marked for their bitterness. . . ." He refused, however, to issue a statement, though pressed to do so, denying his alleged frivolity when visiting the Antietam battlefield after the bloody encounter there. And it took a Treasury Department official to give the lie to the charge that the President insisted on having his salary paid in gold while Union soldiers received inflated greeenbacks. Through it all, though, Lincoln (like Harry Truman years later) withstood the heat in the kitchen without complaining. And like Jefferson and Jackson before him, he triumphed on election day despite all the mud-slinging.[8]

The scurrilousness of old-time campaigns surely exceeded that of present-day contests. It is important to note, however, that none of the candidates themselves—Jefferson, Jackson, the Adamses, Lincoln, McClellan—engaged personally in the brick-throwing and mudslinging that went on at election time. The character assassination dominating 19th-century contests was the work of their supporters—campaign managers, party workers, local politicians, partisan newspaper editors and writers—not of the presidential candidates themselves. Until the 20th century, indeed, most aspirants to the presidency carefully refrained from hitting the campaign trail themselves. George Washington, the first President, had done no campaigning in 1789 and 1792, and the way he stood above the fray set an example for his successors. For years it was considered demeaning for a man seeking the highest office in the land to go out hustling for votes. Those few who did so—William Jennings Bryan, for example, running as a Democrat in 1896—were criticized as boorish and undignified. Even Theodore Roosevelt, seeking reelection in 1904, sat on the sidelines during the contest.

It wasn't until the 20th century that it became acceptable for presidential candidates to go out on the stump to plead their case in person. In 1908, when Bryan, running on the Democratic ticket for the third time, went out on a campaign tour, as he had done twice before, William Howard Taft, the dignified Republican nominee, decided to make some campaign speeches too. Originally he had planned to run a "front-porch" campaign, that is, receive delegations of various organizations (sponsored by his campaign managers) at his home in Cincinnati, and utter a few platitudinous words of welcome (the way McKinley had in 1896) when they made their formal calls on him. By the fall of 1908, however, the Democrats were doing so well (they registered a gain of 32 percent in Vermont's September elections and did well in Maine, too) that Republican leaders began urging Taft to take to the stump to meet Bryan's challenge. With great reluctance, he finally yielded; he regretfully cut short a fishing vacation, fully convinced that "the necessity for stirring up interest in the campaign is so imperative that I am willing to run the risk of breaking a precedent. . . ."[9]

Taft's decision to break a precedent and do some electioneering produced no headlines and elicited no finger-pointing. His solid conservatism (unlike Bryan's passionate populism) seems to have legitimated the action once for all. (Bryan sarcastically pointed out that it was "demagogic to run around hunting votes in 1896 and 1900" the way he had done, but was "now, proper, because Taft was going to do it.")[10] The speeches Taft gave around the country drew large crowds and received favorable comments, and although he felt ill at ease at first, he gradually hit his stride and even began making improvisatory remarks to voters the way Bryan was doing. Taft and Bryan exchanged heated comments on the issues, mainly economic, during the campaign, but neither dreamed of stooping to petty personal attacks on each other. And on election day Taft won by a comfortable margin even though he lacked Bryan's oratorical gifts and had delivered far fewer speeches than the "Great Commoner."

In 1912, Taft took to the stump again (the first President to do so) in his quest for re-election. His challengers that year—Woodrow Wilson, the Democratic candidate, and Theodore Roosevelt, running as a Progressive—also went on speech-making tours, and, like Taft, they both thoughtfully expounded their philosophies of government. It was all on a very high level. The three candidates disagreed strongly about the issues, but none of them descended to personal attacks on his opponents. After the 1912 election (which

Wilson won because the Republicans split their votes between Taft and T.R.), active campaigning by presidential candidates became fully acceptable, but with it went the expectation that the candidates would behave with dignity and decorum on the campaign trail. Neither Warren G. Harding in 1920 nor Calvin Coolidge in 1924 did much campaigning, but both Herbert Hoover and Al Smith went out on the stump in 1928 and so have all the presidential candidates ever since.

Mudslinging did not of course disappear with the new way of conducting presidential campaigns. The rule seemed to be that party workers might lie, steal votes, smear the opposition, and roll in the gutter, as of old, but that the candidates themselves (and their running mates) concentrate on policies and avoid personalities. Voters, it was assumed, would not want to see a candidate make it to the White House who had shown himself to be mean, petty, and malicious.

In 1964, when Republican candidate Barry Goldwater's campaign managers came up with a particularly vicious documentary to use against President Lyndon Johnson, who was seeking re-election, the doughty Arizonian sharply turned his thumbs down on it. "It is nothing but a racist film," he exploded. "If they show it, I will publicly repudiate it."[11] And in 1980, when President Jimmy Carter, running for a second term, implied at one point that his Republican challenger, Ronald Reagan, was a kind of "mad bomber," he was chided for his hyperbole. "Mr. President," exclaimed Barbara Walters, in an interview for ABC News, "in recent days you have been characterized as vindictive, hysterical, and on the point of desperation." Carter meekly admitted that he had "gotten carried away on a couple of occasions" and promised to speak "with more reticence in the future" and avoid name-calling. "Well," smiled Reagan, when he heard about the exchange, "I think that would be nice if he did . . . if he decided to straighten up and fly right, that'll be fine."[12]

Like Carter, George Bush, Reagan's successor, didn't always "fly right" in 1988 and 1992 (on occasion he made personal attacks on his opponents), but this may have been the exception, not the new rule for presidential campaigning. It may well be that the style originally set by Taft and Bryan in 1908—emphasizing policies, not personalities—will come again to characterize the strategies of presidential hopefuls in their bid for votes. After all, from 1800 onward, there have always been enough political activists willing to roll in the gutter during the presidential campaigns without the candidates themselves feeling obliged to engage in the mudslinging.

CHAPTER 42

Presidential
Wives

Hillary Rodham Clinton has been by far the most assertive President's wife in American history.

Not really. In a cover story about Mrs. Clinton in May 1993, *Time* proclaimed her "the most powerful First Lady in history," but this was hyperbolic journalism.[1] Several of Mrs. Clinton's predecessors in the White House were almost as activistic as she and two or three of them were in some ways even more influential.

Mrs. Clinton has been undoubtedly one of her husband Bill's chief advisers, but there is nothing new about that. Abigail Adams, the second President's wife, discussed policies and measures with her husband, John, made suggestions for his speeches, and saw to it that material favorable to his administration got into the hands of newspaper editors. Sarah Polk, James K.'s bright and conscientious wife, was also a partner of her husband in the White House ("he set me to work"); she toiled diligently at his side, giving advice on patronage, bringing information appearing in newspapers and magazines to his attention, and making suggestions for speeches. Abraham Lincoln's wife Mary gave generous (and frequently unsolicited) advice on her husband's appointments, and so, too, did Julia Grant when the "General" (as she called Ulysses) was the nation's chief executive. When Grant decided not to run for a third term in 1880, he made an end run around Julia—informed the public before telling her—because he was afraid she would persuade him to change his mind. Even Bess Truman, a very private person who stayed out of the limelight as much as she could, expected her husband to talk over his policies with her while he was President. Once she read him the riot act after several months of neglect. "She was my chief adviser," said Truman some years after he retired.[2]

Mrs. Clinton took to the campaign trail for her husband during the 1992 campaign, but so did President Bush's wife, Barbara. And neither was the first presidential candidate's wife to do so. Even Bess Truman, who disliked public appearances, stood at her husband's side in 1948 when he made a barnstorming trip by train across the country in his quest for re-election. Mrs. Truman didn't much like it, but the crowds that came to hear the President's little speeches from the rear platform of the campaign train howled with glee whenever he introduced his wife as "the Boss." Dwight D. Eisenhower made a similar trip across the country when seeking election in 1952, and he always got a warm response when he introduced his wife Mamie to the crowd after making a few pungent remarks from the train platform. (Mrs. Eisenhower, however, unlike Mrs. Truman, loved it.) After 1952, all the presidential candidates, Republican or Democratic, utilized their wives—Jackie Kennedy, Lady Bird Johnson, Pat Nixon, Betty Ford, Rosalynn Carter, Nancy Reagan, Barbara Bush—at campaign rallies and receptions. In addition, some of the candidates' wives made little speeches themselves during the campaigns, and two of the wives—Lady Bird Johnson and Rosalynn Carter—even went on speech-making tours of their own to push for their husband's elections. Mrs. Clinton participated actively in her husband's campaign for the presidency in 1992; Barbara Bush was equally busy in her husband's bid for a second term. The Republicans, in fact, featured Mrs. Bush at their nominating convention in Houston in August, and saw to it that she gave one of the convention's major speeches. In some ways Mrs. Bush (who spoke for the moderates in the party) played a more prominent role at her party's convention than Mrs. Clinton did at hers.

With Bill Clinton's election in 1992 and his inauguration in 1993, Mrs. Clinton moved into the White House with every intention of playing an important part in her husband's administration. Her first major job: heading up a task force appointed by her husband to formulate a plan for national health insurance for submission to Congress. Some of Clinton's critics grumbled about his entrusting such a weighty responsibility to his wife, but in the end Congress failed to approve the health plan unveiled by the Clintons in 1994, and Mrs. Clinton thereafter assumed a lower profile in her husband's administration, though she remained his close partner and continued to speak out on health-care reform. But there was nothing unprecedented about her activities on behalf of national health care. All President's wives since Jacqueline Kennedy (who redesigned the White House to emphasize its historical background) had picked special projects to work on while they were in the White House: highway beautification (Lady Bird Johnson), volunteerism, that is, private charity work on behalf of the underprivileged (Pat Nixon), women's rights (Betty Ford), mental health (Rosalynn Carter), drug abuse (Nancy Reagan), literacy (Barbara Bush). But three of Mrs. Clinton's predecessors did much more than this: Edith Wilson, Eleanor Roosevelt, and Nancy Reagan. They were in certain respects far more influential than Mrs. Clinton.

Edith Wilson—Woodrow Wilson's second wife—was a special case. Thoroughly traditional in her social outlook (she even opposed woman suffrage), she ended up, by a sudden twist of fate, playing a crucial role in her husband's administration from 1919 to 1921. In October 1919, President Wilson suffered a massive stroke that left him paralyzed on one side. With his collapse, Mrs. Wilson faced a problem no other President's wife had even confronted: should she insist that he resign his office (and let the Vice President, Thomas R. Marshall, take over), or should she find some way of helping him carry on with his responsibilities as President until he recovered his health? Her husband's doctors advised the latter. The President's mind was as good as ever, they told her, and they were sure he would make a good recovery if she shielded him against "every disturbing problem" while he was convalescing. If he resigned his office, they warned, he might lose the will to live.

The doctors convinced Mrs. Wilson. On their advice she launched what she called her "stewardship." In order to protect her husband's health, she kept everyone, even the highest officials, out of his bedroom until he got better; and to enable him to continue his work as President while bedridden, she became his intermediary with Senate leaders, Cabinet heads, diplomats, secretaries, and advisers. Every day she went over the letters and papers coming to his office for action, picked out what she thought were the most important ones, made summaries of them, took them to his bedside, and then relayed his instructions to the appropriate officials. As Wilson slowly recovered, he was able to dictate notes to her for transmission to his associates; at times, too, he instructed her to get in touch with Senators who were leading the fight for ratification of the Treaty of Versailles in order to convey his suggestions on strategy for them to follow in the Upper Chamber. "I, myself," Mrs. Wilson wrote in her memoirs years after his death, "never made a single decision regarding the disposition of public affairs. The only decision that was mine was what was important and what was not, and the very important decision of when to present matters to my husband."

Despite Mrs. Wilson's disclaimer, it is clear that until Wilson was well enough to take up the reins of office again, his wife's power in the White House was unprecedented. Deciding "what was important," as she put it, surely represented a grave responsibility. It is not surprising that Mrs. Wilson's "stewardship" provoked considerable criticism, particularly among Republicans in Congress and in the press. There were complaints about the "Mrs. Wilson regency" and the "Petticoat Government" in Washington. Some people even began referring sarcastically to Mrs. Wilson as the "Presidentress" and saying that Wilson himself had been demoted to the position of "First Man."[3]

While Edith Wilson's "stewardship" was unique in the history of the presidency, in many respects Eleanor Roosevelt was even more influential than Mrs. Wilson during her twelve years in the White House. Mrs. Roosevelt advised her husband, of course, the way Abigail Adams and Sarah Polk did, and Franklin Roosevelt welcomed, even solicited her advice. Roosevelt didn't always agree with her, but he liked to use her as a sounding board for ideas he was kicking around in his mind, and he sometimes played devil's advocate with her in order to draw her out and clarify his own thinking during the exchanges. She discussed major New Deal projects with him, made suggestions about programs, and sometimes pushed her favorites (like the National Youth Administration) with him. She also saw to it that he got to meet specialists in various fields whom he might not have come to meet without her recommendation. And she testified before the House District of Columbia Committee on conditions in the District and pushed for slum-clearance legislation. "Mrs. Roosevelt," exclaimed the committee chairman, "you are the first First Lady of the land who has appeared before a Congressional

Committee. I can assure you that we are deeply appreciative of your presence. . . ." Later on she appeared before another Congressional committee to talk about the plight of migrant workers in the United States.[4]

In addition to serving as FDR's New Deal partner, Eleanor Roosevelt became famous as the White House's indefatigable peregrinator. Since FDR was physically handicapped and didn't move about easily, she traveled widely on his behalf, studying social and economic conditions around the country and visiting New Deal projects, and then reporting her observations to him in some detail when she returned to Washington. She became a special champion of the blacks, too, at a time when it was not politically feasible for FDR to take up their cause openly, and she worked hard to see that they got a fair break in New Deal programs and in the armed forces. During World War II, at FDR's request, she flew to the front on several occasions to visit and boost the morale of America's fighting forces. And amid all these activities she had a radio program, went on lecture tours, sponsored a subsistence homestead community for unemployed coal miners in West Virginia, taught American history and literature at a young women's school in Manhattan, wrote a daily newspaper column ("My Day") about her activities, had monthly columns in the *Woman's Home Companion* and the *Ladies' Home Journal*, and published her autobiography, *This is My Story* (1937). As a journalist, Mrs. Roosevelt became a seasoned professional who could have lived comfortably on her earnings if she had had to. (She gave them all to charity.) She was, in short, the first President's wife to have a career of her own in addition to her activities as her husband's partner.

Mrs. Roosevelt never went on the campaign trail for her husband the way some of her successors did, but she did appear at the Democratic convention in 1940 to defend her husband's selection of Henry Wallace, Secretary of Agriculture, as his running mate, and, with her grace and charm, she succeeded in winning over the reluctant delegates (who thought Wallace too starry-eyed) to FDR's choice. For a time, she served as deputy director of the Office of Civil Defense (OCD), without salary (the first President's wife to hold a government job), but resigned after anti-New Deal members of Congress made her a major target of their animosities. During the Roosevelt years some reactionaries hated her even more than they did her husband, in great part because of her efforts on behalf of American blacks. But FDR encouraged her to do what she thought was right even if it got him into trouble. "I can always say, 'Well, that is my wife; I can't do anything about her,'" he told her playfully. There was a joke at the time, though, that FDR had a nightly prayer: "Dear God, please make Eleanor a little tired."[5]

Despite Mrs. Roosevelt's almost unbelievably busy schedule, she always played down her influence on FDR. "I never urged on him a specific course of action, no matter how strongly I felt," she wrote in her memoirs, *This I Remember* (published in 1949), "because I realized he knew of factors in the picture as a whole of which I might be ignorant." In retrospect, she decided that on occasion she had "acted as a spur, even though the spurring was not always wanted or welcomed." But her main objective at all times, she insisted, was to further her husband's own objectives. "I was one of those," she said matter of factly, "who served his purposes."[6]

Nancy Reagan served her husband's purposes too. She was no Eleanor Roosevelt; nor was she an Edith Wilson, though sometimes compared to the latter. But in her own way she ranked with Mrs. Roosevelt and Mrs. Wilson when it came to activism in the White House. For eight years she was heavily involved in her husband's scheduling, his speech-making, his campaigning, and his travel plans. From the outset, moreover, she had strong opinions about the people he chose as his chief advisers, and whenever she got the impression they were hurting rather than helping him, she began to press for their dismissal. One by one, under her prodding, they fell by the wayside: campaign workers, counselors, White House staffers. She also pushed for the resignations of William Casey, CIA director; Pat Buchanan, speechwriter, whose ideas, she snorted, were not her husband's; Raymond Donovan, Secretary of Labor; and Margaret Heckler, Secretary of Health and Human Services. She cut passages about abortion from one of her husband's State of the Union addresses ("I don't give a damn about the right-to-lifers"), fought unsuccessfully against her husband's plan to visit Bitburg, Germany, where members of Hitler's elite guard were buried, and insisted on rescheduling dinners, speeches, interviews, and travel arrangements which Donald T. Regan, Reagan's Chief of Staff, had made for the President. "In my two years in the White House," recalled Regan bitterly, "the First Lady was a constant telephone presence in my work." He thought she was unduly influenced, moreover, by friends like Katherine Graham, the liberal publisher of the *Washington Post,* and Robert Strauss, former chairman of the Democratic National Committee.[7]

Donald Regan resented Nancy Reagan from almost the beginning. She "regarded herself," he complained, "as the President's alter ego not only in the conjugal but also in the political and official dimension, as if the office that had been bestowed upon her husband by the people somehow fell into the category of worldly goods covered by the marriage vows." Sometimes Mrs. Reagan called him so often to make demands that he found himself "spending two or three times as much time talking to her as to the President." Once, when he suggested there be someone on the President's staff for her to call, she said icily: "When I need something, I'll call you directly." Of course the inevitable breaking point finally came. At the height of one angry argument, Mrs. Reagan charged, her husband's Chief of Staff suddenly hung up on her. "That may be true," Regan said later, "but if it is it is only because I was quicker than Mrs. Reagan. At the time it seemed to me that it was a race between two angry people to slam down the receiver. I don't know who won." In any case it was their last confrontation. Mrs. Reagan insisted her husband fire his Chief of Staff forthwith. This was not so easy; President Reagan liked Don Regan and had always found it difficult to get rid of people on his staff he liked. But Mrs. Reagan seems to have pressed hard. At one point, according to a report in the *Washington Post* (which Mrs. Reagan denied), President Reagan yelled at her: "Get off my goddamned back!" In the end, though, he let Regan go. "I thought I was Chief of Staff to the President, not to his wife," Regan told Reagan when he finally agreed to bow out. Reagan then murmured that he would "make sure that you go out in good fashion."[8]

In Regan's memoirs, *For the Record* (1988), he tried to get even with the intractable First Lady. Not only did he deplore her influence in the Reagan administration; he also tried to make her look silly by revealing her dependence on astrology in scheduling her husband's activities. It was an astrologer in San Francisco whom she referred to as the "Friend," who, he recalled, provided lists of "good, bad, and iffy days" for the President's scheduling. But Mrs. Reagan was determined to have the last word. In *My Turn* (1989), a book of memoirs which appeared soon after she left the White House, she seemingly evened the score by pointing out Regan's shortcomings as her husband's Chief of Staff, minimizing her dependence on astrology, and denying that she had been a real power in the White House.[9]

But Donald Regan had it right: Mrs. Reagan was a powerful presence in the Reagan administration. She herself admitted that as the President's wife she thought there were times when somebody had "to step in and say or do something," and she added: "And I've had to do that sometimes—often." Her influence wasn't limited to her husband's appointments. She had much to say about his policies too. Her main concern seems to have been his hard-line attitude toward the Soviet Union in the early years of his presidency. She wanted him to go down in history as a peace-maker, not a warmonger, and she continually encouraged him to work for an arms-control agreement. "It was Nancy who pushed everybody on the Geneva summit," according to Reagan aide Michael Deaver. "She felt strongly that it was not only in the interest of world peace but the correct move politically." As she herself once put it: "With the world so dangerous, I felt it was ridiculous for these two heavily armed superpowers to be sitting there and not talking to each other." Hardliners in the administration groused about "Nancyism," but she seemed to have gotten through to her husband. "Nancy is determined I will go down in history as the President of peace," Reagan once remarked gaily, and after 1984 he stopped talking about the "evil empire" and took a more conciliatory approach to the USSR. The time came when he and the new Soviet leader Mikhail Gorbachev got along famously. Mrs. Reagan, like Mrs. Wilson and Mrs. Roosevelt, played down her influence. "If Ronnie hadn't wanted to do it," she said, "he wouldn't have done it." Still, there is no question but that she became an influential force for peace in the White House.[10]

Mrs. Reagan's activism—like Mrs. Wilson's and Mrs. Roosevelt's—came under sharp attack. The *New Republic*'s Fred Barnes called her the White House's "chief honcho," and the *New York Times*'s William Safire complained that President Reagan was "being weakened and made to appear wimpish and helpless by the political interference of his wife." But the American public seemed not to mind. In the spring of 1987, a Gallup poll reported that 62 percent of the people polled believed that Mrs. Reagan had more influence on the President than any other President's wife ever had, and that 59 percent approved of the way she was handling her role as "First Lady."[11]

Like Nancy Reagan—and Edith Wilson and Eleanor Roosevelt—Hillary Rodham Clinton has received a great deal of flak for her activities while she has been in the White House. From almost the beginning, in fact, Hillary-bashing was the vogue among President Clinton's political foes, and at times the assaults on Mrs. Clinton turned mean and nasty and came close to bordering on the pathological. But the assaults on Abraham Lincoln's wife Mary were just as brutal, even though Mrs. Lincoln, unlike Mrs. Clinton, assumed no public responsibilities while she was in the White House. And the attacks on Eleanor Roosevelt, who spent twelve years in the White House, were even greater. Despite the sound and fury roused in certain circles by Mrs. Clinton's activities, Mrs. Roosevelt (whom one columnist regularly referred to as "La Grande Boca") is to date the most vilified presidential wife in American history.

CHAPTER 43

Presidential
Scandals

It would be easy to write a lengthy book about the sexual she-
nanigans of the American Presidents.

Not really.

The majority of our Presidents, the record shows, were good and
faithful husbands. Only a few strayed from the beaten path while
they were in the White House.

George Washington had a crush on Sally Fairfax, a neighbor's
wife, when he was a young man, but it got him exactly nowhere, and
though in later years he looked back on her as the love of his life, he
had a good (if unexciting) relationship with Martha, whom he married when he was thirty. Washington had an eye for pretty women,
but he never cheated on Martha. The Adamses—John and
Abigail—had a far more romantic attachment. They were superbly
matched and their love and respect for each other were deep and
abiding. The letters they exchanged whenever separated from each
other are a joy and delight to read; they liked each other immensely
and went in for a lot of affectionate teasing in their exchanges.

Thomas Jefferson had a good marriage, but he became a widower
long before he became President. When stationed in Paris as U.S.
Minister to France in the 1780s, he fell deeply in love with a married
English woman, Maria Cosway, and wrote her extremely romantic
letters (unusual for him), but nothing seems to have come of it.
After he became President, his political foes accused him of having
had an affair with Sally Hemings, one of his slaves, but the charge

was almost certainly false. Jefferson's friend (and successor as President) James Madison found just the right woman when he met Dolley Payne, a widow, in 1798, and he had sense enough to know it. Dolley herself had misgivings about the match on the eve of the wedding, but the marriage turned out to be a good one for both of them, and they would never have dreamed of betraying each other. The charge by Madison's political enemies that Dolley was Thomas Jefferson's mistress was of course preposterous. Unlike Madison, Andrew Jackson sowed a lot of wild and woolly oats as a young man, but when he met and married Rachel Donelson in 1791, he became the most loyal of husbands. There was some irregularity in Rachel's divorce from her first husband and for a time there was gossip about bigamy and adultery. But Jackson fiercely defended his wife, threatened to shoot her detractors, and, in fact, actually fought a duel and killed a young man who made some nasty remarks about her. Jackson never really got over Rachel's death from a heart attack (shortly after his election in 1828 as President), triggered, he insisted, by slanders of his political enemies during the 1828 campaign.

Not all the presidential marriages were idyllic. John Quincy Adams and his wife Louisa had severely strained relations from time to time that made both of them miserable, but neither of them dreamed of seeking a divorce or of looking for companionship outside the marriage. The Lincolns—Abraham and Mary—experienced stresses and strains in their marriage, too (though nothing like those of JQA and Louisa), but on the whole they were a deeply devoted couple. James A. Garfield had a fling with a married woman in New York City years before he became President, but, overwhelmed with guilt, he told his wife Lucretia ("Crete") about it, and she crestfallenly decided to forgive him. (Years later she confessed to her children that her coldness as a young wife had been very hard on her passionate husband.) Grover Cleveland took up with a merry widow, Maria Halpin, when he was a young bachelor in Buffalo, New York, and there was a baby boy for whom he secretly provided financial support for years. The story of his youthful escapade hit the headlines when he was running for President in 1884, but he won the election anyway. Soon after his inauguration he married an attractive young woman, Frances Folsom, twenty years his junior, and settled into a long and comfortable marriage. Jimmy Carter once told *Playboy* he sometimes lusted in his heart, but his wife Rosalynn did not need to worry; the lust stayed in the heart.

And so it went. Most of the presidential marriages lacked the kind of spice that sets radio and TV talk shows a-twitter. Simply to think of the Theodore Roosevelts or the Tafts or the Coolidges or the Hoovers of violating the conventionalities is to think the unthinkable. As for Harry Truman, when he was in Potsdam for a Big Three conference in July 1945, and a young army officer who was showing him around offered to get him "Anything, you know, like women," Truman snapped: "Listen, son, I married my sweetheart. She doesn't run around on me and I don't run around on her. I want that understood. Don't ever mention that kind of stuff to me again."[1] That was that.

What about the two-timers?

Was Woodrow Wilson really "Peck's Bad Boy"? He did, his first wife Ellen knew, enjoy the company of attractive and vivacious women, but she liked all his favorites, too, and shared his friendships with them. For a time he was much taken with Mrs. Mary Allen Hulbert Peck, a bright and lively woman, separated from her husband, whom he met in 1907 and with whom he exchanged letters for several years. But he seems to have kept the relationship within bounds, saw to it that Mrs. Peck became Ellen's friend, too, and eventually apologized to his wife for temporary infatuation. "These letters," he later wrote of his exchanges with Mrs. Peck, "disclose a passage of folly and gross impertinence in my life. I am deeply ashamed and repentant. Neither in act nor even in thought was the purity or honor of the lady concerned touched or sullied, and my offense she has generously forgiven. Neither was my allegiance to my incomparable wife in anyway in the least jot abated. She, too, knew and understood and has forgiven, little as I deserved the generous indulgence." Still, gossipers called him "Peck's Bad Boy" (the title of a popular comedy based on stories about a mischievous boy written by humorist George W. Peck), and his attachment to Mrs. Peck actually did bother his wife. She once confessed to Dr. Cary Grayson, the family doctor, that it was the only occasion for unhappiness in all her years with Wilson.[2]

Stories about Mrs. Peck made the rounds in 1912, when Wilson ran for President the first time, and again in 1916, when he ran for a second term. (When Theodore Roosevelt heard the gossip, he snorted that nobody would believe that Wilson, "cast so perfectly as the apothecary's clerk, could ever play a Romeo!") After the death of Ellen in 1915, when Wilson began courting his second wife, Edith Bolling Galt, a Washington widow, the stories resurfaced, and Wilson told her about Mrs. Peck, assured her their relations had been platonic, that Mrs. Peck had been Ellen's friend, too, and that the three of them had frequently socialized together. "I am not afraid of any gossip or threat," Edith told him, "with your love as my shield." Wilson had a good second marriage.[3]

Warren G. Harding's marriage was not so good. W-u-r-r-e-n, as his wife Florence ("the Duchess") called him, seems to have been born with a roving eye, and even during the courtship she had to work hard to keep him from going off on tangents. How much she knew about his clandestine love affairs after their marriage, it is impossible to say. For a time Harding had two affairs going on at the same time. One was with Carrie, the wife of his good friend James E. Phillips, a businessman in Marion, Ohio, his hometown; he had fallen in love, apparently for the first time in his life, with Carrie in 1905, and was still deeply attached to her when he ran for President in 1920. The other was with Nan Britton, a young Marionite who had gotten a big crush on him when she was in high school, taken the initiative, and succeeded in getting him to visit her regularly in New York City when he was in the Senate to engage in what she called "love's sweetest intimacy." He also wrote her sixty-page love letters dripping with romantic effusions.[4]

Until 1920, Florence Harding seems not to have known about Carrie; the Hardings and the Phillipses saw a great deal of each other in Marion through the years and traveled abroad a couple of times without either Florence's or Jim's realizing what was going on. But Harding saw Carrie secretly whenever he could, and when he couldn't, he exchanged fervent love letters with her (the way he did with Nan) in which he was "Constant" and she was "Sis." As for Nan Britton, she had made her crush on Harding so obvious in Marion (she liked to write, "I love Warren Harding" on the high school blackboard) that Mrs. Harding regarded her with suspicion from the beginning. But apparently she knew nothing about Nan's baby girl, born in October 1919, for whom Harding made generous provision.[5]

Neither of Harding's dalliances came to light during the 1920 presidential campaign, though Republican officials, suspecting something, sent the Phillipses abroad on a fact-finding mission until Harding won the election. After he became President, Harding continued to see Nan; he sneaked her in and out of the White House, with the help of friendly Secret Service men, and enjoyed blissful moments with her in the coat closet adjoining his main office. One afternoon Florence returned home unexpectedly and almost caught him at it, but Harding, forewarned by the Secret Service, managed to get Nan out of the building in time. When Nan published *The President's Daughter* (1927), a tell-all exposé, filled with details about her involvement with the President, both the Hardings were long gone. But Harding's relatives continued for a time to contribute to the upkeep of Nan's daughter.

About the time Warren Harding took up with Nan Britton, Franklin D. Roosevelt, then Assistant Secretary of the Navy in the Wilson administration, got involved with Lucy Page Mercer, an attractive young Maryland woman who was his wife Eleanor's social secretary. Mrs. Roosevelt found out about the affair by accident. In September 1918, when FDR returned from a trip to Europe with pneumonia, she was unpacking his trunk and suddenly, to her horror, came across letters revealing that for the past year or so he had been having an affair with Lucy. The discovery almost wrecked the Roosevelt marriage. "The bottom dropped out of my own particular world," E.R. told a close friend years later, "and I faced myself, my surroundings, my world, honestly for the first time. I really grew up that year." Mrs. Roosevelt offered FDR his freedom, but when he thought over the consequences of divorce—the effect on the children, on Lucy, a devout Catholic who could not marry a divorced man, and on his own political future—he decided not to accept it. Instead, there was a reconciliation. Mrs. Roosevelt forgave her husband and he in turn agreed to break off relations with Lucy and never see her again. Lucy went on to marry Winthrop Rutherfurd, a Washington businessman, in 1920.[6]

FDR seems to have kept his promise until World War II. Then he began seeing Lucy again, now a middle-aged but attractive widow (her husband died in 1944). It came as a shock for Mrs. Roosevelt to learn that Lucy had been with FDR when he died in Warm Springs, Georgia, in April 1945, and that he had been seeing her from time to time during the war. She also found out to her dismay that her daughter Anna had occasionally invited Mrs. Rutherfurd to the White House when she was out of town. Anna never denied that she thought Lucy's friendship was good for her father, but she insisted that the relationship was "open, aboveboard, not hanky-panky or whatever you want to call it." Still, her mother felt that FDR betrayed the promise he had made years before never to see Lucy again, and she was cool to Anna for a few weeks and then seemed to put the matter out of her mind.[7]

In her memoir of her White House years, *This I Remember*, appeared in 1949, Eleanor Roosevelt said nothing about Lucy, of course, but there are passages toward the end of the book which unquestionably reflect the deep hurt she still felt about her husband's companionship with Lucy. She admitted that she had had an "almost impersonal feeling" about FDR's death and that in trying to understand why this was so she suggested that it may have grown out of the fact that "much further back I had had to face certain difficulties until I decided to accept the fact that a man must be what he is" and that "life must be lived as it is. . . ." She then reflected: "All human beings have failings, all human beings have needs and temptations and stresses. Men and women who live together through long years get to know one another's feelings, but they also come to know what is worthy of respect and admiration in those they live with and in themselves."[8]

Several years after Mrs. Roosevelt's death in 1962, two of her sons engaged in speculation about her relations with their father that would undoubtedly have upset her. In a book appearing in 1974, Elliott Roosevelt portrayed his mother as so sexually inhibited that FDR was driven, almost in spite of himself, to have an affair with Lucy Mercer, and, later on, with Marguerite ("Missy") LeHand, his companionable young White House secretary. But Elliott's brother, James, begged to differ. In a book published in 1976, he agreed that his mother was repressed (he quoted her as telling his sister Anna, "Sex is an ordeal to be borne"), but he doubted that his father was able to have sexual relations after his bout with polio in 1921. FDR's romance with "Missy" LeHand, who became his private secretary in 1921, and his relations with Lucy Rutherfurd while he was President were, he insisted perforce, "affairs of the spirit," not of the flesh. "I traveled the world with him," he wrote, "and slept in the same room with him at times. From my observation it would have been difficult for him to function sexually after he became crippled from the waist down from polio. He had some use of his lower body and some sensation there, but it was extremely limited."[9]

On one point, however, James agreed with his brother Elliott: like Woodrow Wilson, FDR enjoyed the company of comely and personable women and he was able to forget the cares of office in their presence. To judge from the testimony of his two sons, Mrs. Roosevelt was always a bit too earnest. She lacked the light touch; she simply couldn't be frivolous. And that was hard on FDR, who needed to lighten up from time to time and forget about the world's big issues. Once, Anna recalled, her mother walked into the room where FDR was enjoying the cocktail hour with some friends, handed him a bunch of papers, and said, "Now, Franklin, I want to talk to you about this." FDR looked up, grabbed the papers, threw them across the desk to Anna, and cried: "Sis, you handle these tomorrow morning." Mrs. Roosevelt got up, stood there for a moment, said, "I'm sorry," and left. "He wanted to tell stories and relax and enjoy himself. . . ," Anna recalled. "I don't think Mother had the slightest realization."[10]

Stories about FDR and Lucy Mercer didn't reach the American public until after Roosevelt's death in April 1945. By that time, however, stories about Dwight D. Eisenhower's relations with Kay Summersby, his chauffeur in Britain during World War II, were making the rounds, though there is serious doubt that they were grounded in fact. Ike knew and liked Kay, to be sure, but she was only one of his jeep drivers, and four of the other drivers, interviewed years later, agreed that if there was an Ike-Kay romance it was one of the best-kept secrets of the war. Ike's naval aide, Harry Butcher, also doubted the Kay tale. "If a romance had been brewing between Ike and Kay," he said, "I could hardly have missed it." Ike's orderly Michael J. McKeogh had his doubts, too. "I woke the General in the morning," he told an interviewer after Ike's death in 1969, "and I never went to bed until my boss was in bed at night. . . . There was never anyone in the General's bed at night but the General. Never, at any time all during the war, wherever we were quartered."

When the stories about Kay first started circulating during World War II, Ike strongly denied them. He assured Mamie that he had *"never been in love with anyone but you,"* and she believed him.

Still, with the tastelessness masquerading as candor that became the vogue, starting in the late 1960s, the American Broadcast System presented a six-hour mini-series in May 1979 centering on Ike's love for Kay, when Mrs. Eisenhower was still alive. A widow in her eighties, living in Gettysburg, Mamie took it all gamely. She even watched the show. "Mickey," she told Ike's old orderly, "it doesn't bother me one way or the other." When a friend deplored ABC's execrable taste in producing the show, she exclaimed: "Now don't you bother your pretty little head about it for one minute. We both know it isn't true." A few days later, when she and a friend got to talking about World War II British Naval commander Lord Mountbatten (whom she and Ike knew), she suddenly exclaimed: "If I had once thought there was an iota of truth in the Kay Summersby affair, I would have gone after Mountbatten, and believe you me, my friend, I could have gotten him!"[11]

If there are doubts about the authenticity of the stories about Ike and Kay, there are none whatever about John F. Kennedy's amorous antics. JFK, by general agreement, was the womanizer par excellence among our Presidents. Even Warren G. Harding seems a bit stodgy by comparison. Though Kennedy had vowed "to keep the White House white," as he put it, before he became President, he was soon straying far and wide from the marital path after his inauguration. "If I don't have a woman for three days," he told British Prime Minister Harold Macmillan in 1961, "I get terrible headaches." As President, he had frequent meetings with Judith Campbell (mistress of Chicago Mafia capo Sam Giancana), a young beauty he met through singer Frank Sinatra during the 1960 campaign; he also saw a lot of Mary Meyer, *Washington Post* editor Ben Bradley's married sister-in-law. He enjoyed, too, the company of a couple of blonde women from the White House secretarial pool whom he called "Fiddle and Faddle" (his wife Jackie called them "the White House dogs"). There were rumors, moreover, about assignations with some of Hollywood's choicest sex queens—Angie Dickinson, Jayne Mansfield, Kim Novak, Marilyn Monroe—to say nothing of countless starlets with whom Frank Sinatra and actor Peter Lawford put him in touch. Jackie tried to ignore her husband's activities, but there is no doubt that she was deeply hurt by it all. Once she handed him a pair of panties she found in her pillow slip and cried, "Here, would you find out who these belong to? They're not my size."

Perhaps to show her resentment she began spending a great deal of time away from the White House on trips around this country and abroad.[12]

Even world crises seem not to have kept JFK's mind entirely off sex. In the fall of 1962, during the Cuban missile crisis, when President Kennedy, along with Cabinet members and the Chiefs of Staff, was anxiously waiting for the Soviet Premier Nikita Khrushchev's response to their proposals for an agreement on Cuba, a good-looking woman suddenly walked into the Oval Office with a bunch of papers, handed them to Secretary of Defense Robert McNamara and scurried out. Kennedy looked up, then looked down, and then looked up again and asked: "Who's that?" "She's filling in today," McNamara told him. "You know, we're really swamped, so they sent her over from Commerce." At this point Kennedy leaned over and said, "Bob, I want her name and number." Then he explained: "We may avoid war here tonight."[13]

Like Kennedy, Lyndon B. Johnson seems to have been an irre-pressible skirt-chaser, but though he bragged to friends about his conquests, his extramarital adventures have been far less conscien-tiously researched than those of JFK. LBJ biographer Robert Caro thought that Alice Glass, the mistress and then wife of a prominent Washington businessman, played an important part in LBJ's life when he was a young Congressman trying to learn the ropes in Washington in the late 1930s. Not all historians agreed with Caro, but most of them took it for granted that LBJ was something of a philanderer. In the middle of the night, according to one popular tale, LBJ cried to a female aide staying in the guest room at his Texas ranch, "Move over, this is your President!" Several years after John-son's death, when the producer of a TV film about LBJ was bold enough to ask Lady Bird about LBJ's reputation as a womanizer, LBJ's widow looked at him for a moment and then said quietly: "You have to understand, my husband loved people. All people. And half the people in the world are women. You don't think I could have kept my husband away from half the people?" Then her eyes moist-ened and she added: "He loved me. I know he only loved me."[14]

After LBJ the tabloids had slim pickings for a while. The Nixons, Fords, Carters, Reagans, and Bushes provided no surprises and no sensations (though Reagan was known to have played the field in Hollywood between marriages to Jane Wyman and Nancy Davis).

Then, during the 1992 presidential campaign, it came to light that Democratic candidate Bill Clinton had cheated on his wife when he was governor of Arkansas, and the revelation almost derailed his quest for the Presidency. But the infidelity issue dropped out of the campaign after Clinton appeared on CBS's *60 Minutes* with his wife Hillary to acknowledge that they had had difficulties in the past in their marriage but it was now going swimmingly.

In 1994, however, with Clinton now in the White House, an Arkansas woman named Paula Jones, with the encouragement of Clinton's enemies, brought a suit against the President for sexual harassment in 1991, when he was governor of Arkansas. It was an unprecedented action. No President had ever been taken to court for his sexual behavior before entering the White House (or even after leaving office). "Press coverage of the private sexual life of the President has a salience that is new," observed historian Arthur M. Schlesinger, Jr., "but every President who stands for change is hated—beginning with Thomas Jefferson." Clinton-haters—and there were many, among religious as well as political conservatives—reveled in the charges against the President, but neoconservative Catholic theologian Michael Novak issued a caveat. Though by no means condoning Clinton's pre-presidential behavior, he had serious reservations about the new form of President-baiting. "Private life should be ruled out of bounds," he declared. "People whose private lives, in a Christian sense, have not been of the highest standard have made significant contributions to the common good."[15] It was, of course, Clinton's great hope that he would make significant contributions to the common good before leaving the White House.

CHAPTER 44

President-Bashing

The American people are a lot harder on their Presidents today than they were in the good old days.

Not so.

From almost the beginning of the republic, the American people have been rough on their Presidents, especially the competent ones. They called John Adams a fool and a criminal, Thomas Jefferson a coward and an atheist, Andrew Jackson a thief and a murderer, Martin Van Buren sly, selfish, and treacherous, James K. Polk mendacious and mediocre, Ulysses Grant a crook, drunkard, and ignoramus, Chester A. Arthur an accomplice in the assassination of James A. Garfield, Grover Cleveland a wife-beater, William Howard Taft a Mr. Malaprop, and Woodrow Wilson a syphilitic. But the Presidents whom most historians today regard as the nation's greatest—George Washington, Abraham Lincoln, Franklin Roosevelt—came in for especially fulgurous obloquy and contumely.

George Washington received a great deal of adulation when he was President, but he was the target of vehement criticism, too, during his eight years as chief executive. His first years in office were largely peaceful, but with the emergence of political parties (not contemplated by the Constitution) in the early 1790s, he was inevitably drawn into the political strife that erupted, even though he tried hard to stay above the fray. His problem was that he tended to side with the Federalists (who backed Alexander Hamilton's centralizing economic policies and favored Britain over France) and thus incurred the wrath of the Jeffersonian Republicans (who opposed Hamilton's program as monarchical in nature and who preferred France to Britain). The Republican press at first gingerly and then with increasing stridency took after Washington, as well as Hamilton and other Federalist leaders who in their opinion put the interests of the few above the interests of the many. It got so that General Washington, once the great hero of the Revolution, became for the Republican opposition practically the villain of the piece.

Philip Freneau's *National Gazette* and Benjamin Franklin Bache's *Aurora* were particularly hard on the old Revolutionary commander. In piece after piece (and in poetry too) they called him arrogant, treacherous, dishonest, despotic, stupid, crooked, and tyrannical, and they belittled his abilities both as commander-in-chief during the Revolution and as the first chief executive of the new nation. The Republicans charged that receptions at the President's House aped the court of George III, deplored the "sycophantic" celebrations of his birthday, accused him of overdrawing his accounts as President, circulated letters forged by the British during the Revolution to prove he was a traitor to his country, and said he fancied himself "the *grand lama*" of the country. "We have given him the powers and privileges of a King," lamented the *Jersey Chronicle* (Mt. Pleasant, New Jersey). "He holds levees like a King, receives congratulations on his birthday like a King, receives ambassadors like a King, makes treaties like a King, answers petitions like a King, employs his old enemies like a King, shuts himself up like a King, shuts up other people like a King, takes advice of his counsellors or follows his own opinion like a King" and "swallows adulation like a King."[1]

The Republican press was particularly incensed when Washington issued a Proclamation of Neutrality upon the outbreak of war between Britain and France (America's old Revolutionary ally) in June 1793. Why, Freneau's *National Gazette* wanted to know, was the President lulled by the "opiate of sycophancy" into his arbitrary and tyrannical assumption of the powers of Congress (which alone could make war) in issuing his proclamation? "I am aware, sir," cried the *Gazette*, "that some court satellite may have deceived you with respect to the sentiment of your fellow citizens. The first magistrate of a country whether he be called king or president seldom knows the real state of a nation, particularly if he be so buoyed up by official importance as to think it beneath his dignity to mix occasionally with the people. Let me caution you, sir, to beware that you do not view the state of the public mind at this critical moment through a fallacious medium. Let not the little buzz of the aristocratic few and their contemptible minions of speculators, tories, and British emissaries, be mistaken for the exalted and generous voice of the American people." There were calls for his impeachment, and one Republican even proposed a toast to "a speedy death to General Washington" at a public dinner in Virginia.[2]

Jay's Treaty, a compromise agreement with Britain which Washington sponsored in 1795 to stave off war with the British, produced even more wrath among the first President's critics. Bache's *Aurora* charged that Washington "had violated the Constitution and made a treaty with a nation abhorred by our people, that he answered the respectful remonstrances of Boston and New York as if he were the omnipotent director of a seraglio, and had thundered contempt upon the people with as much confidence as if he had sat upon the throne of Industan." There were renewed calls for his impeachment, and Republican newspapers showered him with abuse: "traitor to the people," "supercilious and arrogant," "usurper," "Political degenerate," "drunk with the idea of his own omnipotence," "in his dotage," "tyrant." One writer warned the President that the American people would "look to death, the man who assumes the character of an usurper." Cried William Duane's *Independent Chronicle*, published in Boston: "Would to God you had retired . . . four years ago, while your public conduct threw a veil of sanctity around you."[3]

Washington's retirement did not, however, mute the criticism. His Farewell Address, so much admired by later generations of Americans, was savaged by his critics when it appeared in September 1796. Bache's *Aurora* charged that the "perfidious" Washington had decided not to run for President again, not from "want of ambition or lust of power," but from a realization that he couldn't win this time. And Bache came up with a kind of farewell of his own for the departing President: "If ever a nation was debauched by a man, the American Nation has been debauched by Washington. If ever a nation has suffered from the improper influence of a man, the American Nation has suffered from the influence of Washington. If ever a nation was deceived by a man, the American Nation has been deceived by Washington. Let his conduct, then be an example to future ages. Let it serve to be a warning that no man may be an idol, and that a people may confide in themselves rather than in an individual. Let the history of the Federal Government instruct mankind, that the masque of patriotism may be worn to conceal the foulest designs against the liberties of a people."[4]

Washington found the attacks on his integrity hard to take, and he periodically exploded in mighty wrath at what he read in the opposition journals. Still, he had an easier time of it than Abraham Lincoln did. Washington at least had a fairly peaceful first term. With Lincoln, the barbs, taunts, sneers, and slurs started coming in right after his election in 1860. By the time he took his oath of office on March 4, 1861, he had already been contemptuously dismissed by newspapers in the North as an ape, demon, beast, baboon, gorilla, simple Susan, and imbecile. A speech he gave in Pittsburgh en route to Washington for the inauguration was ridiculed as "crude, ignorant twaddle, without point or meaning." When he started growing a beard at the suggestion of a little girl he met on his trip to the nation's capital, one journalist reported snidely: "Mr. Lincoln having brought his brilliant intellectual powers to bear upon the cultivation of luxuriant whiskers . . . has now . . . concentrated his mental energies upon the question—what hotel shall he stop at in New York."[5]

The sniping continued, even increased, after Lincoln's inauguration: "You cannot fill his . . . empty skull with brains"; "A respectable mule would have done better"; the North "fights without a General, without a Statesman"; "Every one is . . . disappointed at the President's course . . . [and] the first man I met . . . this morning in a rage declared that if a speedy change . . . did not occur, he hoped some Brutus would arise and love his country more than he did his President. . . ." Soon after Lincoln launched his presidency, he seemed to become almost loathsome to just about everybody: abolitionists, state's righters, strict constructionists, Negro-haters, radical Republicans, Democrats, conservative Republicans. One New York newspaper got in the habit of referring to him as "that hideous baboon at the other end of the avenue" and suggested that "Barnum should buy and exhibit him as a zoological curiosity." "*Honest Abe forsooth!*" sneered one editor. "Honest Iago! Benignant Nero! Faithful Iscariot!" Even Lincoln's hometown newspaper joined the assault: "How the greatest butchers of antiquity sink into insignificance when their crimes are contrasted with those of Abraham Lincoln!"[6]

Lincoln's prose, much acclaimed by lovers of the English language, then and now, left his critics unimpressed. Of the Gettysburg Address, the *Chicago Times* had this to say: "The cheek of every American must tingle with shame as he reads the silly, flat and dishwatery utterances of the man who has to be pointed out to intelligent foreigners as the President of the United States." In Harrisburg, Pennsylvania, The *Patriot and Union* was similarly scornful. "We pass over the silly remarks of the President," it declared; "for the credit of the nation, we are willing that the veil of oblivion shall be dropped over them and that they shall no more be reported or thought of." Of Lincoln's Second Inaugural Address (which the *Spectator,* a London journal, called "the noblest political document known to history"), the *Chicago Times* had only contempt: "We did not conceive it possible that even Mr. Lincoln could produce a paper so ship-shod, so loose-jointed, so puerile, not only in its literary construction, but in ideas, its sentiments, its grasp." The *New York News* felt the same way. "We shall not attempt to analyze Mr. Lincoln's address," wrote the editor, "because the intention of its author evidently was to deliver so many words without expressing any idea, suggesting anything, or asserting any facts. He has succeeded."[7]

There was little that the Lincoln-haters overlooked in their denigration of the Civil War President. They charged that his wife was secretly aiding the Confederate cause, that his 20-year-old son Bob had cunningly made over half a million in war contracts, and that Lincoln himself was a drunkard, as well as being dumb, dishonest, and dictatorial. One Baltimorean put all his venom in doggerel:

> With a beard that was filthy and red,
> His mouth with tobacco bespread,
> Abe Lincoln sat in the gay white house,
> Awishing he was dead —
> Swear! Swear! Swear!
> Til his tongue blistered o'er,
> Then in a voice not very strong

He slowly whined the Despot's song;
Lie! Lie! Lie!
I've lied like the very deuce!
Lie! Lie! Lie!
As long as lies were of use;
But now that lies no longer pay,
I know not where to turn,
For when I the truth would say,
My tongue with lies will burn!
Drink! Drink! Drink!
Till my head feels queer!
Till I get rid of all fear!
Brandy, and Whisky, and Gin,
Sherry, and Champagne, and Pop,
I tipple, I guzzle, I suck 'em all in,
Till down dead drunk I drop.

The plain fact that Lincoln did not drink, smoke, or use profanity was for his despisers utterly irrelevant.[8]

In 1864, when Lincoln ran for a second term, the lies about him became even more outrageous. One of the meanest was the charge that he took his salary as President in gold while insisting the Union soldiers be paid in greenbacks, worth fifty cents on the dollar. "Isn't this patriotic and honest in Old Abe Lincoln?" cried his enemies, "and ought not he to be re-elected to another four years' hard money for himself, and of largely depreciated money for the people?" Lincoln, who usually kept his temper, was furious at the charge; he said he hoped the scoundrel who got that story started would "boil here-after." But when the story began spreading from newspaper to newspaper, producing a spate of shocked editorials, F. E. Spinner, United States Treasurer, finally felt obliged to issue a public statement flatly denying the allegation.[9]

The Antietam story—that Lincoln visited the battlefield soon after the bloody encounter there and laughed and joked and had a friend sing a frivolous song—was even nastier. But when Marshal Ward Hill Lamon pressed Lincoln to issue a public denial, Lincoln told him to "let the thing alone" and added: "If I have not estab-lished character enough to give the lie to this charge, I can only say that I am mistaken in my own estimate of myself. In politics, every man must skin his own skunk. These fellows are welcome to the hide of this one. Its body has already given forth its unsavory odor." Lamon went ahead anyway and drafted a statement setting the record straight, which Lincoln edited to tone down and then neglected to make use of after all. In the end, though, he won his bid for re-election despite the venom spewed forth by his enemies. Mudslinging failed to do him in.[10]

Mudslinging didn't demolish Franklin D. Roosevelt either. FDR-bashing rivaled, perhaps even exceeded, Washington-bashing and Lincoln-bashing, but it did not prevent Roosevelt from being elected President four times in a row and occupying the White House for twelve years. FDR was luckier, though, than Lincoln. Like Washington, he enjoyed a couple of years of peace and harmony after he took office in March 1933 in the depths of the Great Depression. As he took vigorous action, working closely with Congress, to pull the economy out of the doldrums during his first months in office and at the same time give the nation's morale a big boost by his jaunty, good-humored, and self-confident manner, he received mostly applause, even from Republicans, even from conservatives, and even from members of the business community who were normally hostile to the idea of an activistic federal government. But as conditions gradually bettered in the land and as it became clear that FDR's New Deal program was developing a welfare state as well as working to revive the economy, the approval in conservative quarters gradually turned to dismay and, then, with some people to fury.

Some of the criticism of what FDR was doing was reasoned and fair-minded. Much of it, though, was mean-spirited and mendacious. "No phenomenon of the times is more disturbing than the persistent hatred of President Roosevelt which finds a more and more poisonous expression among a considerable section of the American people," noted Marquis Childs in the *New Republic* in September 1938. "No slander is too vile, no canard too preposterous, to find voice among those who regard the President as their mortal enemy. And what is more not a little of this slander finds its way into print. . . . Men and women who appear to be themselves normal take pleasure in wishing the President every kind of ill. The word assassination is used in a reckless and willful way by persons who seem at least relatively familiar with the ordinary decencies of human conduct." The ad hominem nature of the attacks on Roosevelt and his policies had the ironic effect of diverting attention from the New Deal itself. The result, as the *Nation* complained in April 1938, was that "there can be no serious discussion of basic issues like a program for meeting the depression or expanding the national income or dealing with the war danger; and even the progressives who care more about these issues than they do about the President are forced into the false position of defending him against the unfair tactics of his opponents."[11]

Some of the attacks on Roosevelt were, to be sure, merely silly. His critics said he was snobbish because he used a cape instead of an overcoat, that he didn't know the value of a dollar, and that he took too many vacations ("the fishingest President that any country ever had"). There were many jokes, too, some of which FDR himself enjoyed. Once he went fishing, according to one tale, and ran out of bait, so he heaved the bare hook into the water, flashed his winning smile, and cried, "My friends!" whereupon "a thousand suckers leaped into the boat." But the criticism turned spiteful after 1934, and soon the "below the belt" files of letters and clippings collected by White House secretaries were bulging with epithets: Franklin "Doublecrossing" Roosevelt, Franklin "Deficit" Roosevelt, Stalin Delano Roosevelt, Roosevelt the Demoralizer, Roosevelt the Tyrant, Roosevelt the Violator, Public Enemy No. 1, Swollen-headed Nitwit, Boozedoggling President, Unprincipled Charlatan, Ham Actor, Simpleton, Svengali, Sorcerer, Imposter, Socialist, Fascist, Communist, Collectivist, Revolutionist. The New Deal, for the disgruntled, was the Raw Deal, the Red Deal, the Pagan Deal, and the New Steal.[12]

As with Lincoln, there were preposterous falsehoods as well as vicious epithets floating around the country. Starting about 1934, Roosevelt-haters put scores of fake stories into circulation. They said Roosevelt entertained one of the country's foremost stamp collectors at the White House one day and then helped himself to the collector's most valued specimens when the man wasn't looking. They also said he made the government pay $100,000 a year in rent to his mother so he could use her house in Hyde Park, New York, as a summer White House. They charged, too, that he diverted funds raised by the March of Dimes birthday balls (which he sponsored to raise money for polio research) to his own use, and that he was involved in both the assassination of Huey Long and in the kidnaping of the Lindbergh baby.

Equally vicious were the falsehoods spread about his physical and mental health. FDR had, indeed, suffered polio in 1921 and was never able thereafter to walk without the use of braces and canes, but he was otherwise in good health when he became President: physically robust, full of energy and good spirits, and able to get around nicely despite his handicap. Still, if he got a common cold, *Newsweek* reported, gossipmongers quickly transmuted it into "a combination of leprosy, epilepsy, congenital insanity, and moral turpitude." One story had it that FDR was found in a coma at his desk, was sneaked out of the White House, and put on a boat headed for southern waters so he could secretly recuperate. Another tale reported that a prominent Senator came upon him cutting out paper dolls in the White House, and, still another, that one of the nation's leading business executives found him in his office babbling to himself, unable to talk coherently. Once he burst into hysterical laughter at a press conference, his enemies said, and went on and on with his mad laughter, as the reporters gaped, until White House personnel finally wheeled him away. He was under constant surveillance by psychiatrists disguised as servants, it was said, and spent ever-longer periods in a straitjacket to keep him from hurting himself. There were also iron bars in the White House windows, people said, to prevent him from jumping out. One rumor had it that one day he went completely berserk, was spirited away, and his place taken by an imposter. "Whom the gods would destroy," intoned Hamilton Fish, Jr., Republican Congressman from FDR's own district, "they first make mad!" When the hatemongers got tired of trashing President Roosevelt, they went after his family, particularly his wife. In time, Eleanor Roosevelt came in for almost as much character assassination by Roosevelt-haters as her husband did. [13]

It was Roosevelt's program—the collection of legislative enactments that came to be called the New Deal—that inspired the pathological hatred for the President that some Americans displayed in the 1930s. They saw the New Deal as basically subversive of the American system and FDR as virtually a traitor to his country as well as to his class. The New Deal (with its roots in 19th-century Populism and 20th-century Progressivism) was about as American as it could be: piecemeal, practical, forward-looking, non-ideological, experimental, improvisatory, and full of contradictions and inconsistencies. (When British economist John Maynard Keynes, who liked some of the things FDR was doing, met the President in 1933, he was surprised and disappointed by the latter's utter lack of interest in theory.) Still, Roosevelt-haters charged that the New Deal was un-American, alien, borrowed from crackpot and dangerous ideas dreamed up in Europe. Former President Herbert Hoover warned against the New Deal's "march to Fascism," and Virginia Senator Carter Glass deplored "the utterly dangerous effort to transplant Hitlerism to every corner of the nation." John T. Flynn, popular writer on economic subjects, published a book in which he, too, took the line that the New Deal was basically fascist in nature. Then he had second thoughts, and came out with another book in which he proved to his own satisfaction that Roosevelt's program smacked of Communism. Most Roosevelt-haters thought Flynn got it right the second time around. In the end, the charge of Communism was probably the commonest charge hurled against the New Deal President after 1934. As newspaper publisher William Randolph Hearst put it in a poem he ran in his newspapers around the country:

A Red New Deal with a Soviet seal
Endorsed by a Moscow hand,
The strange result of an alien cult
In a liberty-loving land.[14]

The books, pamphlets, articles, speeches, handbills, and editorials charging that the New Deal was a Communist plot were legion. In the Senate, Minnesota's Thomas D. Schall said that during the 1932 campaign Russian newspapers published a picture of FDR with the caption "the first communistic President of the United States." (The American Communists in fact called FDR a "social fascist" in 1932 and ran their own candidate for President that year.) Governor Eugene Talmadge of Georgia announced that New Deal programs came from "the Russian primer." In *The Roosevelt Red Record* (1936), Red-hunter Elizabeth Dilling revealed that a "Red ruling clique" was running the government, with the "full approval and cooperation" of Roosevelt. In a pamphlet entitled "Is the New Deal Communistic?" a man named Colonel Sanctuary listed thirty-five objectives of Karl Marx's "1848 program" to show the similarity of New Deal programs to Marx's prime desiderata. One book, *Frankie in Wonderland* (1934), was dedicated to "the American Eagle, that noble bird before it was turned into a Soviet Duck." Of one New Deal bill, Senator Henry Hatfield of West Virginia lamented: "Had Karl Marx risen from the grave to write the bill, the triumph of his idea could not have been more complete. . . . The wonder is that Stalin . . . has not called his congratulations to the White House, because this bill flaunts the label, 'Made in Moscow.'"[15]

And so it went throughout the 1930s. Percy Crosby, creator of the comic strip "Skippy," published a 500-page diatribe, *Three Cheers for the Red, Red and Red* (1936), blistering FDR as a Communist. Pennsylvania Congressman Robert F. Rich charged that Roosevelt was not only "socializing the country" but also "Russianizing" it. In the pages of the *Chicago Tribune* the Roosevelt-as-Red-baiting was bitter and unremitting. Owner Col. Robert R. McCormick, very early decided that FDR was soft on Communism and thereafter made no secret of his hatred of the President in the pages of his newspaper. "MOSCOW ORDERS REDS IN U.S. TO BACK ROOSEVELT" went a typical *Tribune* headline. During the 1936 campaign, when FDR sought a second term, the *Tribune,* the Hearst papers, and Roosevelt's enemies in general ran presumably factual news stories reporting that Moscow was backing the New Deal candidate and that the American Communist Party was helping FDR out on his campaign. The fact that CP, USA ran its own presidential candidate, Earl Browder, that year, didn't faze FDR's enemies. Browder, explained Hearst's *New York Journal,* was the "titular nominee" of CP, USA, but "the real candidate—the unofficial candidate of the Comintern—is Franklin D. Roosevelt." Even Al Smith, once a liberal and a friend of FDR, but now anti-New Deal, joined the chorus. In a speech to the reactionary Liberty League in January 1936, he announced that it was all right with him if the New Dealers "want to disguise themselves as Karl Marx or Lenin and the rest of that bunch," but "I won't stand for their allowing themselves under the banner of Jefferson or Jackson or Cleveland." H. L. Mencken, who should have known better, called FDR "a blood brother of Lenin" and compared him to "Holy Joe" Stalin. (But Mencken could be amusing too; he once said that if Roosevelt thought cannibalism would get him votes, he would begin fattening up a missionary in the White House backyard.)[16]

Not least among Roosevelt's enemies were the bigots: anti-Semites and racists. Fringe groups that made no secret of their admiration for Hitler called Roosevelt "the Kosher President," referred to his administration as "Roosevelt Red Democracy: New Deal Government by and for Jews," and charged that Roosevelt was part of a gigantic Jewish-Communist conspiracy to take over the United States and then the planet and establish a world state under Jewish domination. Some of the extremist groups added American blacks to the Great Conspiracy. With FDR's approval, they said, the Jews hired "big, black niggers" to rape white women in the South, utilized diseased black prostitutes to infect Gentile public officials, and planned to use the blacks as executioners ("just as Stalin used his Chinese") when they finally came to power. Popular among the paranoid right was the following doggerel:

> You kiss the negroes
> I'll kiss the Jews,
> We'll stay in the White House
> As long as we choose.[17]

Unlike Washington and Lincoln, FDR on occasion talked back to his detractors, at press conferences, in public addresses, and in letters to his critics. More often, though, he made use of people in his administration—especially the sharp-tongued Interior Secretary Harold L. Ickes—to take on his calumniators. But he realized there was nothing new in President-baiting. In a speech at a Jackson Day dinner in 1936, he recalled that Andrew Jackson hadn't had an easy time of it when he was in the White House. "An overwhelming proportion of the material power of the Nation was arrayed against him," he pointed out. "The great media for the dissemination of information and the molding of public opinion fought him. Haughty and sterile intellectualism opposed him. Musty reaction disapproved of him. Hollow and outworn traditionalism shook a trembling finger at him. It seemed sometimes that all were against him but the people of the United States." History, FDR, reminded his audience, "so often repeats itself."[18]

Half century after FDR's death history was still repeating itself—

and busily innovating, too, as was its wont. If Roosevelt-baiting was rife in the 1930s, "Clintonophobia" was the rage in the 1990s. Because Bill Clinton, the Arkansas governor who became President in 1993, was at times disingenuous when answering questions during the 1992 race about his personal behavior, he was a tempting target for those who resented the return to liberal activism after the conservative presidencies of Ronald Reagan and George Bush. Above all, the new President's broad-mindedness about sex—he behaved like a playboy before running for President, opposed barring gays from the military, and favored choice when it came to abortion—shocked and enraged many Americans and produced an outpouring of venom that astonished even some of Clinton's political opponents. "There are some hard, hard, hard-core Clinton haters," acknowledged Clinton political adviser James Carville. "This guy gins up more feelings and pulls them from greater extremes than any politician I know."

Among the extremists spreading hatred for the President far and wide were a handful of mealy-mouthed televangelists, reactionary talk-show hosts, and nutty computer bulletin-board aficionados. Not only did these people besmirch his character and make fun of his wife and daughter; they also blamed him for scores of beatings, suicides, and murders around the country. A former Republican Congressman circulated a list of twenty-four people with some connection to the President who had died "under other than natural circumstances." An Indianapolis lawyer publicized a list—"The Clinton Body Count: Coincidence or the Kiss of Death?"—containing the names of thirty-four people with ties to the Clinton family who she believed had died mysteriously, though she admitted there was "no direct evidence" of Clinton's involvement. Clinton finally took note of the slander, complained angrily that he was being subjected "to more assault than any previous President," but insisted he could "live with it." To his pleasure, though, he had one sturdy defender from the Old Right: former Republican Senator Barry Goldwater of Arizona. So appalled was Goldwater by the demagoguery of extremists in his party that he emerged from retirement to write OpEds urging the Republicans to "get off [Clinton's] back and let him be President" and lamenting that "the radical right has nearly ruined our party."[19]

President-baiting was, to be sure, an old American sport. But there were new elements in the Clinton-bashing that got under way soon after Clinton's inauguration in January 1993. For one thing, radio and TV talk shows, which had a powerful impact on the American people's perception of reality in the last decade of the 20th century, were mostly hostile to the new President. (The publisher of *Talkers*, the talk-show industry's trade journal, declared that Clinton was "the most criticized figure in the history of modern talk radio.") For another, Clinton's enemies, in a new twist, arranged for an Arkansas woman to bring suit against the President in 1994 for sexual harassment when he was governor of Arkansas in hopes of destroying his administration. [20]

Clinton was not the first President to be sued while in office. In 1962, President Kennedy faced a lawsuit brought by a Mississippi delegate to the 1960 Democratic convention (who was injured in an automobile JFK lent him) and reached a settlement out of court. And President Nixon was sued for damages by Ernest Fitzgerald, a Pentagon employee who was fired for whistleblowing (Nixon took responsibility for the dismissal), but took the case to the Supreme Court, which held that the President was absolutely and forever safe from lawsuits attacking his official acts. In *Nixon v. Fitzgerald* (1982), Chief Justice Warren Burger warned that uncontrolled litigation, used as "a mechanism of extortion," could encourage a President's political opponents to file suits simply to distract him from his duties. [21] Whether the President is immune while in office from lawsuits relating to private matters, as the Clinton administration contended, remained unsettled in 1994. It was clear, however, that the sexual-harassment lawsuit was damaging to Clinton's presidency and that it set a mischievous precedent for the future of President-bashing.

Notes

Preface

1. Paul Fussell, *Thank God for the Atom Bomb and Other Essays* (New York, 1988), 10.

Chapter 1. Columbus and the Flat-Earthers

1. Jeffrey Burton Russell, *Inventing the Flat Earth: Columbus and Modern Historians* (New York, 1991), 26.
2. Ibid., 16.
3. Washington Irving, *Life and Voyages of Christopher Columbus*, John Harmon McElroy, ed. (Boston, 1981), 48.
4. Ibid., 49–51.
5. Ibid., xciv; Samuel Eliot Morison, *Admiral of the Ocean Sea: A Life of Christopher Columbus* (Boston, 1942), 88–89.
6. John W. Draper, *History of the Conflict Between Religion and Science* (New York, 1876), 158–61.
7. Andrew D. White, *A History of the Warfare of Science with Theology* (New York, 1925), 108–9.
8. Russell, *Inventing the Flat Earth*, 44.
9. Ibid., 76.

Chapter 2. Pre-Columbian America

1. Kirkpatrick Sale, *The Conquest of Paradise* (New York, 1991); Arthur M. Schlesinger, Jr., "Was America a Mistake?," *Atlantic Monthly* (September 1992): 20; Alvin M. Josephy, Jr., ed., *America in 1492* (New York, 1991), 6.

2. Paul W. Valentine, "Are We Dancing with Myths About Indians?," *Washington Post*, reprinted in *Fort Worth Star-Telegram*, April 28, 1991, p. B7.

3. Stephan Thernstrom, "Hello, Columbus," *American School Board Journal* (Oct. 1991), 23; Josephy, *America in 1492*, 162; Paul Valentine, "Who Doomed the Maya?," *New York Times*, Nov. 19, 1991, pp. C1, C10.

4. Elmer Kelton, "Politically Correct or Historically Correct?," *The Roundup Magazine* (Sept.–Oct. 1993), 7.

5. Thernstrom, "Hello, Columbus," 21.

6. Oliver LaFarge, "Myths That Hide the American Indian," *American Heritage* 7 (Oct. 1956): 7; Valentine, "Are We Dancing with Myths About Indians?," B7; Olivia Vlahos, *New World Beginnings* (New York, 1970), 224–26.

7. Kelton, "Politically Correct or Historically Correct?," 6.

8. Alvin M. Josephy, Jr., *The Indian Heritage of America* (Boston, 1991), 28.

9. LaFarge, "Myths That Hide the American Indian," 8.

10. Kelton, "Politically Correct or Historically Correct?," 6.

11. Ibid., 7, 9.

12. Inga Clendinnen, *Aztecs: An Interpretation* (Cambridge, Eng., 1991), 87–110, 261–62.

13. Josephy, *America in 1492*, 193.

14. Hugh Thomas, *Conquest: Montezuma, Cortés, and the Fall of Old Mexico* (New York, 1993), xiii.

15. Schlesinger, "Was America a Mistake?," 22.

16. Ibid., 18.

Chapter 3. The Puritans and Religious Freedom

1. Perry Miller and Thomas H. Johnson, *The Puritans* (New York, 1938), 195–99.

2. James Kendall Hosmer, ed., *Winthrop's Journal*, 2 vols. (New York, 1908), II: 637–39.

3. Harry R. Warfel, Ralph H. Gabriel, and Stanley T. Williams, eds., *The American Mind*, 2 vols. (New York, 1947), I: 19.

Chapter 4. Roger Williams's Soul Liberty

1. Vernon L. Parrington, *Main Currents in American Thought*, 2 vols. (New York, 1954), I: 62–75.

2. Ibid., 71; James Ernst, *Roger Williams: New England Firebrand* (New York, 1932), 432–43; Cyclon Covey, *The Gentle Radical: A Biography of Roger Williams* (New York, 1966), 139–46.

3. In *Roger Williams: His Contribution to the American Tradition* (Indianapolis, 1953), Perry Miller was one of the first to challenge the Parrington approach to Williams. Edmund S. Morgan, *Roger Williams: The Church and the State* (New York, 1967), contains penetrating insights into Williams's religious outlook.

Chapter 5. Sex and the American Puritan

1. Martin E. Marty, *Righteous Empire: Protestantism in the United States* (New York, 1986), 88.

2. Meade Minnigerode, *The Fabulous Forties* (New York, 1924), 105–6, 213; Carl N. Degler, "What Ought To Be and What Was: Women's Sexuality in the Nineteenth Century," *American Historical Review* 79 (Dec. 1974): 1467.

3. Seymour Martin Lipset and David Riesman, *Education and Politics at Harvard* (New York, 1975), 22, 35–36.

4. Carl N. Degler, *Out of Our Past* (New York, 1959), 11–12.

5. Ibid., 14.

6. Daniel Walker Howe, ed., *Victorian America* (Philadelphia, 1976), 17.

7. Frances Trollope, *Domestic Manners of the Americans*, Donald Smalley, ed. (New York, 1949), 91–92, 136.

8. Ibid., 134–35.

9. Ibid., 135–36n.

10. Ibid., 159.

11. Degler, *Out of Our Past*, 14.

Chapter 6. The Second and the Fourth of July

1. L. H. Butterfield, ed., *The Book of Abigail and John: Selected Letters of the Adams Family, 1762–1784* (Cambridge, Mass., 1975), 142.

2. Carl Becker, *The Declaration of Independence* (New York, 1922), 3–4.

3. L. H. Butterfield, ed., *Diary and Autobiography of John Adams,* 4 vols. (Cambridge, Mass., 1962), III: 336; Charles Francis Adams, ed., *The Works of John Adams,* 10 vols. (Boston, 1850–56), II: 514; Becker, *Declaration of Independence,* 135–36.

4. Becker, *Declaration of Independence,* 230–31; Jefferson to Dr. John Manners, June 12, 1817, *The Works of Thomas Jefferson,* 12 vols. (Federal Edition, New York, 1905), XII: 66.

5. Vaclav Havel, "The New Measure of Man," *New York Times,* July 8, 1994, OpEd page.

Chapter 7. George Washington's Prayer at Valley Forge

1. M. L. Weems, *The Life of George Washington* (29th ed., Frankford near Philadelphia, 1826), 184.

2. Paul F. Boller, Jr., *George Washington and Religion* (Dallas, Tex., 1963), 9–10.

3. B. F. Morris, *Christian Life and Character of the Civil Institutions of the United States* (Philadelphia, 1864), 297.

4. Dr. James Abercrombie to Origen Bacheler, Nov. 29, 1831, *Magazine of American History* 13 (June 1885), 597.

5. Paul Leicester Ford, ed., *The Works of Thomas Jefferson,* 12 vols. (New York and London, 1904), I: 352.

6. The Papers of George Washington, Library of Congress, CCCXXXVI: 282.

Chapter 8. George Washington's False Teeth

1. Letter, Margaret Keys Saunders, *New York Times,* March 11, 1991, p. A16.

2. Ann Pasquale Haddad, "Washington's Last Tooth Rests in New York," *New York Times,* March 30, 1991, p. 12.

3. James Thomas Flexner, *George Washington: Anguish and Farewell,*

1793–1799 (Boston, 1969), 308–9; John C. Fitzpatrick, ed., *The Writings of George Washington*, 39 vols. (Washington, D.C., 1931–44), XXXVII: 29–30n.

4. Flexner, *Washington*, 317; James Thomas Flexner, *Gilbert Stuart: A Great Life in Brief* (New York, 1955), 124.

Chapter 9. The Founding Fathers and Democracy

1. Max Farrand, *The Records of the Federal Convention of 1787*, 4 vols. (New Haven, Conn., 1937), I: 299.
2. *Notes on Debates in the Federal Convention of 1787 Reported by James Madison* (Athens, Ohio, 1966), 308–9.
3. Ibid., 305. I have changed "worse possible" to "worst possible."
4. Ibid., 42; Charles A. Beard, *An Economic Interpretation of the Constitution of the United States* (New York, 1913), 204.
5. *Notes on Debates*, 39.
6. Beard, *Economic Interpretation*, 202; Richard Hofstadter, *The American Political Tradition* (New York, 1948), 4.
7. Charles A. Beard, *The Republic* (New York, 1943), 29–33.
8. Ibid., 33.

Chapter 10. The Declaration and the Constitution

1. Steven Greenhouse, "A Small-Business Federation Looms Large Against Clinton," *New York Times*, Sept. 17, 1993, p. A1.
2. Paul F. Boller, Jr., *American Transcendentalism, 1830–1860: An Intellectual Inquiry* (New York, 1974), 87.
3. Paul F. Boller, Jr., *Freedom and Fate in American Thought* (Dallas, Tex., 1978), 48–53.

Chapter 11. The Religion of Thomas Paine

1. Molly Ivins, "Faith Alive, Well in Public Discourse," *Fort Worth Star-Telegram*, Sept. 14, 1993, p. A21.
2. For a fuller discussion of Paine's views, see Paul F. Boller, Jr., "Changing 18th-Century Religious Attitudes," in Howard H. Quint and

Milton Cantor, eds., *Men, Women, and Issues in American History*, 2 vols. (Homewood, Ill., 1975), I: 55–61; Boller, *Freedom and Fate in American Thought* (Dallas, Tex., 1978), 29–31.

3. Thomas Paine, *Age of Reason*, Alburey Castell, ed. (New York, 1957), 3.

4. Ibid., 3, 7, 42.

5. Ibid., 4, 15, 22, 54.

6. Ibid., 24, 25–26.

7. Boller, "Changing 18th-Century Religious Attitudes," 60–61.

Chapter 12. Thomas Jefferson and Sally Hemings

1. Fawn M. Brodie, *Thomas Jefferson: An Intimate History* (New York, 1974).

2. Virginius Dabney, *The Jefferson Scandals: A Rebuttal* (New York, 1981), 6, 10–11.

3. Ibid., 18, 38, 45–53; Dumas Malone, "The Miscegenation Legend," *Jefferson and His Time*, 6 vols. (Boston, 1948–81), IV: 494–98.

4. Dabney, *Jefferson Scandals*, 79–80.

5. Ibid., 76, 78–79.

6. Ibid., 81–82.

7. Willard Sterne Randall, *Thomas Jefferson: A Life* (New York, 1993), 477.

Chapter 13. Thomas Jefferson on Government

1. Introduction, *United States Magazine and Democratic Review* 1 (Oct.–Dec. 1837): 6.

2. Albert E. Bergh, ed., *The Writings of Thomas Jefferson*, 18 vols. (Washington, D.C., 1904), III: 320.

3. "Annexation," *United States Magazine and Democratic Review* 17 (July–Aug. 1845): 5.

4. Bergh, ed., *Writings of Jefferson*, III: 377.

5. Thomas A. Bailey, *A Diplomatic History of the American People* (New York, 1964), 126.

Chapter 14. James Madison and Congressional Power

1. Theodore Draper, "Presidential Wars," *New York Review of Books,* Sept. 26, 1991, p. 64.
2. *The Federalist Papers,* Frederick Quinn, ed. (Washington, D.C., 1993), 121.
3. *Works of Fisher Ames,* Seth Ames, ed., 2 vols. (Boston, 1854), I: 35.
4. *A Compilation of the Messages and Papers of the Presidents,* 19 vols. (New York, 1897–1917), II: 490.

Chapter 15. The War of 1812 and Vietnam

1. Dec. 11, 1811, 12th Cong., 1st sess., *Annals of Congress* (1811–12): I: 457.
2. Feb. 1810, 11th Cong., 1st and 2d sess. (1809–10): I: 580; May 1812, 12th Cong., 1st sess. (1811–12): II: 397.
3. Glenn Tucker, *Poltroons and Patriots,* 2 vols. (Indianapolis, 1954), II: 567, 584, 594–95.
4. John M. Blum et al., *The National Experience: A History of the United States* (New York, 1977), 172; Tucker, *Poltroons and Patriots,* II: 432.
5. Tucker, *Poltroons and Patriots;* Blum, *National Experience,* 173.
6. Paul F. Boller, Jr., and Jean Tilford, *This Is Our Nation* (St. Louis, Mo., 1961), 201.
7. Theodore Dwight, *History of the Hartford Convention* (New York, 1833), 368.
8. George Dangerfield, *The Era of Good Feelings* (New York, 1952), 88; Joan Rezner Gunderson et al., *America's Changing Times* (New York, 1982), 208.
9. Tucker, *Poltroons and Patriots,* II: 670.

Chapter 16. President Fillmore's Bathtub

1. H. L. Mencken, "A Neglected Anniversary," *A Mencken Chrestomathy,* H. L. Mencken, ed. (New York, 1949), 592–96.
2. Vilhjalmur Stefansson, *Adventures in Error* (New York, 1936), 288–89.

3. Mencken, "Hymn to the Truth," *Prejudices: Sixth Series* (New York, 1927), 194–201.

4. William Seale, *The President's House: A History*, 2 vols. (Washington, D.C., 1986), I: 196–201, 315–17.

Chapter 17. William H. Seward and the Higher Law

1. Archibald H. Grimké, *William Lloyd Garrison: The Abolitionist* (New York, 1891), 354.

2. *The Works of William H. Seward*, George E. Baker, ed., 3 vols. (New York, 1853), I: 74–75; Paul F. Boller, Jr., *Congressional Anecdotes* (New York, 1991), 86.

3. Paul F. Boller, Jr., *Freedom and Fate in American Thought* (Dallas, Tex., 1978), 123–25.

Chapter 18. Uncle Tom as a Black Hero

1. Harriet Beecher Stowe, *Uncle Tom's Cabin* (Bantam ed., New York, 1981), 403.

2. Ibid., 21.

3. Ibid., 92, 183.

4. Ibid., 349.

5. Ibid., 300.

6. Ibid., 37, 53, 92.

7. Ibid., 395.

8. Ibid., 304.

9. Ibid., 354–56.

10. Ibid., 354–55.

11. Ibid., 377–78, 388–89.

12. Ibid., 394.

13. Ibid., 410, 412, 414–19.

14. Thomas F. Gossett, *Uncle Tom's Cabin and American Culture* (Dallas, Tex., 1985), 247, 254.

15. See Staughton Lynd, ed., *Nonviolence in America: A Documentary History* (Indianapolis, 1966), 25. On Martin Luther King, Jr., and other Christian non-resisters, see 25–31, 379–96, 461–81.

16. Stowe, *Uncle Tom's Cabin*, 414.

Chapter 19. Abraham Lincoln and James Buchana

1. Michael John Sullivan, *Presidential Passions* (New York, 1991) also Thomas P. Lowry, *The Story the Soldiers Wouldn't Tell: Sex in the War* (Mechanicsburg, Pa., 1994), 114–18.

2. Stephen B. Oates, *With Malice Toward None: The Life of Abrah Lincoln* (New York, 1977), 44.

3. See Paul F. Boller, Jr., "Mary Todd Lincoln," in Boller, *Presidentia Wives* (New York, 1988), 109–27.

4. Sullivan, *Presidential Passions,* 218.

5. Merle Miller, *Plain Speaking* (New York, 1974), 356. See, Boller, *Presidential Wives,* p. 170, for Cleveland's distrust of women's clubs, which he thought encouraged wives and mothers to neglect the home.

6. Philip Shriver Klein, *President James Buchanan* (University Park, Pa., 1962), 28–33; "James Buchanan and Ann Coleman," *Pennsylvania History* 21 (Jan. 1954): 1–20.

7. Carl Anthony, *First Ladies: The Saga of the Presidents' Wives and Their Power* (New York, 1990), 162.

8. Ibid., 136, 137; Klein, *Buchanan,* 111; Shelley Ross, *Fall from Grace: Sex, Scandal and Corruption in American Politics from 1702 to the Present* (New York, 1988), 87–89.

9. Klein, *Buchanan,* 220.

10. Anthony, *First Ladies,* 159.

11. Ibid., 167.

Chapter 20. Abraham Lincoln's Defense of His Wife

1. William O. Stoddard, *Inside the White House in War Time* (New York, 1890), 35.

2. *Lincoln Lore,* no. 1643 (Jan. 1975): 1–4.

Chapter 21. Abraham Lincoln's Religion

1. David H. Donald, *Lincoln's Herndon* (New York, 1948), 256–57.

2. Ward Hill Lamon, *The Life of Abraham Lincoln* (Boston, 1872), 39–40; William J. Wolf, *The Religion of Abraham Lincoln* (New York, 1963), 38–40.

3. Wolf, *Religion of Lincoln,* 51.

4. "Abraham Lincoln's Religion: His Own Statement," *Abraham Lincoln Quarterly* 2 (March 1942): 1–4.

5. William Herndon, *Herndon's Life of Lincoln* (New York, 1930), 67; Carl Sandburg, *Abraham Lincoln: The Prairie Years*, 2 vols. (New York, 1926), I: 93, 336–37.

6. *Stories and Speeches of Abraham Lincoln* (Chicago, 1900), 49–50.

7. Henry Deming, *Eulogy upon Abraham Lincoln Before the General Assembly of Connecticut* (n.p., 1865), 42.

8. *Collected Works of Abraham Lincoln*, 9 vols. (New Brunswick, N.J., 1953–55), VII: 281–83.

9. "Address at Gettysburg, Pennsylvania," Nov. 19, 1863, *Abraham Lincoln: Speeches and Writings, 1859–1865* (New York, 1989), 536.

10. Richard V. Pierard and Robert D. Lindner, *Civil Religion and the Presidency* (Grand Rapids, Mich., 1988), 98; "Annual Message to Congress," Dec. 1, 1862, *Lincoln: Speeches and Writings*, 415.

11. Wolf, *Religion of Lincoln*, 22, 30, 128–29; Frederick Carpenter, *The Inner Life of Abraham Lincoln: Six Months at the White House* (New York, 1868), 209; Carl Sandburg, *Abraham Lincoln: The War Years*, 4 vols. (New York, 1939), III: 381.

12. Sept. 1862, *Lincoln: Speeches and Writings*, 359.

13. Ibid., 686–87.

14. Ibid., 687, 689.

Chapter 22. Senator Lodge and the League of Nations

1. William C. Widenor, *Henry Cabot Lodge and the Search for an American Foreign Policy* (Berkeley, Calif., 1980), 76, 111, 114.

2. Ibid., 112, 121.

3. Thomas A. Bailey, *A Diplomatic History of the American People* (New York, 1964), 540–41; James E. Hewes, "Henry Cabot Lodge and the League of Nations," *Proceedings of the American Philosophical Society* (Philadelphia, 1970), 246.

4. Widenor, *Lodge*, 250–52, 255–56.

5. Ibid., 285.

6. Ibid., 292, 298, 304.

7. Ibid., 228; "A League of Nations," May 27, 1916, in Edgar E. Robinson and Victor J. West, *The Foreign Policy of Woodrow Wilson, 1913–1917* (New York, 1918), 325–29.

8. Hewes, "Lodge and League," 245; Widenor, *Lodge*, 291n.

9. Hewes, "Lodge and League," 249; Widenor, *Lodge*, 337–38, 306n.

10. Hewes, "Lodge and League," 252.

11. Ibid., 250, 252; Widenor, *Lodge*, 346.

12. Ibid., 346–47.

13. Ibid., 271, 285, 297n, 331.

Chapter 23. President Harding's Strange Death

1. Gaston B. Means, *The Strange Death of President Harding* (New York, 1930); see Paul F. Boller, Jr., *Presidential Wives* (New York, 1988), 249–50.

2. May Dixon Thacker, "Debunking the Strange Death of President Harding," *Liberty*, Nov. 7, 1931, pp. 8–11; Robert K. Murray, *The Harding Era: Warren G. Harding and His Administration* (Minneapolis, 1969), 491.

3. Andrew Sinclair, *The Available Man: The Life Behind the Masks of Warren Gamaliel Harding* (New York, 1965), 283; Robert H. Ferrell, "Medical Coverups by Seven Presidents," *Miller Center Report* (Univ. of Virginia) 9 (Summer 1993): 4.

4. Edmund W. Starling, *Starling of the White House* (Chicago, 1956), 200–201; Harry Daugherty, *The Inside Story of the Harding Tragedy* (New York, 1932), 272; "Mrs. Harding Dies After Long Fight," *New York Times*, Nov. 22, 1924, p. 3; Evalyn Walsh McLean, *Father Struck It Rich* (Boston, 1936), 274.

5. Elizabeth Jaffray, *Secrets of the White House* (New York, 1927), 92; "Mrs. Harding Dies After Long Fight," 3.

Chapter 24. Herbert Hoover and the Great Depression

1. Charles A. and Mary Beard, *America in Midpassage*, 2 vols. (New York, 1939), I: 88–90.

2. Special Session Message, Sept. 4, 1837, *A Compilation of the Messages and Papers of the Presidents*, James D. Richardson, ed. (New York, 1897), 1543, 1546.

3. Ibid., 1561–62.

4. Beard and Beard, *America in Midpassage*, I: 90.

5. Walter Lippmann, "The Permanent New Deal," in Richard M. Abrams and Lawrence W. Levine, eds., *The Shaping of Twentieth-Century America* (Boston, 1965), 428, 439.

Chapter 25. Justice Holmes and President Roosevelt

1. Catherine Drinker Bowen, *Yankee from Olympus: Justice Holmes and His Family* (Boston, 1944), 414.

2. James MacGregor Burns, *Roosevelt: The Lion and the Fox* (New York, 1956), 156–57.

3. Gary J. Aichele, *Oliver Wendell Holmes, Jr.: Soldier, Scholar, Judge* (Boston, 1989), 136, 159; Richard A. Posner, *The Essential Holmes* (New York, 1992), 65.

4. *Holmes-Pollack Letters*, Mark DeWolfe Howe, ed., 2 vols. (Cambridge, Mass., 1941), II: 64.

Chapter 26. Presidential Ghostwriters

1. Proposed Address to Congress, April 1789, *The Writings of Washington*, John C. Fitzpatrick, ed., 39 vols. (Washington, D.C., 1931–44), XXX: 296–308.

2. Ibid., 296–97; James Thomas Flexner, *George Washington: Anguish and Farewell, 1793–1799* (Boston, 1969), 162–63, 183–84.

3. W. W. Abbot, ed., *The Papers of George Washington*, Presidential Series, II: April–June 1789 (Charlottesville, 1987), II: 152–54; Irving Brant, *James Madison: Father of the Constitution, 1787–1800* (Indianapolis, 1950), 258; Ralph Ketcham, *James Madison: A Biography* (New York, 1971), 284.

4. Victor Hugo Palsits, *Washington's Farewell Address* (New York, 1935), 9–20.

5. Fitzpatrick, *Writings of Washington*, XXXV: 48–61.

6. Palsits, *Washington's Farewell Address*, 247–50.

7. Ibid., 250–51; Flexner, *George Washington*, 295–302; Felix Gilbert, *To the Farewell Address: Ideas of Early American Foreign Policy* (Princeton, N.J., 1961), 115–36.

8. John A. Carroll and Mary W. Ashworth, *George Washington: First in Peace* (New York, 1957), 402–3.

9. Palsits, *Farewell Address*, 75–94.

10. Jim Wright, "A Morn When History Was Made," *Fort Worth Star-Telegram*, June 5, 1994, p. C3.

Chapter 27. FDR and Soviet Recognition

1. This is an adaptation of Paul F. Boller, Jr., "The 'Great Conspiracy' of 1933: A Study in Short Memories," *Southwest Review* 39 (Spring 1954): 97–112.

Chapter 28. Franklin Roosevelt and Pearl Harbor

1. Richard Hofstadter, *The American Political Tradition* (New York, 1948), 343n.
2. *The Public Papers and Addresses of Franklin D. Roosevelt*, 13 vols. (New York, 1938–50), VI: 406–11.
3. Ted Morgan, *FDR: A Biography* (New York, 1985), 488.
4. Thomas A. Bailey, *A Diplomatic History of the American People* (New York, 1964), 736.
5. Ralph M. Ketcham, *The Borrowed Years, 1938–1941: America on the Way to War* (New York, 1989), 682, 689.
6. Ibid., 696.
7. Ibid., 698.
8. Robert E. Sherwood, *Roosevelt and Hopkins* (New York, 1948), 421; Morgan, *FDR*, 609–10.
9. Ibid., 611.
10. Ibid., 613–14.
11. Forrest C. Pogue, *George C. Marshall: Ordeal and Hope* (New York, 1966), 173; Ladislas Farago, "Spies and Codebreakers," in George M. Waller, ed., *Pearl Harbor: Roosevelt and the Coming of War* (Lexington, Mass., 1976), 211–12; Leonard Mosley, *Marshall: Hero for Our Times* (New York, 1982), 165.
12. Sherwood, *Roosevelt and Hopkins*, 425–26.
13. Morgan, *FDR*, 616.
14. Ibid., 617; interview, White House butler Alonzo Field, National Public Broadcasting, "The American Experience: FDR," 2 parts (1994), produced by David Grubin, Part 2.
15. Joseph R. Conlin, *The American Past* (New York, 1993), 706.
16. Bailey, *Diplomatic History*, 740.
17. Morgan, *FDR*, 622.
18. Gordon W. Prange, *At Dawn We Slept* (New York, 1981), 35–36.
19. *Time*, Dec. 8, 1941, p. 15; Ketcham, *Borrowed Years*, 682; Paul F. Boller, Jr., *Quotemanship* (Dallas, Tex., 1967), 134–35.

20. Stanley Weintraub, *Long Day's Journey into War: December 7, 1941* (New York, 1991), 525.

21. Thomas A. Bailey, *Probing America's Past,* 2 vols. (Lexington, Mass., 1973), II: 702.

Chapter 29. Eleanor Roosevelt's Love Life

1. Paul F. Boller, Jr., *Presidential Wives* (New York, 1988), 306; Joseph P. Lash, *Love, Eleanor: Eleanor Roosevelt and Her Friends* (Garden City, N.Y., 1982), 200–201; Geoffrey Ward, "Outing Mrs. Roosevelt," *New York Review of Books,* Sept. 24, 1992, pp. 52–53.

2. William H. Chafe, "Biographical Sketch," in Joan Hoff-Wilson and Marjorie Lightman, eds., *Without Precedent: The Life and Career of Eleanor Roosevelt* (Bloomington, Ind., 1964), 15; Ward, "Outing Mrs. Roosevelt," 52.

3. Boller, *Presidential Wives,* 306; Ward, "Outing Mrs. Roosevelt," 54n.

4. Boller, *Presidential Wives,* 305.

5. William T. Youngs, *Eleanor Roosevelt: A Personal and Public Life* (Boston, 1985), 147–66, 178–80, 199–202.

6. Blanche Wiesen Cook, *Eleanor Roosevelt* (New York, 1992), 458–93; Lash, *Love, Eleanor,* 134, 135, 137; Doris Faber, *The Life of Lorena Hickok: Eleanor Roosevelt's Friend* (Garden City, N.Y., 1980), 152.

7. Henry Mitchell and Megan Rosenfield, "A Vulnerable Woman of Intimacy and Affection," *Washington Post,* Nov. 23, 1979, p. C1.

8. Carroll Smith-Rosenberg, "The Female World of Love and Ritual," in Nancy F. Cott and Elizabeth H. Pleck, eds., *A Heritage of Her Own: Toward a New Social History of American Women* (New York, 1979), 311–13.

9. Ward, "Outing Mrs. Roosevelt," 52; Hoff-Wilson and Lightman, *Without Precedent,* 17–18; Lash, *Love, Eleanor,* xiv.

10. Hoff-Wilson and Lightman, *Without Precedent,* 16.

11. Faber, *Lorena Hickok,* 170, 186.

12. Ibid., 238–39; Lash, *Love, Eleanor,* 201.

13. Ward, "Outing Mrs. Roosevelt," 55; Faber, *Lorena Hickok,* 373–74.

14. Lash, *Love, Eleanor,* 459.

15. Ibid.

Chapter 30. FDR and Yalta

1. Paul F. Boller, Jr., "An American Irrelevance: CP, USA," *Southwest Review* 45 (Autumn 1960): 294.

2. Ibid., 296.

3. "Do Not Seek or Expect Utopia Overnight," Washington, D.C., Feb. 10, 1940, *Public Papers and Addresses of Franklin D. Roosevelt*, 13 vols. (New York, 1938–50), IX: 92–93; Joseph P. Lash, *Eleanor and Franklin* (New York, 1971), 605–7.

4. Boller, "American Irrelevance," 297.

5. Paul F. Boller, Jr., *Quotemanship* (Dallas, Tex., 1967), 28–29, 190–92.

6. Ibid., 29. For the Sheen quote, see Irving Howe and Lewis Coser, *The American Communist Party: A Critical History* (Boston, 1957), 433.

7. James F. Byrnes, *Speaking Frankly* (New York, 1947), 33; Hugh Gregory Gallagher, *FDR's Splendid Deception* (New York, 1985), 206.

8. W. Averell Harriman, *Special Envoy to Churchill and Stalin* (New York, 1975), 399.

9. Ted Morgan, *FDR: A Biography* (New York, 1985), 755.

10. Byrnes, *Speaking Frankly*, 45; *Chicago Tribune*, Feb. 13, 1945, p. 2.

11. Paul F. Boller, Jr., *Presidential Wives* (New York, 1988), 299.

Chapter 31. Harry Truman and the Vice Presidency

1. Paul F. Boller, Jr., *Congressional Anecdotes* (New York, 1991), 270.

2. "Billion Dollar Watchdog," *Time*, March 8, 1943, pp. 13–15; David McCullough, *Truman* (New York, 1992), 285–86.

3. Margaret Truman, *Souvenir—Margaret Truman's Own Story* (New York, 1956), 64; Robert H. Ferrell, *Truman: A Centenary Remembrance* (New York, 1984), 45.

4. Grace Tully, *F.D.R.: My Boss* (New York, 1949), 275–76; Jim Bishop, *FDR's Last Year* (New York, 1974), 99–100, 107; Leon Friedman, "Election of 1944," in Arthur M. Schlesinger, Jr., ed., *A History of American Presidential Elections*, 4 vols. (New York, 1971), IV: 3015–17.

Chapter 32. Hiroshima and the American Left

1. Paul Fussell, *Thank God for the Atom Bomb and Other Essays* (New York, 1988), 5.
2. David McCullough, *Truman* (New York, 1992), 442.
3. The present chapter is based on material appearing in Paul F. Boller, Jr., "Hiroshima and the American Left," *International Social Science Review* 57 (Winter 1982): 13–26.
4. Sidney Hook, *Out of Step: An Unquiet Life in the 20th Century* (New York, 1989), 322.

Chapter 33. Losing China

1. Michale Schaller, *The United States and China in the Twentieth Century* (New York, 1979), 75.
2. Ibid., 93–94.
3. Ibid., 98.
4. Theodore White and Annalee Jacoby, *Thunder Out of China* (New York, 1946), 201–2.
5. *China White Paper* (Stanford, Calif., 1967), 382.
6. Ibid., Introduction, p. 10.
7. June 24, 1949, 81st Cong., 1st sess., *Congressional Record*, Vol. 95, pp. 8296–97.
8. *China White Paper*, xvi.
9. Schaller, *United States and China*, 114.

Chapter 34. McCarthy and the Commies

1. *Washington Post*, March 25, 1954, quoted in Thomas C. Reeves, *The Life and Times of Joe McCarthy: A Biography* (New York, 1982), 587.
2. Robert Goldston, *The American Nightmare: Joseph R. McCarthy and the Politics of Hate* (Indianapolis, 1973), 56.
3. Ibid., 71–75, 102; *New York Times*, July 18, 1950, pp. 1, 17; "A Woman's Conscience," *Time*, June 12, 1950, p. 17; Frank Graham, Jr., *Margaret Chase Smith: Woman of Courage* (New York, 1964), 73–86.
4. Reeves, *McCarthy*, 372; June 14, 1951, 82nd Cong., 1st sess., Vol. 97, pp. 6556–6603.
5. Author's recollection.

6. Goldston, *American Nightmare*, 125, 152–53, 157.

7. Ibid., 163–67; "The Gauge of Recklessness," *Time*, June 21, 1954, pp. 21–22.

8. Reeves, *McCarthy*, 663.

9. Ibid., 206, 308.

Chapter 35. JFK and Vietnam

1. *Public Papers of the Presidents of the United States*, John F. Kennedy, 1963 (Washington, D.C., 1964), 652, 673.

2. Ibid., 659; Richard Reeves, *President Kennedy: Profile of Power* (New York, 1993), 449–50.

3. *Washington Post*, May 12, 1963; Noam Chomsky, *Rethinking Camelot: JFK, the Vietnam War, and U.S. Political Culture* (Boston, 1993), 72.

4. Ibid., 80–81.

5. Ibid., 33, 46, 81; *Public Papers*, Kennedy, 1963, pp. 652, 660, 673, 889, 892.

6. *Public Papers*, Kennedy, 1963, p. 11.

7. Chomsky, *Rethinking Camelot*, 72.

8. Ibid., 77, 78; *Public Papers*, Kennedy, 1963, p. 828; Jack Raymond, "G.I. Return Waits on Vietnam Talk," *New York Times*, Nov. 15, 1963.

9. Chomsky, *Rethinking Camelot*, 48.

10. George Ball, "JFK's Big Moment," *New York Review of Books*, Feb. 13, 1992, p. 20.

11. *New York Times*, March 23, 1968; "The Rationalist in Power," *New York Review of Books*, April 22, 1993, p. 35.

Chapter 36. The Kennedy Assassination

1. Priscilla Johnson Macmillan, *Marina and Lee* (New York, 1977), is one of the most knowledgeable and perceptive studies of Oswald's formative years.

2. Max Holland, "Cuba, Kennedy and the Cold War," *Nation*, Nov. 29, 1993, p. 650; *The Warren Commission Report: Report of the President's Commission on the Assassination of President John F. Kennedy* (New York, n.d.), 414–15.

3. Margaret Leech, *In the Days of McKinley* (New York, 1959), 597;

A. Wesley Johns, *The Man Who Shot McKinley* (South Brunswick, N.J., 1970), 244, 248.

4. *Warren Commission Report*, 10, 379–80; George Lardner, Jr., and Walter Pincus, "A Man on the Edge," *Washington Post National Edition*, Nov. 29–Dec. 5, 1993, p. 8.

5. Gerald Posner, *Case Closed: Lee Harvey Oswald and the Assassination of JFK* (New York, 1993), 6, 53, 91; *Warren Commission Report*, 391–92.

6. *Warren Commission Report*, 183–87, 404–6; Posner, *Case Closed*, 106, 116.

7. *Warren Commission Report*, 413; Posner, *Case Closed*, 116, 165.

8. Daniel Schorr, "All Things Considered," National Public Radio, Nov. 15, 1993, transcript, p. 8; Macmillan, *Marina and Lee*, 485.

9. Posner, *Case Closed*, 221–22.

10. *Warren Commission Report*, 5, 63–64, 143–46; Howard Brennan and J. Edward Cherryholmes, *Eyewitness to History* (Waco, Tex., 1987), 13–15, 56.

11. Posner, *Case Closed*, 304–42.

12. Ibid., 397, 399, 400.

13. William Manchester, *The Death of a President* (New York, 1967), xix; Alexander Cockburn, "Beat the Devil," *Nation*, Nov. 29, 1993, p. 647.

14. *I. F. Stone's Bi-Weekly*, Dec. 9, 1963, p. 8.

Chapter 37. President Nixon's Domestic Politics

1. George Will, "Ambition, Tenacity and Nixon," *Fort Worth Star-Telegram*, April 28, 1994, p. A33; Theodore Draper, "Nixon Redivivus," *New York Review of Books*, July 14, 1994, p. 28. See also Joan Hoff, *Nixon Reconsidered* (New York, 1994).

2. Michael A. Genovese, *The Nixon Presidency* (Westport, Conn., 1990), 72.

3. State of the Union Address, Jan. 22, 1970, *Public Papers of the Presidents of the United States, Richard Nixon, 1970* (Washington, D.C., 1971), 13.

4. Tom Wicker, *One of Us: Richard Nixon and the American Dream* (New York, 1991), 518.

5. Genovese, *Nixon Presidency*, 79.

6. Ibid.; Wicker, *One of Us*, 538; Richard M. Nixon, "Health Care Now," *New Republic*, Sept. 19 and 26, 1994, p. 11.

7. Wicker, *One of Us*, 493.

8. John Ehrlichman, *Witness to Power: The Nixon Years* (New York, 1982), 235.

9. Wicker, *One of Us*, 486–87.

10. Ibid., 504; see also Herbert S. Parmet, *Richard Nixon and His America* (Boston, 1990), 602–4.

Chapter 38. Watergate

1. Samuel Dash, *Chief Counsel: Inside the Ervin Committee-The Untold Story of Watergate* (New York, 1976), 109.

2. John W. Dean, *Blind Ambition* (New York, 1976), 138–39.

3. Stanley I. Kutler, *The Wars of Watergate: The Last Crisis of Richard Nixon* (New York, 1990), 99.

4. Dean, *Blind Ambition*, 107; Carl Bernstein and Bob Woodward, *All the President's Men* (New York, 1974), 26.

5. Ibid.

6. *Public Papers of the Presidents of the United States*, Richard Nixon, 1972 (Washington, D.C., 1974), 276; ibid., 1973, pp. 299, 326–28, 552, 691–92, 956.

7. Ibid., 1974, p. 621.

8. Dean, *Blind Ambition*, 392.

9. Ibid., 201; Dash, *Chief Counsel*, 206; Stanley I. Kutler, *The Wars of Watergate: The Last Crisis of President Nixon* (New York, 1990), 604.

10. J. Anthony Lukas, *Nightmare: The Underside of the Nixon Years* (New York, 1976), 559; Dash, *Chief Counsel*, 264–65; Garry Wills, "Nixon in Heaven," *Esquire* (July 1994), 43–44.

Chapter 39. The Pledge of Allegiance

1. "Bush Expands Pledge Not to Increase Taxes," *New York Times*, June 25, 1988, p. 7.

2. "Socialist Pledge?," *U.S. News & World Report*, Sept. 26, 1988, p. 13; Michael Kinsley, *New Republic*, July 11, 1988, p. 4; "Taking the Pledge," *Time*, Sept. 5, 1988, p. 15.

3. Kinsley, p. 4.

4. "Taking the Pledge," 14.

5. Maria Recio, "Texas Lawmaker's Criticism of Pledge Upsets Colleagues," *Fort Worth Star-Telegram*, June 30, 1993, p. A6.

Chapter 40. Presidential Salutes

1. Paul F. Boller, Jr., "No Need to Salute the Troops, Sir! You're the Civilian Boss," *Fort Worth Star-Telegram*, March 27, 1992, p. A27; Ronald Reagan, *An American Life* (New York, 1990), 388–89.

2. Edward C. Lathem, ed., *Meet Calvin Coolidge* (Brattleboro, Vt., 1960), 109.

3. This information comes from the staffs of the presidential libraries of Truman, Eisenhower, Kennedy, Johnson, Ford, and Carter.

4. "Hails from the Chief," *Time*, March 1, 1993, p. 9; "Conventional Wisdom," *Newsweek*, March 22, 1993, p. 4; Richard L. Berke, "Unaccustomed Role for Clinton in Captain's Seat," *New York Times*, March 13, 1993, p. 7.

5. Maureen Dowd, "Clinton Faces Heroes: Judgment Day," *New York Times*, June 4, 1994, p. 5.

6. Maureen Dowd, "Retracing History: Clinton's 20-Something Aides," *New York Times*, June 6, 1994, p. A4.

7. Christopher Matthews, "Drop the Salute, Mr. President," *Liberal Opinion*, March 29, 1993, p. 31.

8. William Lee Messick, *America's Fighting Presidents* (Summerland, Calif., 1993), 48–49; Gerald Emmanuel Stearn and Albert Fried, eds., *The Essential Lincoln* (New York, 1962), 135–36.

9. Ulysses S. Grant, *Personal Memoirs*, 2 vols. (New York, 1885), I: 53.

Chapter 41. Presidential Campaigns

1. Paul F. Boller, Jr., *Presidential Campaigns* (New York, 1985), vii.
2. Ibid., 18.
3. Ibid., 12.
4. Ibid., 12–13, 18.
5. Ibid., 44–45.
6. Ibid., 45–46.
7. Ibid., 117.
8. Ibid.

9. Donald F. Anderson, *William Howard Taft: A Conservative's Conception of the Presidency* (Ithaca, N.Y., 1973), 47.

10. Paolo E. Coletta, *William Jennings Bryan*, 3 vols. (Lincoln, Nebr., 1964–69), I: 417.

11. Boller, *Presidential Campaigns*, 318–19.

12. Ibid., 359.

Chapter 42. Presidential Wives

1. "At the Center of Power," *Time*, May 10, 1993, p. 29.

2. Carl Sferrazza Anthony, *First Ladies*, 2 vols. (New York, 1990–91), I: 135; Paul F. Boller, Jr., *Presidential Wives* (New York, 1988), 321.

3. Boller, *Presidential Wives*, 226–29.

4. Anthony, *First Ladies*, I: 466.

5. Boller, *Presidential Wives*, 308–9; Doris Kearns Goodwin, *No Ordinary Time: Franklin and Eleanor Roosevelt: The Home Front in World War II* (New York, 1994), 164, 629.

6. Boller, *Presidential Wives*, 301.

7. Ibid., 463–64; Donald T. Regan, *For the Record: From Wall Street to Washington* (New York, 1988), 77, 86.

8. Ibid., 84, 101, 109, 321, 326; Boller, *Presidential Wives*, 464.

9. Regan, *For the Record*, 76; Nancy Reagan, *My Turn* (New York, 1989).

10. Lou Cannon, *President Reagan: The Role of a Lifetime* (New York, 1991), 507–8; Kitty Kelley, *Nancy Reagan: The Unauthorized Biography* (New York, 1991), 477; Reagan, *My Turn*, 336–37.

11. Boller, *Presidential Wives*, 462, 464.

Chapter 43. Presidential Scandals

1. David McCullough, *Truman* (New York, 1992), 435.

2. Paul F. Boller, Jr., *Presidential Wives* (New York, 1988), 221.

3. Ibid., 224.

4. Ibid., 247.

5. Ibid.

6. Ibid., 289.

7. Ibid., 300; Hugh Gregory Gallagher, *FDR's Splendid Deception* (New York, 1985), 142.

8. Boller, *Presidential Wives*, 300.

9. Ibid., 301.

10. Doris Kearns Goodwin, *No Ordinary Time* (New York, 1994), 504.

11. Ibid., 340–41, 348.

12. Ibid., 365–66; Richard Reeves, *President Kennedy: Profile of Power* (New York, 1993), 290.

13. Larry King, *Tell It to the King* (New York, 1988), 93–94.

14. Boller, *Presidential Wives*, 391–92.

15. H. Brandt Ayers, "The Death of Civility," *New York Times*, July 16, 1994, p. 11.

Chapter 44. President-Bashing

1. Donald H. Stewart, *The Opposition Press of the Federalist Period* (Albany, N.Y., 1969), 212; John A. Carroll and Mary W. Ashworth, *George Washington: First in Peace* (New York, 1957), 321n.

2. Samuel E. Forman, *The Political Activities of Philip Freneau* (Baltimore, 1902), 68, 71, 231; Carroll and Ashworth, *Washington*, 231.

3. James E. Pollard, *The Presidents and the Press* (New York, 1947), 17; Stewart, *Opposition Press*, 525, 528.

4. Stewart, *Opposition Press*, 533.

5. J. G. Randall, "The Unpopular Mr. Lincoln," *Abraham Lincoln Quarterly* 2 (June 1943): 257.

6. Ibid., 257–58; Paul F. Boller, Jr., *Presidential Anecdotes* (New York, 1981), 127.

7. Robert S. Harper, *Lincoln and the Press* (New York, 1951), 263, 287–88; Edmund Fuller and David E. Green, *God in the White House* (New York, 1968), 115; Pollard, *Presidents and Press*, 388.

8. Carl Sandburg, *Abraham Lincoln: The War Years*, 4 vols. (New York, 1939), II: 138–39.

9. Pollard, *Presidents and Press*, 350.

10. Ibid., 380–81; Paul F. Boller, Jr., *Presidential Campaigns* (New York, 1985), 119–20.

11. Marquis W. Childs, "They Still Hate Roosevelt," *New Republic*, Sept. 14, 1938, p. 147; "Number One Obsession," *Nation*, April 30, 1938, p. 492.

12. George Wolfskill and John A. Hudson, *All But the People: Franklin D. Roosevelt and His Critics, 1933–1939* (London, 1969), 24–25; Stephen T. Early, "Below the Belt," *Saturday Evening Post*, June 10, 1939, pp. 7, 111–12.

13. Ibid.; Childs, "They Still Hate Roosevelt," 148; Wolfskill and Hudson, *All But the People*, 6–7, 12, 14.

14. Wolfskill and Hudson, *All But the People*, 111, 214, 245; Pollard, *Presidents and Press*, 95.

15. Wolfskill and Hudson, *All But the People*, 93, 150.

16. Ibid., 106, 166, 188, 194, 210, 213, 216; Patrick Gerston and Nicholas Cords, *Myth in American History* (Encino, Calif., 1977), 234.

17. Gerston and Cords, *Myth in American History*, 25, 68, 92.

18. Ibid., 306; Jan. 8, 1936, *Public Papers and Addresses of Franklin D. Roosevelt*, 13 vols. (New York, 1938–50), V: 40.

19. "Whatever It Is, Bill Clinton Likely Did It," *U.S. News & World Report*, Aug. 8, 1994, pp. 29–32; *Fort Worth Star-Telegram* July 31, 1994, p. A-16; Anthony Lewis, "Merchants of Hate," *New York Times*, July 15, 1994, p. A-13; Ann Devroy, "At Least He Isn't Boring," *Washington Post National Weekly Edition*, May 30–June 5, 1994, p. 13; "President Says He Has Been Under Assault," *New York Times*, May 10, 1994, p. A-10.

20. "Talk Radio Gets a Spirited New Voice from the Left," *New York Times*, May 9, 1994, p. C7.

21. "Why Paula Jones Should Wait," *Time*, June 27, 1994, p. 40.

Index